John Marshall:
The Final Founder

JOHN MARSHALL: THE FINAL FOUNDER

A Biography and Thoughts on the Issues of American History He Inspired

ROBERT STRAUSS

Guilford, Connecticut

An imprint of The Rowman & Littlefield Publishing Group, Inc.
4501 Forbes Blvd., Ste. 200
Lanham, MD 20706
www.rowman.com

Distributed by NATIONAL BOOK NETWORK

British Library Cataloguing in Publication Information available

Library of Congress Cataloging-in-Publication Data

Names: Strauss, Robert, 1951– author.
Title: John Marshall : the final founder / Robert Strauss.
Description: Guilford, Connecticut : Lyons Press, An imprint of The Rowman
  & Littlefield Publishing Group, Inc., [2021] | Includes bibliographical
  references and index. | Summary: "A biographical history of Chief
  Justice John Marshall, one of the Founding Fathers of the United
  States"— Provided by publisher.
Identifiers: LCCN 2020044801 (print) | LCCN 2020044802 (ebook) | ISBN
  9781493037476 (hardback) | ISBN 9781493037483 (epub)
Subjects: LCSH: Marshall, John, 1755-1835. | Judges—United
  States—Biography. | United States. Supreme Court—Officials and
  employees—Biography.
Classification: LCC KF8745.M3 S84 2021 (print) | LCC KF8745.M3 (ebook) |
  DDC 347.73/2634 [B]—dc23
LC record available at https://lccn.loc.gov/2020044801
LC ebook record available at https://lccn.loc.gov/2020044802

CONTENTS

INTRODUCTION

WE DID NOT TRAVEL MUCH WHEN I WAS YOUNG, BUT ALL OUR TRIPS seemed thematic. At least every few months, we would visit my father's sisters in Brooklyn or his cousin in Maryland, near Washington, DC. Since my father was an active alumnus at Rutgers, we would often go to Rutgers football games, mostly in New Brunswick in central New Jersey, about sixty miles north of our home, but sometimes away in places like Quantico, Virginia; Cambridge, Massachusetts; Storrs, Connecticut; or, most every year, Princeton, only forty miles from the house. The other trips, and in fact, often these as well, all had to do with American history, whether it was close by in Philadelphia or nearby New Jersey or Pennsylvania to see some Revolutionary War site, or a day trip to DC and all the monuments and museums an afternoon could fill.

Our one epic excursion, at least by our family standards, came at Christmas time in 1961. My father, a solo practicing attorney, had a case he was settling in the town of Tarboro, North Carolina, so we motored through North Carolina and Virginia to celebrate the Centennial of the Civil War, as well as seeing as many Jeffersonian parcels as we could accommodate in a week. It did beat our usual late December visit to Aunt Cele or Aunt Freda up in Brooklyn.

At each juncture on any of these history jaunts, my father would seek out the plaques and signs indicating where we were and how, in a few sentences, we could find out why. I was instructed to read, aloud, the few sentences that usually took up the markers. I was his only child and he was not going to waste his own enjoyment in seeking the trivia of American history without having me as a companion in tow.

Dad had mahogany bookshelves built on every wall and in every cranny of our split-level's downstairs recreation room. Most of his books were either the history of religion or American history, all arranged in some arcane order that often got me in trouble when I took down a book whose return location parameters I couldn't quite figure out. I am frankly not sure that he read most of the books, but they were sacred nonetheless. I remember one summer in high school or college, my friend Noah was working in a book distribution warehouse in a nearby town. Noah came over one day and, I am certain, half-kiddingly, told my father he had seen some volumes of Woodrow Wilson's papers on the warehouse shelves. My father went into near-apoplexy.

"You have got to get me them," he babbled. "Whatever they cost, please let me know."

So far as I know, Noah might have put them inside his jacket and spirited them out as secretly as if they were the Dead Sea Scrolls. Decades later, they are now on my living room bookshelf, *The Papers of Woodrow Wilson*, volumes one, two, three, four, five, and fourteen—Noah's warehouse work having some holes in it. I wonder if Noah also got him the second volume of James Polk's papers a few presidents to the left of Wilson on my shelf, though, as with Wilson, it is alone, sans any other volume, another piece of a probably-never-complete set.

My dad was also a joiner. I do not know whether he thought his solo law practice in Camden, the county seat, was enhanced by his memberships in the Lions, the Shriners, the Masons, and even the Tall Cedars of Lebanon, and his various alumni associations, but he and my mom seemed always to be going to some dinner or dance for these.

American history, too, had him joining, and maybe even creating places to join. My mother's cousin was a Ben Franklin scholar and ran, for a time, the Friends of Independence Park, so Dad, with that familial in, made those meetings. He was a member of the Lincoln Civil War Society, which as I remember met in the second floor of a bookstore in, shall we say, the Tenderloin part of Philadelphia. I still have some of his missives as an officer of the Commodore John Barry Day Committee. Many visitors think the statue at the back of Independence Hall pointing to the future is one of the Main Guys, like Washington or Jefferson or Franklin, but, no, it is Barry, who is buried a few blocks away[1], and who was said to be the Father of the United States Navy, an Irishman seeking fortune on the colonial seas. Barry never did get his Day, despite my father's greatest efforts, but when they built a bridge in the 1970s to replace the Chester-Bridgeport Ferry across the Delaware River between those Pennsylvania and New Jersey towns, it became the Commodore John Barry Bridge. I can't find any citations to prove it one way or the other, but I always pronounce, when I drive over it, that this is my father's historical legacy.

When I speak on historical subjects, I always bring along the first book I remember my father giving me, *Facts About the Presidents*, by Joseph Nathan Kane.[2] Its pages are so yellow they are Crayola Burnt Sienna colored now, and the paperback binding is in terrific disrepair, but it always pleases me to leaf through it. It is *Moneyball* or the *Bill James Baseball Abstract* for presidents. So those early readings about, for instance, James Monroe's mother's birthdate, and Calvin Coolidge's hobbies (mechanical bull riding and throwing Indian clubs) and the most wondrous presidential stat of them all—that John Adams and Thomas Jefferson both died on July 4, 1826, the fiftieth anniversary of the Declaration of Independence—served as a good foundation for my love of the lives of the presidents, substantive and trivial.

Dad also bought me a set of the Marx toy company's two-and-three-quarter-inch-high white plastic figurines of the presidents—albeit at the time of the gift, only going up to John F. Kennedy. I maniacally gave them for her youth to my younger daughter, whom I believe used them for preteen playlets ("William Howard Taft Among the Thin Ones," perhaps), before I spirited them back to my own shelves, with the cigar box my mom had saved them in, some years ago.

American history, I admit, is personal to me. I want it my way, with a slightly chipped George Washington plastic figurine and missing volumes of Polk's and Wilson's papers. On that 1961 trip, my father berated an employee behind the desk in the special collections section at the University of Virginia library until the guy brought out Thomas Jefferson's will from the archives. Why the will and not something else? There is no one to tell me now. My father photographed it and self-framed it for his office. The two framed pieces of "art" are propped up on the floor behind me in my office as I write this. I am sure anyone can find a better copy of these pages on any number of websites today, but few can have a better laugh about theirs than I.

On that same trip, too, my father wanted to stop at Woodrow Wilson's birthplace in the out-of-the-way southwestern Virginia burg of Staunton. He could not contain his eagerness when we got to the modest house—Wilson's father was a local Presbyterian minister—and Dad practically sprinted to the door from his parking space a block away. By the time my ten-year-old legs could catch up, his face had turned a horrific shade of glum and he was trudging back to the car. When I got there, I noticed that on the door was a typewritten index card saying the birthplace would be closed that day, December 28, 1961, not because it would have been Wilson's 105th birthday, which it would have, but because Edith Galt Wilson, the president's second wife, had died earlier that day. It was as if Ponce de León had been turned away from the Fountain of Youth, or the Tin Man from Oz.

Yet, I am sure if Dad knew in the future there would be such as the Barry Bridge or the incomplete papers of Polk or, even, the next day, December 29, 1961, which was when he manically photographed Jefferson's will, he would have had a chuckle. He was his kind of history buff, and I only wish he would have known I could be his type of history-book writer. I turned from a career in journalism to write the contrarian *Worst. President. Ever.*, a biography not of Jefferson, or even as later in these pages, John Marshall, but the (fortunately) inimitable James Buchanan.

Other historians have similar youthful stories. C-SPAN in 2019 put out a book, *The Presidents*, based on a survey the network did of historians, rating the presidents from top to bottom. Buchanan, to be sure, was that bottom-dweller, and a portion of the interview C-SPAN founder Brian Lamb did with me on the network in 2016 about *Worst. President. Ever.* appeared in the book.

To kick off the promotion of *The Presidents*, C-SPAN had several others whose interviews captured each president in the book do a panel at

George Washington's home, Mount Vernon. Douglas Brinkley was there for his work on Theodore Roosevelt, and Richard Norton Smith for his book on Herbert Hoover, *An Uncommon Man.*

Brinkley said it was his mother, a schoolteacher, who dragged him, not so unwillingly on his part, into history.[3]

"I was born in Atlanta, Georgia, and when I was young, my mom and dad would go to Callaway Gardens," said Brinkley during that panel at Mount Vernon. "Near the gardens was the little White House for FDR State Park. I could not believe that the president had lived in such a small, little cottage house, and that he died while somebody was painting his portrait only half-done."

Brinkley has written more than twenty books and appears all over TV as a presidential expert, like an ingenue of history. His most recent book, as of this writing, is about the American race to the moon. He became even more obsessed with the space race as an adolescent, he said, when he found out that, after his family moved to northwest Ohio, Neil Armstrong lived not more than an hour away.

Brinkley became a history major at The Ohio State University— contrarian that I am, I did not, becoming instead a philosophy major, great training for my first jobs as an argumentative sportswriter. But, Brinkley said, it was all based on the wonder his mom instilled in him.

"It is a big deal—we call [Ohio] the Mother of Presidents," he said, pausing slightly on the word *mother*, perhaps in honor of his. "We claim seven of them. . . . There was a great bit of pride in that.

"My mom was a teacher and all of that in high school," said Brinkley. "We would take our car, a station wagon actually—we had a twenty-four-foot Coachman trailer—and we would go all over the country visiting presidential sites and Civil War battlefields, national parks. I have a lot of photos from when I am young at the graves of presidents."

Smith's parents, too, indulged and enhanced his youthful history bug.

"People don't do this any more," Smith speculated. "I must have been about eight . . . the polite word is precocious, but I had four siblings [who might disagree].

"We used to go for a month every summer. We would get in the station wagon and do a section of the country—the Midwest, the Deep South. And guess who gets to set the itinerary?" he said, pointing at himself, mimicking the eight-year-old still in him after writing a slew of books about American history, mostly biographies.

"It was all set around presidential gravesites, that sort of thing," he said with a chuckle. "We found out where [Wendell] Willkie was buried. We had to pay our respects.

"The only concession that we made to the others was they got a swimming pool in the evening," he said. "There is nothing quite like being there. Andrew Jackson, who is not on my hit parade of presidents—go to the Hermitage and you will walk away from there with a much more vivid sense of who he was, including his limitations."

My dad died in 1981, a little too early for my taste, perhaps, but he gave me a way of viewing American history I hope I have passed on to my readers—that thinking about the past, especially our marvelous American past, need not be ponderous, but better with a wink at pretension and a smile at the wonder of it all.

—◆—

Those looking for the definitive biography of John Marshall on these pages will be, sadly, disappointed. There have been two deeply researched Marshall biographies published in the three years or so before this book: *Without Precedent* by Joel Richard Paul (2018), and *John Marshall* by Richard Brookhiser (2018), not to mention Jean Edward Smith's *John Marshall* from 1996, and the first real biography of Marshall by Albert Beveridge, which won a Pulitzer Prize for Biography in 1920, *John Marshall*.

All the above are fair and honest biographies of the subject, comprehensive—even annoyingly so. Every page is dense with Marshall, but the books seem too dense to explore the legacy Marshall left, and the impact his legacy has had.

This volume will instead use Marshall's life to illustrate or lead into thoughts about the nature of American history. Marshall may seem an odd figure to "tell" this story. Why not George Washington, Thomas Jefferson, Ben Franklin, or James Madison?

Only Madison, among the major Founders, outlived Marshall, but Madison retired to his Virginia home well before his death, while Marshall kept working as the chief justice through to his own death in 1835. Aaron Burr, too, outlived Marshall, and while he had a good career early on, he was discredited after his duel with Alexander Hamilton. From the time Marshall and his father set off to join George Washington's ailing army early in the Revolutionary War, Marshall led himself on a path of succeeding jobs, lauded by some and vilified by others, but often solving problems necessary to the new nation.

This book, then, will follow Marshall's life but connect to other questions about those early years for our nation: When did the Founding of the nation end? Who else could have been president, for better or worse? What were the worst Supreme Court decisions? I will find that Marshall either came out on the right side, or accepted his losses. He knew, and often clashed with, pretty much every one of the nation's Founders, and even knew well the few actual ex-presidents by his time and how they treated their successors and challengers. Marshall was, indeed, everywhere—and for decades—and is a perfect man to ride through the wilderness of early American politics.

CHAPTER ONE

Marshall's Early Years

WOODY ALLEN CREATED A CURIOUS CHARACTER, LEONARD ZELIG, FOR his 1983 mockumentary movie, *Zelig*. Throughout, Zelig appears in vintage photographs and actual historic events during the mid-twentieth century. Zelig preternaturally assumes the demeanor and style of those who inhabit these famous scenes, becoming a patrician with refined tones among the affluent, at a formal dinner, say, and then going to the kitchen to become folksy and coarser in speech among the back of the house.

The famed and the observant comment on Zelig in the movie—Susan Sontag, Saul Bellow, Bruno Bettelheim, and the musician Bricktop among them. A psychiatrist played by Mia Farrow discovers that Zelig is a transformative character, and is all the more so because of his desire to please those, the noted and the not, around him in these vaunted circles.[1]

John Marshall may well be the Zelig of the Founding Era. He apparently lived through precisely the right years, and was at the right age at the right times, to be just about everywhere of note. From the early Virginia frontier, to service at Valley Forge, to the debates over the ratification of the Constitution by his home state of Virginia, to the XYZ Affair in France, to the Adams Cabinet and, most assuredly, the chief justiceship of the Supreme Court in its most crucial decades, Marshall had quite a resonant six decades or so of adulthood in the American political pantheon.

Marshall's ubiquity in those heady decades is, in itself, a good reason to study him, and his movements, both physical and cerebral. To be everywhere and to do everything was a lot easier in the late eighteenth and early nineteenth centuries than in the fictional Zelig's time and certainly today. The population in the colonies and later states and territories was in the low seven figures most of Marshall's lifetime, and only white men got to do much of note. Today, with the population up more than a hundred-fold from those days, and communication and technology keeping everyone apprised of that cache of "everything," what may have been a relatively normal life like Marshall must have thought he had, at least early on, would be a Renaissance existence today.

The colonies were comfortably British when Marshall was born on September 24, 1755[2], but the first tremors of their eventual schism from the empire were just being felt. In the summer just prior to his birth, a formidable force of about five thousand British regulars was routed in an ambush in the far reaches of Pennsylvania along the Monongahela River by a combined French and Indian force. The British leader, Major General Edward Braddock, was the commander in chief of British troops in the colonies, and any move he had planned to push farther west to capture land was thwarted, at least for the time being.

But for the impending birth of his new son, Thomas Marshall, John's father, would probably have been on the scene. Thomas's friend and schoolmate from childhood, George Washington, all of twenty-three years old, was the leader of the Virginia division serving under Braddock. News of the British summary defeat, not to mention Braddock's death in the battle, almost certainly got back to the Marshalls quickly. The conclusion of those frontiersmen like Marshall no doubt was that the colonists could no longer trust the British regulars to defend them from Indians and the French, much less drive those enemies back so that the population could continue its move west.[3]

The road up the social ladder had few rungs in those days, even in the most populous colony, Virginia. A trade, some moxie, hard work, and a reasonable lineage in the colonies—maybe two generations—all qualified for status in mid-eighteenth-century America. There was plenty of land, and thus the chance to be of status and largesse. Thomas Marshall had attended school for a time in Washington Parish with George, and both served as surveyors for the properties that kept being subdivided for new settlers.

While Washington preferred to stay on the Tidewater estate his family had been building upon, Marshall moved to the west, at the foot of the Blue Ridge Mountains in the small community of Germantown in Fauquier County.[4] The Marshalls on John's father's side had been in the colonies at least two previous generations, coming over from Wales at some point in the late seventeenth or early eighteenth centuries. On his mother's side, though, they were of what would become Virginia aristocracy. There, his ancestors actually came from a measure of Scottish nobility, sailing over to Jamestown, the first permanent Virginia community, as early as 1635. By the late seventeenth century, the Randolphs and the Ishams, Marshall's two matriarchal clans, both well landed and into colonial politics in a big way, had intermarried. Tenuous as it may have been, the Marshalls were tied together in the same large family web with the Lees (Henry and eventually Robert E.), the Randolphs (all over the political map), and the Jeffersons (including Marshall's lifelong nemesis, his second cousin Thomas).

Thomas Marshall made the most of his income as a surveyor and land agent for the British Lord Fairfax, whose holdings, based on a royal bequest, of more than five million acres covered about a fourth of the current boundaries of Virginia and a good portion of West Virginia. Fairfax picked what he considered the most beautiful part of his realm, the Shenandoah Valley estate of Greenway Court, as his principal home. What made Fairfax unusual, and perhaps made Virginia more attractive than the other colonies, is that he was the only person of English peerage to make his home in the colonies.

Fairfax routinely served as a mentor of sorts to Washington and Marshall—and no doubt others in his employ. He had a large library, most of which he brought over from England, and a lot of intellectual capital in the relative backwoods of Virginia, having studied at the premier college of the English-speaking world, Oxford. Thomas Marshall, who at least had a modicum of schooling in his youth, gravitated to Fairfax's library when he was at Greenway Court, and Fairfax encouraged that.[5]

Thomas Marshall had more status than money when his first child John was born, and the details of his life are fairly robust because the younger Marshall became someone of note. In actuality, several of the fifteen children Thomas sired did well, and, unusually for the age, all reached adulthood. The Founders must have been aware that they were doing something of significance, since so many of them saved their papers and correspondence back even before the United States was on firm ground. Thus, when we have a peek at the Founders' forebears, like Thomas Marshall, we may get a skewed idea of what became the United States in the previous generation. We know much more of what we do about Washington's and Jefferson's and Marshall's fathers because of the sons' remembrances than we do from contemporaneous accounts.

The Founders' families tended to be more well off and of status than the average family, at least by mid-eighteenth-century standards. Many of their fathers owned a considerable amount of land, supplemented by fruitful marriages to women whose lines were equal, and often greater, in wealth and status. Thomas Marshall had at least twenty-two hundred acres during John's early childhood, for example. Few Founders started penniless and without resources—even Alexander Hamilton, who was born out of wedlock in Nevis in the Caribbean, had "sponsors" who got him through to college at King's (later Columbia) College and a push on his way.

So John Marshall was, too, a beneficiary of his father's relative wealth, and certainly status as a favorite of Lord Fairfax and a willing conscript into military service. As the oldest son, he was destined to inherit if not all the land, at least the prestige of the Virginia Marshall clan. What the younger Marshall got most from his father, though, was the can-do frontier spirit. In the late eighteenth century, just the idea of being in America meant that those there had taken a chance, a flyer on a different kind of future. The first explorers and settlers in the seventeenth century were adventurous, to be sure, but many had come to escape persecution and did not have a good idea of what they might accomplish.

By the time of John Marshall's birth, America was balancing between stability and adventure. There were governments, colonial and local, with ordinances and rules, but they were as fluid as the population, which always seemed to be in motion. There was a little more than a century of history in the colonies, but little of precedent. New ideas abounded. Where it was dangerous, the colonists looked to see how they could make their homes safer. There were hundreds of microclimates and soil variations, so new crop methods, and certainly new crops, took hold. Roads were hacked through woodlands and streams bridged and dammed. Disease was rampant, but so was the search for cures.

Land, though, was what could cure most things. If this parcel would not work, well, maybe the next one would. Too much rock to plow through? No matter, just over that ridge might be pliable soil. George Washington and Thomas Marshall did not just take up surveying and hope to have a lifelong business in the profession. They looked through their instruments to the lands just beyond their clients' properties. Out there, Washington and Marshall saw their futures, and it was in land, plenty of it. They may not have known exactly where the American continent ended, but they were sure there was plenty of it for themselves and their progeny. If Lord Fairfax could have five million acres, surely there would be a few thousand for the Washingtons and the Marshalls.

Even in the cities there was land to be had. The largest of the colonial cities, Philadelphia, had but forty thousand residents, most of them crowded into a mile-square area hugging the Delaware River. Ben Franklin, for instance, perpetrated his famed lightning experiment on what is now 12th Street, only a mile from the Delaware.[6] What would become Central Park—central now on Manhattan Island—was far off to the north, and Breed's Hill, the site of the first great battle of the Revolutionary War—known to later generations as Bunker Hill—now firmly in the downtown part of the city, was exurban Boston then.

There was little thought of how military careers might advance colonists' destinies, though, and only after the war with France progressed over the Atlantic in the form of the so-called French and Indian War, did they even become a real possibility. The military had been the provenance of the British shipped in from abroad. If there were rebellions to quell, expeditions to be made, or protection to be fostered, it was generally British regulars, trained in Europe and sailed over for the duty. It is not that there were no militias or people ready to defend themselves from such threats as Indian raids, but there was no hierarchy, no major general's post to get to, no ongoing uniformed career structure.

After Washington's strategic retreat—one of many he would have in the next couple of decades as a military commander—and the reports of his militia's valor in western Pennsylvania following the British army's disaster there, there was a shift among at least a certain group of men. Not only did it seem there would be a need for more local military with a knowledge of the countryside, but the idea that the British soldiers were invincible was crushed. Further, there was the inkling of an idea that maybe, just maybe, the colonists could, and should, have more self-rule.

Thomas Marshall realized this early on, and his devotion to Washington solidified his belief that at best, there needed to be some kind of militia at the ready, either in case the colonies wanted some kind of break from the mother country, or at least needed to have better security from outside enemies, be they European powers or Native Americans. His eldest son, John, thus became equally interested in this kind of future for himself.

Despite Thomas Marshall's true attempts at erudition, especially in Lord Fairfax's library, he apparently gave little thought to his eldest son's opportunities for formal schooling. The young Marshall had been enamored of his father's friend Washington, presumably because Thomas Marshall admired him so. Formal schooling, though, at least in the hinterlands, was understood to be difficult, so the lack of it was not disqualifying in early American elite circles. Even the two great Renaissance men of the founding age, Ben Franklin and Thomas Jefferson, were pretty much self-taught, if ultimately curious.

When his good friend, Supreme Court justice Joseph Story, was writing a review of John Marshall's book, *History of the Colonies*, in 1827, Marshall acquiesced to giving Story a few autobiographical notes, such as he could remember. His father, Marshall said, always wanted to improve himself, and was not going to allow his eldest son to stray from that proscription.

"He superintended my education, and gave me an early taste for history and poetry. At the age of twelve I had transcribed Pope's *Essay on Man*, with some of his *Moral Essays*," wrote Marshall to Story.[7]

Thomas sent his son about one hundred miles away to Washington Parish for a year when he was fourteen to study with Reverend Archibald Campbell—he met James Monroe there—and then brought in the new pastor of the local church to live with the family for a year, tutoring John and his siblings. When that was over, Marshall told Story, "I continued my studies with no other aid than my dictionary. My father superintended the English part of my education, and to his care I am indebted for anything valuable which I may have acquired in my youth. He was my only intelligent companion; and was both a watchful parent and an affectionate friend." Marshall called his contemporary friends "entirely uncultivated" and their time together was mostly athletic and not intellectual.

By the time John Marshall was born, though, Thomas had clearly established himself as a substantial force in Fauquier County. There were no Jeffersons, Randolphs, or Washingtons to compete with him there, but nonetheless Marshall made the most of the absence of that kind of competition. He became sheriff and tax collector, which was one and the same, and divided the county into its initial tax districts. He got to keep a portion of the tax receipts, slowly and incrementally increasing his finances, most of which he plowed back into land purchases. He became the county's first magistrate and was elected to the House of Burgesses, serving there until the Revolutionary War.

Thomas and Mary Marshall had eight girls and seven boys, none of whom died in childhood, a remarkable feat anywhere in the world in the eighteenth century, but even more so in the rural mountain reaches of North America, where there was scant, if any, formal medicine practiced. Several cousins, including future Kentucky senator Humphrey Marshall, who married John's second sister Mary, also did well. Among the other Marshall children, James married the daughter of wealthy Founding

Father (until he lost money in speculation) Robert Morris; Lewis was a doctor who became president of Washington (now Washington and Lee) College; Alexander and Thomas became prominent lawyers; and several of the daughters married into money and/or political fame.

Marshall often said his mother, who was only eighteen when she started having all these children, taught him the basis of good character: "If the agency of the mother in forming the character of her children is, in truth, so considerable as I think it—if she does so much toward making her son what she would wish him to be—how essential is it that she should be fitted for the beneficial performance of these important duties."

That John Marshall spent a lot of his educational adolescence copying Alexander Pope's essays and poems would not have been unusual even in the American frontier. Pope, though he died in 1744, was the most revered writer of his age in England, a sort of bridge between Shakespeare, an edition of whose work Pope edited, and the Romantics—a master of satire, long-form poetry, and translation. Thus, if there were one book, in addition to the Bible, most likely on the shelves of a colonist, it would probably have been a collection of Pope. The patricians also were Pope-a-holics. George Washington, for instance, had a six-volume set of Pope's writing, and Ben Franklin would get editions regularly from Philadelphia publishers.

By the time Marshall was eighteen, though, his father decided his family's prominence should be outwardly displayed, so Thomas built a house he called Oak Hill—with seven rooms certainly the largest one for miles around—on seventeen hundred acres he bought next to North Cobbler Mountain ten miles farther northwest from their former, already remote, smaller home. It was said to have the first glass windows in the area and was the house viewed by the Marshall clan as the family's ancestral home.

Within mere months, though, John Marshall ceased to view his life as study and athletics, Revolutionary fever burning within him.

"The controversy between Great Britain and her colonies had assumed so serious an aspect as almost to monopolize the attention of the old and the young," Marshall told Story many years later. "I engaged in it with all the zeal and enthusiasm which belonged to my age . . . [concentrating more on] learning the first rudiments of military exercise in an Independent company of the gentlemen of the county, to training a militia company in the neighborhood, and to the political essays of the day, than to the classics."[8]

Virginia was the largest colony both by physical size and population, but most of it was rather rural. It was split mostly along the lines of the cash crop, tobacco. Those who grew it, primarily in the Tidewater region, were more dependent on England and, frankly, were far more like the gentry in the old country. They were primarily Anglican and almost entirely from England itself originally. The markets for both their tobacco going out and the slaves coming in to tend it were English traders. Their land debt was from British banks, but their economic rules and political mindsets were based on English norms.

More often than not, votes in the House of Burgesses, the representative legislative body of the colony, would follow what was good for the planter class. At best, the other Burgesses had some popular men—like George Washington and George Mason—but the opposition was more diffuse and remote, given the effort it took just to get around their own county, let alone to the capital. It was not until a young representative from Louisa County, an upland area, claimed his place in the House of Burgesses that things started to change. Soon thereafter, that young man, Patrick Henry, personally took on the Tidewater oligarchy, which had tried to set up a loan fund primarily to help plantation scions gain footing. Henry convinced his outlander colleagues, and a few conscientious Tidewater types, to defeat the measure by one vote.

When, later in the spring of 1765, news of the Stamp Act, the tax the British Parliament put on newspapers and some other products, basically to pay for the military protection in the colonies, got to Williamsburg, Henry was ready to strike again. On May 24, 1765, his own twenty-ninth birthday, Henry made the first serious resolutions of colonial independence, saying that the House of Burgesses, not Parliament, had the "sole exclusive right and power to lay taxes ... upon the inhabitants of this colony." He then gave the first of what would become decades of rousing speeches, the kind for which Mason, no slouch himself in the oratorical realm, called Henry "by far the most powerful speaker I have ever heard."[9]

His voice changing timbre from moment to moment, he came finally to his full throat: "Tarquin and Caesar had each his Brutus. Charles the First, his Cromwell. George the Third ..." and the Speaker of the House, John Robinson, a Tidewater leader, shouted, "Treason! Treason!" Henry, though, hesitated only for effect and looked squarely at Robinson, "—may profit by their example. If this be treason, make the most of it."

A landmark peroration, yes, but only barely. Henry again won his measure by just one vote, but a win was a win. Thomas Jefferson, then a law student at William & Mary College up the street, was said to have been listening to the vote from the House doorway. Peyton Randolph, his and Marshall's cousin, but then the king's attorney, was quoted by Jefferson as lamenting, "By God, I would have given five hundred guineas for a single vote."

From then on, though, the House of Burgesses turned mainly defiant of Parliament and the king. By 1774, Peyton Randolph was a member of the Virginia delegation to the Continental Congress in Philadelphia and the hope of the Tidewater planters was not a renewed British takeover, but merely a compromise settlement.

When the rumblings of battle came to Massachusetts in 1775, Virginia was a ready seconder. As Marshall wrote later, the skirmishes at Lexington and Concord, "however trivial in itself, was the commencement of a long and obstinate war, and had no inconsiderable influence on that war, by increasing the confidence the Americans felt in themselves."

The House of Burgesses called itself into a special session in Richmond, much closer to the upcountry members. Henry put forth a motion: "That this colony be immediately put into a state of defence." It won only by sixty-five to sixty, showing again that what later generations seem to have assumed a landslide was close to being the other way. Even then, most Burgesses were willing to wait and see where things were going. That is, until Henry rose to speak.

"What is it that gentlemen wish? What would they have?" he said rhetorically. "Is life so dear, or peace so sweet, as to be purchased at the price of chains and slavery? Forbid it, Almighty God! I know not what course others may take, but as for me, give me liberty, or give me death."

Though there is no transcript of Henry's words, they were generally believed to be so, and in any case, the effects were everlasting. John Marshall later said his father, in the House of Burgesses at the time, called it "one of the most bold, vehement, and animated pieces of eloquence that had ever been delivered."

Albert Beveridge, an early Marshall biographer, said even in Henry's early days, the young Marshall hung on his father's relating of the orator's skills. "The heart of his son thrilled, we may be sure, as he listened to his father reciting Patrick Henry's words of fire and portraying the manner, appearance, and conduct of that master orator of liberty. So it was that John Marshall, even when a boy, came into direct and living touch with the outside world."[10]

Beveridge then paints a mythic scene of coming home to Oak Hill after Henry's speech and the passage of the militia bill.

"He knew that it meant war; and he also knew what war meant," Beveridge writes. "The same decision that made him cast his vote for Henry's resolutions also caused Thomas Marshall to draw his sword from its scabbard. It inspired him to do more; for the father took down the rifle from its deerhorn bracket and the hunting knife from its hook, and placed them in the hands of his first born. And so we find father and son ready for the field and prepared to make the ultimate argument of willingness to lay down their lives for the cause they believed in."[11]

CHAPTER TWO

Marshall Becomes a Revolutionary and a Sense of Time and Distance

LIKE A MODERN DAD TEACHING HIS SON THE RUDIMENTS OF SWITCH-hitting in baseball or the proper spin on a basketball jump shot, Thomas Marshall started instructing his son, John, in the art of warfare.

When the call came for volunteers in Virginia in May 1775, young Marshall was eager to join up. When the presumed lieutenant did not show up at the first muster, Marshall, whose father's training was known, was appointed lieutenant instead. The nineteen-year-old Marshall started teaching the volunteers, many younger than he. They were mostly simple drills—moving a rifle around and marching in unison.

He seemed the right guy to be a leader among youths. He was tall for his era, perhaps six feet or a little more, but walked erect, so his thin body was not as apparent. He had a big face and a ruddy complexion, with "raven black" hair and intense eyes. He had brought clothes so no one could doubt his identification—a purple hunting shirt, and pants of the same color fringed in white. His hat was a simple round black one, except he had attached a buck's tail to it for effect.

In that first command of sorts, he drilled the company for a time and then asked them that if they wanted to hear more about what had already transpired in the war to gather around him and he would tell them in the form of a speech—that form, to be sure, in the style he had heard his father describe as Patrick Henry's. Biographer Albert J. Beveridge is a bit melodramatic, but he tries to capture the young Marshall in his first semi-military phase.[1]

"Lively words they were, we may be sure, for John Marshall was as ardent a patriot as the colonies could produce," writes Beveridge. "He had learned the elementary truths of liberty in the school of the frontier. His soul was on fire with the burning words of Henry. And he poured forth his immature eloquence not to a company of peaceful theorists, but to a group of youths read for the field. Its premises were freedom and independence. Its conclusion was action."[2]

In his youth Marshall was ultra-competitive when it came to athletics. Like a colonial era Jim Thorpe, he challenged anyone, particularly other soldiers his age, to contests. He felt all throughout that this kept his charges both fit and in good spirits. He was often the fastest of the young recruits in sprints, but also, incongruously, had the patience and hand-eye coordination to be a quoits savant. (Quoits is a horseshoe-like game, save that the things thrown are circular with a hole in the middle.) He also reveled in being a master tumbler and, thus, a high-jump champ, for which he was later, under Washington's command at Valley Forge, nicknamed Silver Heels.[3]

By fall, Patrick Henry had been put in charge of all Virginia militias and the British governor, Lord Dunmore, had taken to retreat from Williamsburg, primarily in the largest city in the state, Norfolk. Henry called the Marshalls' unit to march across the state to see what could be gained. Though Dunmore offered freedom to enslaved Blacks if they would enlist with the British, he ended up retreating anyway, and had Norfolk burned to the ground after a short skirmish with the Virginians, at what was sometimes called the Battle of Little Bunker Hill nearby.

By March 1776, there seemed little fighting ahead, at least in Virginia, so Henry released the Culpepper Minute Men, as the group came to be called, and the Marshalls headed for home, at least temporarily.[4]

Soon enough, though, Revolutionary Fever infected anew. The Virginia legislature installed Thomas Marshall as major of the Third Virginia Regiment. By July 30, 1776, his son John, barely twenty-one years old, became a lieutenant in his father's troop. The Marshalls now were no longer backwoodsmen, their jaunty bucktails and fringes almost de rigeur, but soldiers in the Continental army, buff and blue uniformed with three-cornered formal hats, and swords and pistols rather than scalping knives.[5]

Marshall and his men marched for several weeks and finally got to serve with Washington as he circled just west of Philadelphia, then held by the British, with a ragtag army, many of whom did not even have firearms, and many of whom were ill clothed. By the late summer of 1777, Washington's choices were becoming limited. He would either have to try to take Philadelphia quickly, or establish some line in vague proximity to the city, set up a winter camp, and try to restock both in manpower and supplies.

The Marshalls were faithful to Washington. All letters and journals during this period—and to be sure, much of their lives—find Washington a hero, even when he is beaten in battle.

"As must ever be the case in new-raised armies, unused to danger and from which undeserving officers have not been expelled, their conduct was uniform. Some regiments, especially those which had served the preceding campaign, maintained their ground with the firmness and intrepidity of veterans, while others gave way as soon as they were pressed,"[6] wrote Marshall after the standoff at Brandywine, his first real battle experience under Washington. He was praising units that Washington had had a chance to drill and form, and hoping that newer soldiers would eventually be able to say the same. He then noted that Washington had to rally these men while they were ill prepared.

"Many of their muskets were scarcely fit for service; and being of unequal caliber, their cartridges could not be so well fitted, and consequently, their fire could not do as much execution as that of the enemy," wrote Marshall in the wake of Brandywine, noting that Washington kept the troops "in good spirits," even as he announced plans for retreat.[7]

The Continental Congress, having fled Philadelphia and landed in York, about fifty miles west, had hoped Washington would mount an attack to get the capital back, which he did by way of Germantown, the northwestern part of the city. They managed to take a large stone house, Cliveden, and set up an encampment around it, but it turned out to be a disaster, as the British burned fields around it and the subsequent smoke and fog caused the troops that couldn't escape to be trapped.

Washington surmised that he could not afford another loss, which most certainly would have happened had he tried to move farther into Philadelphia. It was time to rest, find some high ground, start rounding up food and supplies from farmers allied with the revolutionaries, and see what funds the Congress could come up with.[8]

Unfortunately, that "high ground" was in a place called Valley Forge.

On December 19, 1777, Washington, after consulting his staff officers, led his mobile city of twelve thousand into the outskirts of the mill town of Valley Forge, about twenty miles west of Philadelphia. Snow had not yet fallen—it was still technically autumn—and the idea was to build log cabins to house the residents. Rather quickly, the troops built as many as fifteen hundred cabins, most fairly solid, if dark and without windows. Some dug in the earth a couple of feet so that more building above was unnecessary. All seemed set for rest and rejuvenation, if not exactly home-like comforts.

There has been much hyperbole, and a lot of inaccuracy, surrounding the dangers and weariness of that winter of 1777-78 at Valley Forge. Not that it was a lounging time on the beach in the Caribbean, but it was a far more typical wintering in place than the bleak enumerations of death and despair Americans have heard of since even its time.

Despite the name, the encampment at Valley Forge was on a high ground, above the Schuylkill River, which ran nearby. Thus, it was a good, if ultimately unnecessary, place to observe British military maneuvers, had they had any. There had already been a quartermaster's depot there, and armaments and other supplies were housed in and around the forges. In the fall, Washington dispatched troops under two Founding-Fathers-to-be, Alexander Hamilton and Henry "Light Horse Harry" Lee, to evacuate the supplies if the British got too close. Unfortunately, a British brigade mounted a surprise attack on September 19, stealing some supplies, but mostly just setting the forges and armaments on fire.[9]

Still, Washington had hopes that replenishment would come as the winter progressed. He set up smaller encampments in other places within striking distance of Philadelphia. About two thousand troops were housed in Wilmington, Delaware, to the south, and the mounted troops went to Trenton along the Delaware River north of Philadelphia. There were also troops in nearby Radnor, a bit down the road toward Philadelphia, and Downingtown, to the south. The hopes were that the rather well-off farmers in those two towns would trade food and building materials with Washington's troops.

The twelve thousand to settle at Valley Forge—making it the fourth largest city in the country—were not just soldiers. Wives of the soldiers were encouraged to come and about four hundred did, earning some money for laundering and tailoring the clothes of nearby townsfolk as well as troops, and were particularly vital as nurses to the sick at the camp. There were a few dozen children housed there, as well as craftsmen to help build the huts and repair the firearms.

Still, disaster struck early, in the form of not being able to get enough food. The land around was hilly and not particularly good for growing such vegetables as tomatoes, onions, and some other more popular crops. Two days before Christmas, Washington wrote that there was "not a single hood of any kind to slaughter, and not more than twenty-five barrels of flour." A typical breakfast became "firecakes," with soggy dough cooked over a strong fire.[10]

Most of the dead at Valley Forge—there could have been upwards of fifteen hundred—were from disease, not starvation or exposure. Supplies were at a premium, but food was not completely unavailable and was severely rationed. Washington had chosen Valley Forge for its high ground and river access, but the winter roads made transport, especially of food and clothing, uneven at best, and unavailable sometimes for a couple of weeks at a time.

On January 7, for instance, Christopher Marshall, no relation, an émigré from Dublin who kept an extensive diary during the war, wrote about "ten teams of oxen, fit for slaughtering, came into camp, driven by loyal Philadelphia women. They also brought two thousand shirts, smuggled from the city, sewn under the eyes of the enemy."[11]

Perhaps the women could smuggle the supplies out of the city because the British occupiers and local loyalists were too busy living the high life. Philadelphia, though occupied, was not leveled by either army and retained its reputation as the most luxurious city, short of London, in the empire. The City Tavern sponsored balls on a regular basis. A few blocks away, the South Street Theater was a see-and-be-seen artistic venue. The Indian Queen, a gourmand's paradise, had all-night dinners often.

"You can have no idea of the life of continued amusement I live in," wrote Rebecca Franks, a Tory, to the beleaguered wife of a Revolutionary. "I can scarce have a moment to myself. I spent Tuesday evening at Sir William Howe's, where we had a concert and a dance. . . . You would have an opportunity of raking as much as you choose at Plays, Balls, Concerts and Assemblies. I have been but three evenings alone since we moved to town."[12]

Whatever paucity there was twenty miles away at Valley Forge, there was little but full larders in Philadelphia. There was so much cheese, it could not all be used. All the parties had copious wine and other liquors. Farmers from miles around were all too happy to supply the British occupiers, and since they were mostly of English descent, they hated the war anyway, and if it had to be, they were on the Tory side. Many, to be sure, also knew what the Americans were doing in their camps and were all too willing to share the information.

As bad as those who stuck it out at Valley Forge had it, the prisoners under guard in Philadelphia were not exactly partaking in the party scene there. The British were harsh with their captives. One account, perhaps a little overwrought, had a prisoner "drove to the last extreme by the rage of hunger, eat his own fingers up to the first joint from the hand, before he died. Others eat the clay, the lime, the stones, of the prison walls. Several who died in the yard had pieces of bark, wood, clay and the stones in their mouths."[13]

There were some sympathetic neighbors for the encampment, though. The Moravians, a German sect which had settled primarily in and near Bethlehem, north of Valley Forge, were Christian socialists, and were willing Samaritans fairly unanimously in favor of independence. A lot of the sick soldiers were transported to the colony, especially for dysentery. "A violent putrid fever," wrote Marshall, who lost three dozen of his regiment to the disease, "swept off much greater numbers than all the diseases of the camp."[14]

Marshall took it upon himself to be the uplifting spirit among the officers at Valley Forge. He was only twenty-two years old, but then there were a lot of militia officers not much older than that. His name appears in several journals and diaries of soldiers written at the time and from memory afterwards.

"If he only had bread to eat," wrote Lieutenant Philip Slaughter, often a messmate of Marshall's, "it was just as well. If only meat, it made no difference. If any of the officers murmured at their deprivations, he would shame them by good-natured raillery, or encourage them by his own exuberance of spirits.... John Marshall was the best tempered man I ever knew."[15]

Sometimes he would pull pranks and often would make fun of himself. He had a pair of silk stockings, which one night burned because the leaves he had used as a pillow caught fire. He made fun of himself, just for having silk stockings in a camp where socks themselves were at a premium.

Beveridge, Marshall's most enthusiastic biographer, wrote that "Valley Forge was a better training for Marshall's peculiar abilities than Oxford or Cambridge could have been. His superiority was apparent, even to casual observers, notwithstanding his merriment and waggishness."[16]

One thing Marshall was apparently conflicted about during the winter in Valley Forge was Washington's harshness to insubordination. Washington ordered captured deserters to receive a hundred lashes, and even one time he ordered a woman to get the same lashing. Washington dismissed a lieutenant for eating with privates and buying a pair of shoes from one of them.

Yet he gave Washington a lot of leeway afterwards. Were it not for Washington staying on top of things—and not coincidentally not falling to illness—Marshall believed that the army would be defeated right then.

Washington, with no battles to fight, became the foresighted administrator. He wrote pleas to the Continental Congress with passion, and maybe some hyperbole, in their tone.

"We should all be considered, Congress and Army, as one people, embarked in one cause, in one interest," Washington wrote in the Valley Forge winter to the Congress. "No history extant can furnish an instance of an army's suffering such uncommon hardships . . . To see men without clothes to cover their nakedness, without blankets to lie on, without shoes, by which their marches might be traced by the blood from their feet, and almost as often without provisions as with them, marching through the frost and snow, and at Christmas taking up their winter quarters within a day's march of the enemy, without a horse or hut to cover them 'till they could be built, and submitting to it without a murmur, is proof of patience and obedience which in my opinion can scarce be paralleled."[17]

Meanwhile, he was working both to shore up his troops and get them ready for the spring's battles. Washington chose General Nathanael Greene, a rival for the top job, to become the quartermaster general, overseeing the vital need to find food, munitions, and clothing, wherever he could.

Then, almost at winter's end, Washington made a swift judgment of a man whom he knew little about, the flamboyant Prussian war veteran, Friedrich Wilhelm Ludolf Gerhard Augustin Von Steuben. Von Steuben had been an army brat, his family moving around central Europe as his father became the army engineer, building fortresses and the like in the pay of Empress Anna of Russia in the middle eighteenth century. Young Friedrich signed up for the Prussian army in 1747 at age fourteen. Von

Steuben moved up the ranks quickly during the Seven Years War, but when it was over in 1763, he was just another unemployed soldier.

Luckily, he met a German prince, Josef Friedrich Wilhelm, of the small state of Hohenzollern-Hechingen. Von Steuben's most important job was finding financing and loans to keep the state afloat. He and the prince were often in France, where a French count introduced him to Benjamin Franklin, thinking the Americans could use a soldier with strict Prussian military training. Unfortunately, Franklin told Von Steuben, the Continental Congress had little money to pay for his service, so Von Steuben politely declined.

When Von Steuben returned to Prussia, he was met with allegations that, during his service to Prince Josef, he had solicited homosexual relations with a number of young soldiers. He quickly escaped back to more libertine Paris, but the rumors dogged him there, too. The count, Claude Louis, now the French minister of war, got Franklin to write a letter of recommendation to Washington, exaggerating Von Steuben's credentials and making him a lieutenant general. By September 26, 1777, he and his secretary, three other potential recruits, and, to be sure, his Italian Greyhound Azor, left Marseilles, bound to find Washington, wherever he might be.

They landed in Portsmouth, New Hampshire, on December 1, 1777, and were immediately arrested as British soldiers, Von Steuben mistakenly having dressed them in red uniforms. When let free, they first made it to Boston, and then on to York, Pennsylvania, where the Congress had escaped when Philadelphia was taken by the British. He and Congress reached a compromise, that Congress would pay him after the war was over, commensurate with his service.

Von Steuben got to Valley Forge only in the late winter—February 23, 1777. Washington sized him up and, perhaps without other alternatives, made him inspector general, in charge of all camp arrangements and military training. It was part of Washington's list of genius moves.

Von Steuben was everywhere. He moved latrines away from soldiers' huts, and on a downhill slope, thwarting disease and unquenchable stench. He inspected every soldier's hut, clothing, and munitions, ordering upgrades where Greene could find them available. Officers and soldiers under their command moved huts to be near each other. Most importantly, he taught them Prussian drill, and even tried to make the haggard troops into showpieces. He formed an honor guard for Washington and would wear full military dress for two-a-day drill practices. Since he did not speak English, he would write down the drills in German, give them to his secretary to translate into French, and a soldier in the army would translate that in English for Washington each night, just in case he would want to change the drills for the next morning.[18]

Marshall was also ingratiating himself with the troops. As the weather started to get a little better, Marshall, always the competitor, arranged for games and sports among the men. He took it upon himself to try to rally the men both to be better physically and to have something to smile about. Quoits being a big at-home sport during the mid-eighteenth century, there were lots of team and individual matches. Then there was running and jumping, Marshall's own expertise.

One of his fellow officers wrote in his journal that Marshall could vault over a pole "laid on the heads of two men as high as himself." Marshall got a box of supplies from home, among its contents being socks, so he decided to run in stocking feet, showing off the whites of his heels to losing competitors. The soldiers nicknamed him "Silver Heels."[19]

By early May, the troops heard of the alliance between King Louis XVI of France and Congress, with men and munitions coming to America, and France pursuing hostilities with England more fervently abroad. It was not just news but a reason for celebration. Valley Forge filled with sounds of cannon fire, songs, sermons, and more enthusiastic marches and drills. Washington did not quell the enthusiasm, but he confided to his officers, Marshall among them, that he feared that Congress would not act to pay more for troops and supplies because the French additions would be enough—in fact, there was nothing coming from the legislature.

What did come was the British deciding to leave Philadelphia. Just before the Redcoats left the capital, there was one big blast of celebration.

Major John Andre, who would eventually be executed as a prisoner, recounted that flower-decked boats plied the Delaware, while soldiers paraded throughout the city. All sorts of theatrical and musical performances took place during the day and dancing was the order of the evening. At midnight, twelve hundred people had dinner, with slaves dressed in Oriental uniforms with silver collars and bracelets.

On June 18, the British started a quick march in the direction of New York. By that time, the Americans were ready to fight, and soon had caught up with the enemy in Monmouth, in the north central part of New Jersey.

Though it was just barely into summer, Marshall wrote of "the intense heat." One observer, full of hyperbole, described that Sunday of battle as "long remembered all over the United States as the most sultry day which had ever been endured since mankind learned to read the thermometer."[20]

Marshall was in the first wave of five thousand men commanded by Charles Lee. They advanced but soon fell into full retreat, Lee apparently fearing a death warrant in being first in. The remainder of the troops, commanded by Washington himself in full regalia on horseback, angrily turned Lee's forces around and charged the British. From ten in the morning until midnight, the battle continued, sometimes hand to hand. The Marquis de Lafayette, always enamored of Washington, was beyond his usual writing to Marshall of their hero at Monmouth:

"Never was General Washington greater in war than in this action. His presence stopped the retreat. His dispositions fixed the victory. His fine appearance on horseback, his calm courage, roused by the animation produced by the vexation of the morning, gave him the air best calculated to excite enthusiasm."[21]

The battle ceased at about midnight, and Washington himself lay with the troops among the fallen. Washington had hoped to continue the fight at daybreak, but when the sun rose, he found that the British had retreated. Though Marshall later wrote in his biography of Washington that he was disappointed to be in the troops who retreated under

Lee, he was invigorated under Washington. The victors had lost only sixty-nine dead, while the British left behind more than 250 on the battlefield.

Three days after the battle, the young Marshall was made a full captain, to go along with his role from Valley Forge as deputy judge advocate. For the next couple of years, Marshall stayed in New Jersey, in various battles won and lost. The storming of Verplanck's Point and Stony Point garrison along the eastern bank of the Hudson River was a futile mission in June 1779, but the assault on Powles Hook, a hill on the west side of the river, in which Captain Marshall also fought, brought a capture of 159 prisoners.

Soon after that, Marshall went home, his enlistment time finished. He did not fight again, though he lamented it at times as the war dragged on, often prominently in Virginia, not all that far from his home. He did back up some of the troops that invaded Virginia in January 1781, but when the British, commanded by the turncoat Benedict Arnold, got to Richmond, they burned some munitions, and just retreated along the James River.

Rather than being satisfied with his military exploits, Marshall became circumspect about how they proceeded. In his writings, he noted that when the fighting went from one state to another, soldiers from a "visiting" state often would not listen to orders given by a home-state officer. They noted that Congress would be slow to supply troops, if they supplied them at all, but when they were near home, residents would be anxious to meet their needs. Marshall was with the troops in their thought that the civil government did not understand the needs of the military, and Valley Forge's trials, without a battle, were also an argument in that regard.

Well before the war ended, though, Marshall himself would be part of that civil authority, and his life would pivot again.[22]

Amazingly the United States formed into a nation and thrived in its early years in spite of the sparseness of effective communication and the harshness and time-consuming nature of traveling just about anywhere.

Richard Henry Lee, for instance, objected to the Constitution's replacement of the Articles of Confederation not because he did not believe that type of government could survive, but he did not believe it could do so in a nation so large.

"Many citizens will be more than three hundred miles from the seat of this [national] government," he wrote in *Letters from the Federal Farmer.* "As many assessors and collectors of federal taxes will be above three hundred miles from the seat of the federal government as will be less."[23]

Lee and others had some measure of confidence that states were big enough to govern themselves, but even then, the hardships of travel to meet, make laws, and adjudicate them was a rough go.

The best road in Virginia in the 1790s was the one from Williamsburg, the former capital near the Atlantic coast, more or less paralleling the James River to the new capital of Richmond. It was only sixty-three miles, but even the speediest journey from point to point took two days—a trip that would be an hour today. Most travel of any distance was on horseback—only slaves actually walked—and there were few coaches, there being not that much call for them.

It is not as if riding those miles on horseback was any treat. Horses regularly broke down, and often died, negotiating the rocky and ill-groomed paths. Most every bridge in Virginia got quickly damaged, which meant fording streams, which sometimes the horse could not make, drowning itself and, often, the rider. Even if the riders tried to hew to the paths that were called "roads," they often reached dead ends, filled with forest.[24]

Of necessity, then, the men in the leadership of the early Congresses, executive branch, and judiciary had a certain amount of wealth, either to afford the means of getting to Philadelphia or being able not to work to make money. About half the contingent who came to the convention that wrote the Constitution in 1787 did not make it there on the specified date. Some did come in carriages—the road to Boston was the showpiece of those times, but even there, ruts caught carriages and the passengers were often called upon to push. And if they could not make it out, the only recourse was to wait until someone else came by to help out.

The bulk of the American population was along the coasts, and if not that, along major rivers like the Delaware, the Hudson, and the James. As late as the early nineteenth century, the largest inland city in the nation was Lancaster, Pennsylvania, with all of six thousand inhabitants.

Even state capitals like Richmond, thought to be ideal both along a river and in the center of Virginia, were ramshackle affairs. In 1782, two years after the capital moved from Williamsburg, Richmond still had fewer than two hundred homes and a year-round population of only twelve hundred. There were no paved streets, and the square where the yet-unbuilt Jefferson-designed capitol would stand—the assembly met in a small former warehouse—and gullies made even walking precarious. Domestic animals grazed there. The few taverns filled their upstairs with beds, smashed together side by side, and even then delegates pleaded for their shelter. No one left, save those who lived in or near town, for it would have taken days, and maybe weeks, to make the journey up and back.

Even more established cities were not all that tidy. In 1795, Talleyrand, the French statesman, who was then living in the United States, visited Baltimore and found that the buildings of what would be downtown "disputing the ground with trees whose stumps have not yet been removed." He found Philadelphia accommodating, but going inland was a major problem. "At less than a hundred and fifty miles distance from the Capital, all trace of men's presence disappeared; nature in all her primeval vigor confronted us. Forests old as the world itself; decayed plants and trees covering the very ground where they once grew in luxuriance."[25]

People who wanted to be remote, or just to have a slice of property, may not have seemed to worry about such things, but remote was truly that in the late eighteenth century. Even with crowded cities, the population of the country was fewer than five persons per square mile. The wheels of justice often rolled depending on distance. Beveridge cites humorously the rich Virginia planter who had a valuable horse stolen from him. Unfortunately, he lived 140 miles from Richmond, where the case would be heard. Everyone knew who the thief was, but the expense and time to go to Richmond was double the value of the horse, so the thief kept his prize.[26]

Almost all crops even in wealthy and innovative Virginia ended up having to be sold locally. Either the price of transport was prohibitive, as with tobacco, or would not have made it to market fresh, as with produce. Bears still inhabited most of the forests of British North America, so stopping to linger along the rough road was ill advised.

Communication itself was a sometime thing. It is a wonder that the patriots in Massachusetts could possibly know what was going on with their compatriots in Virginia. It took at least six days for a letter to get from Boston to New York. Even important folks like Jefferson and Madison had little luck, Madison noting in return mail—and not in irony—that a letter Jefferson had written him in 1794 reached from Monticello to Philadelphia in a mere nine days. Letters from Richmond to New York, when it became the first capital under the Constitution, often took two months to get there. New Yorkers only heard of Massachusetts ratifying the Constitution eight days after it had taken place.

Even more incredible is how folks like John Adams or Thomas Jefferson or even John Marshall, in his case of what would become the XYZ Affair in Paris, could communicate what was going on. John Jay tried to ask for orders while he was negotiating the peace treaty with the British, and he thought himself lucky that his letters home reached across the Atlantic in eight weeks. Sometimes, he noted, it could take five months for post to cross the sea—and four weeks would have been close to a record. The news of Washington's death, on December 14, 1799, did not reach his most prominent acolyte in the capital of Philadelphia, Marshall, until December 18, even with the fastest rider carrying the letter.

Even so, post generally came to proper settlements and cities. Postmasters regularly opened mail—some for sinister reasons, and others just hoping to read news from important people abroad. During the first year of the official government Post Office department, 1791, there were only eighty-nine post offices in the entire country. Even in the well-traveled and populated state of New Jersey there were only six post offices, and none south of Trenton.[27]

There were few newspapers, and even then, they were local to big cities, most being published, even if irregularly, in Philadelphia, Boston, or New York. Certainly they had the same problem of distribution—only four people of twelve hundred living in Ridgefield, Connecticut, subscribed to a newspaper. Virginia, the most prosperous and largest state, had only one newspaper in 1784, and it came out in Richmond only twice a week.

So those opened letters from postmasters were for the most part the source of news in the early republic—given the prejudices and supposed accuracy of the writer, much like following someone on social media in the twenty-first century.

Still, some places had better communications than others, and when they did not, some found a way to be cultivated on their own. Quaker farmers on the outskirts of Philadelphia still made black walnut furniture and were able to have linen the same quality as in the city. In Massachusetts, there were a lot of mill towns and others with nascent industry. Settlers farther away actually disdained "cultural" items. For them, the idea of being "rustic" was just the point of being in America. It took a long time for anyone to get to their doorsteps, but that is how they wanted it. America meant ultimate freedom. As Secretary of War Henry Knox wrote to Washington, they opposed the Constitution "from deadly principle levelled at the existence of all government whatever."[28]

Given the treacherous travel, any schooling at all was another luxury. Marshall barely had lessons from teachers—one year at a small boarding school and one year being tutored at home by a nascent minister. Most people, though, on the ridges of the Appalachians like the Marshalls, were simply educated at home in what was necessary, and often that meant manual labor, not Alexander Pope, Marshall's personal literary hero. Many landowners were illiterate, and others knew so little about science as to believe the Earth was flat. A century after it was founded, only thirty students were matriculating at William and Mary College, as Washington's term as president was winding down. Washington himself had had a magnificent career, and he was unschooled, so there was no real rush to expand the system.

Despite the obvious need for better infrastructure, little upgrading happened in the initial half-century of the nation. Henry Clay, from the time he was a young man getting into politics, pressed the need for roads and canals in and to his home state of Kentucky. For him, proper transportation trails were the key to expanding the economy and culture of the still-new nation. Those whom it might most benefit, those living in the now westward-moving interior, were none too high on the national government treading on their territory. Only a small fraction of those young adult males, unlike Marshall, saw service during the Revolutionary War, and were too busy just trying to get things done day to day to worry about the philosophical polemics, like *The Federalist Papers*, written by Hamilton, Madison, and John Jay, to promote support for the Constitution and the nation itself.[29]

Still, whatever improvements were to come, walking and horses were still the primary mode of transportation, until at least 1807, when the *Clermont*, Robert Fulton's steamboat, started making pilgrimages up and down the Hudson from New York to Albany. Even that took the better part of two days one way. The Erie Canal, which went from Albany to Buffalo, opened in 1825, but the first railroads went on line only in the early 1830s. Even then, most of the lines were short, and in the South especially, used only for freight. Sailing ships did ply ports on the Atlantic and Gulf coasts, but their use was problematic, dependent on the wind and other weather, so the passenger list was small as well.

It is worth remembering, too, that what moderns might consider "progress" was pretty slow even in the nineteenth century. Samuel Morse set up the first telegraph system between Baltimore and Washington in 1844, but a message could not have been sent from Atlantic to Pacific until 1861. The Pony Express, which ran for only eighteen months between

Missouri and California—most of that during the Civil War—still only got a piece of mail delivered in ten days. The transcontinental railway had to wait until after the Civil War in 1869—and even then went west only to Sacramento, where paddle steamers actually transported passengers to San Francisco.

So the federal government operated much more slowly and cautiously in its first century at least. Politics cleaved to that pace. There was no direct campaigning, for instance, for president—surrogates and pamphleteers did the talking for the man running. The Supreme Court often met only twice a year, and as few as a couple dozen cases met the scrutiny of the justices each of the early terms. Taxes were minor and collected almost entirely locally with no regular federal income tax until the Sixteenth Amendment passed in 1895.

The vastness of America was something not seen before—Russia and Canada were bigger in land mass, but much of that land was untenable or not populated, even by the equivalent of the American frontier families and Native Americans. It took a long time to get to here and there, to make friends with other like-minded folks in another state, or even to know what those people would be like or find important.

The boldness of America, then, is that it was the ultimate in seat-of-the-pants thinking. It did not have so much a ruling class as one in which everyone seemed to know everyone else. There was not always compromise, but there was grudging admiration, starting from those early days in Philadelphia. Happenstance in the way the city lay, mostly along the Delaware River and about a mile west from it, forced those men known as the Founding Fathers to actually meet each other daily in both social and professional manners. There were only so many boardinghouses or taverns at which to stay, and they were primarily within walking distance of the State House. Ben Franklin had numerous get-togethers at his house. The dirty water issues in Philadelphia forced taverns to serve a "breakfast beer," a somewhat lighter and smaller mug, so conviviality reigned even before the daily grind of country-making. It would have been hard to just slough off the guy from South Carolina or the young delegate from

Connecticut after drinking toasts with him from dawn to late-night. Letters from home came a couple weeks late, but gossip with a man whose interests were similar, with a glass of Madeira, was to be had easily.

American democracy, then, was not as much about winning the war, but being sane about the peace, a breakfast beer in hand, the silent majority otherwise minding their own business on the frontier.[30]

CHAPTER THREE

Marshall Moves up the Ladder in Virginia, and the World Shakes as America Comes to Be

WHEN JOHN MARSHALL LEFT THE ARMY AFTER HIS ENLISTMENT WAS up, he was at a loss where to go. He could always trundle back to Fauquier County and figure out something to do—maybe go into politics or become a surveyor like his father. While there was a bit of wanderlust, though, he decided to head to Yorktown—ironically where the war would end about three years hence—where his father had a small command assignment.

As he was coming there, stories swirled about him, especially among the young ladies and families who had young ladies in them. One of those families was the one headed by Jacquelin Ambler, formerly one of the richest men in Yorktown. His businesses, though, had failed him, and the family was now living in a small house, conveniently next door to Colonel Thomas Marshall's headquarters.

Ambler had a bit of history in the upper classes. His wife, Rebecca Burwell, stopped dating Thomas Jefferson to marry Ambler. Jefferson's letters are replete with mentions of her or allusions from literature about characters that reminded Jefferson of her.[1]

The Ambler daughters were, then, desirable belles, but since there were fewer men available, many having gone to the army, the idea of one coming to visit was enticing. They and their friends decided that there should be a ball for his benefit. Whatever young women and, mostly, army officers in town were on the invite list, none could compare to the young John Marshall, son of the esteemed colonel, hero of Brandywine and Germantown, Monmouth, and Valley Forge, who rode under General George Washington himself.

"Our expectations were raised to the highest pitch," wrote Eliza, the eldest Ambler sister in remembrance of the night. "The little circle of York was on tiptoe on his arrival. Our girls particularly were emulous who should be first introduced."[2]

Then, stunningly, the shy and somewhat sardonic Mary Ambler, not yet fourteen by a few weeks, told her sister, "we were giving ourselves useless trouble, for that she, for the first time, had made up her mind to go to the ball, though she had not even been at dancing school, and was resolved to set her cap at him and eclipse us all."[3]

When John Marshall arrived, though, hearts sank around the room. He was not the warrior knight of their dreams, but a gangly guy with a dubious hat and ill-fitting clothes. He was smart enough, but with only rural manners, and a bit shy.

"I, expecting an Adonis, lost all desire of becoming agreeable in his eyes when I beheld his awkward figure, unpolished manners, and total negligence of person," wrote Eliza Ambler in that letter.[4]

Mary Ambler, true to her word, set her wiles on Marshall, and he reciprocated, allegedly falling in love immediately, and resolved to stay on at Yorktown a while, on the pretense of helping his father. Not quite knowing how to handle his stay, the families of Yorktown all invited him for a meal or a visit and, to their surprise, they found him charming. His shyness belied his inner confidence, and he was always polite and charming, so much so that even his rural dress was no longer an issue.

Still, his main evening address was the Ambler home next to the command post. He would tell the teenaged Mary about the war, to be sure, and apparently, from her sister's letters, read poetry to her ad nauseam. He won over the rest of the Amblers, too.

"Under that slouched hat, there beamed an eye that penetrated at one glance the inmost recesses of the human character," wrote Eliza to her sister Nancy, perhaps a bit over the top. "Beneath the slovenly garb there dwelt a heart complete with every virtue. From the moment he loved my sister, he became truly a brother to me.... Our whole family became attached to him, and though there was then no certainty of his becoming allied to us, we felt a love for him that can never cease."[5]

Marshall signed up for the law lectures of George Wythe at William and Mary College, about twelve miles from Yorktown. Wythe was the premier teacher of law in Virginia, if not the entire new country. He also practiced law and was off and on involved in politics. Thomas Jefferson, Marshall's antagonist in later years—not to mention his second cousin— was one of those who studied with Wythe. Marshall was clearly a little older than most of the students, entering school as a twenty-four-year-old veteran in the spring of 1780. He was immediately elected to Phi Beta Kappa, the honorary scholastic excellence fraternity started at William and Mary. He was on the Phi Beta Kappa debate team and did a little moot court, a favorite project of Wythe.

By his notebook, though, it seems he was clearly attending William and Mary to be close to Yorktown. Over the pages of some of his lecture notes were scrawls, "Miss Maria Ambler," "Miss M. Ambler"; upside down "Miss M. Ambler—J. Marshall" and "John Marshall, Miss Polly Am"; then "John, Maria," "John Marshall, Miss Maria," and "Molly Ambler."[6] While Miss Ambler was by this time fourteen and maybe appropriately writing things like this, Marshall was nearing his twenty-fifth birthday. It was not entirely out of place to be courting a teenager, but it must have turned heads in Yorktown to have a man who had already seen life in battle to be so taken with someone just past puberty.

Still, that is the way it was for Marshall. He was not the kind to give up on a desire, in war, later the law, and now in love. As it happened, Jacquelin Ambler was made treasurer of the state of Virginia in early summer of 1780 and the family moved to Richmond. On the way, they stopped in Williamsburg and there was a ball given to celebrate. Marshall, to be sure, attended, and spent the entire time with Miss Ambler, whom he eventually called not Maria, but Polly.

That was that for George Wythe and William and Mary. Marshall headed off to Richmond and spent his first two weeks there with the Amblers. The prerequisites for the bar in Virginia had little to do with actually studying the law, but more about who would sign a license. In this case, it was the governor, Thomas Jefferson, certainly not knowing of the antagonism between the cousins that was to come in the decades ahead. Marshall went back to his home in Fauquier County and was admitted to the bar on August 28, 1780, a whirlwind of a life in early America in just a few months. Marshall still thought he might get command of some troops, but by 1781, he gave up and looked to the law.[7]

During this time, though, he did something that added to the Marshall myth. He had decided to get inoculated for smallpox. The way of getting inoculated in Virginia was complex—neighbors for two miles around had to consent to it happening—so Marshall went off to Philadelphia. By foot.

Marshall claimed that he covered the route in thirty-five miles a day. This would be a decent journey on the modern roads of the twenty-first century. It would be next to impossible in the late eighteenth century, when infrastructure, especially in western Virginia, but even just outside any big city, was vague at best. Often going a few miles in a day, given brush and rocks and fording streams, was a triumph. If Marshall did do his trek in the time he alleged, it still would have taken seven days.

The myth goes on to say that when he reached Philadelphia and went to a tavern, with his long beard and disheveled clothes, he was denied entrance. When he appeared later in Philadelphia as a congressman and secretary of state, he would go to the tavern and remind the proprietors of their error nearly twenty years before.[8]

Still, however it worked out, Marshall got his inoculation and hurried back to figure how he would next pursue Miss Ambler.

He decided his next move in courting Ambler was to run for a seat in the House of Delegates from Fauquier County and be part of the legislature in Richmond. The Marshall name still held sway in Fauquier out west and by 1782, Marshall was elected and became a new member of the Virginia legislature.

Within two months of his installation in Richmond, on January 3, 1783, John Marshall was wed to Mary Willis Ambler: she, sixteen and he, now twenty-seven. Thomas Marshall gave the couple their first slave and three horses, and soon took the rest of his family off to Kentucky, allegedly on the advice of George Washington, acquiring some land, and staying there the rest of his life in comfort.[9]

John Marshall was now ready to set himself up as a lawyer in the capital. Richmond, from Eliza Ambler's letters, was a bit of a Potemkin village—the capital in name, but a rough-hewn place to say the least. No home windows had curtains, no streets were paved or had sidewalks. Not even Main Street was paved, so it was dusty when it was dry and so muddy when it rained that wagons often could not ply it. Even a small stream crossed Main Street. There were no brick or stone buildings, and the Capitol itself was little more than a barn. There was one church and only one tavern, owned by an Italian immigrant, with two rooms downstairs and two up, so accommodations for the visiting legislators were commonly in private homes. Good liquor was available, and visitors were often well heeled, so everyone had ample funds to drink, play cards, and carouse.[10]

Marshall began keeping an account book soon after arrival in Richmond, and it shows he had a hard time earning money for his first year there in 1783. In fact, he earned more gambling on whist and backgammon than lawyering. He clearly tried to keep expenses low, buying oats and coal by the bushel and keeping his and Polly's wardrobes spare. He did buy rum and wine in the fall—which was not at all unusual all over America, where alcohol had replaced water as the drink of choice—and even bought a cow in January 1784. He recorded payment for his "service in the Assembly": more than thirty-four pounds by July 5, 1784. By August, their first child was born, inducing more expenses, and that summer Marshall also bought what appears to be at least five slaves, perhaps some for specific services and not permanent.[11]

His law practice grew in the proportions that might have been expected, with some good fees and some paltry. He also made new friends, some to be important as time went on. One was a young man of twenty-two who emigrated from Switzerland in 1784, Albert Gallatin, who would eventually become secretary of the treasury under Virginians Thomas Jefferson and James Madison. Marshall had a liking for Gallatin and took him into his office without charging him. Gallatin later characterized Marshall as "almost at the head of the bar in 1786,"[12] after only three years in practice.

By 1786, Marshall had enough of a reputation that his cases were big enough to get reports in the ledger of the Virginia Court of Appeals. The first was his defense of lands that were originally in the hands of his father's benefactor, Lord Fairfax. Such cases would consume a lot of his time throughout his legal career, and he became a specialist in them, sometimes getting land as payment. It was also in this first case that he argued against Virginia's attorney general Edmund Randolph, whom he would cross paths with many times—when Randolph was governor of Virginia; during the deliberations on whether Virginia would accept the US Constitution; as the first US attorney general; and most famously when Randolph defended Aaron Burr at Burr's treason trial in front of Marshall in the Richmond circuit court in 1807.

In the meantime, Marshall spent what time he needed to in the legislature. Despite the reputations the legislators had later, or at the time in some cases, it was a disorganized, not an august, body.

Several times, two of its most prominent members, Thomas Jefferson and Patrick Henry, had to be corralled by men of the sergeant at arms and delivered to Richmond because they deemed the sessions less valuable than what they were doing at home.[13] James Madison was forever fed up with his colleagues. In July of 1784, Madison wrote to Jefferson, who had recently gone to France as a diplomat, that things had become chaotic at best.

"Nothing can exceed the confusion which reigns throughout our revenue department," wrote Madison. "This confusion indeed runs through all of our public affairs, and must continue as long as the present mode of legislating continues."[14]

A letter to George Washington two years later, just as the Constitution was being debated, proved to Madison nothing had changed in his home state.

"The proceedings of the Assembly are, as usual, rapidly degenerating with the progress of the session," he wrote to Washington. "Our Assembly has been ... employed ... chiefly in rectifying some of the mistakes of the last, and committing new ones for emendations at the next."[15]

Marshall liked his colleagues more than Madison did. As early as 1783, he could see the light, writing to a friend: "It is surprising that Gentlemen of character cannot dismiss their private animosities, but will bring them in the Assembly."[16]

Nonetheless, Marshall refused to shy away from any position he could find. He was on several committees, but most importantly, he was on what was called the Council of State. He came to the Assembly with good lineage, his father having been a member and his father-in-law, Jacquelin Ambler, being state treasurer. Not many twenty-seven year olds were members of this almost invulnerable body, made up mostly of judges and long-term representatives.

The Council had eight members elected by the legislature, who did not have to have been in the elected body. It served as the governor's Cabinet, so Marshall was both in the legislative and executive end of things. The Council approved the governor's appointments, and he consulted with it on all other executive matters. It was first run by Patrick Henry and then Thomas Jefferson, so its methods were perfected by supple minds. Marshall got to know the real run of government, from appointing surveyors to business inspections to making sure justices of the peace were helping make every outpost in the state secure.

After two years, Marshall resigned from the Council but ran again for the legislature and won from Fauquier. Marshall was one of those late members to get to Richmond, and so the sergeant-at-arms had orders to take him into custody—corralling him and four other legislators, seating them in their places, and charging them a fine as well. Sardonic viewers today may like this idea enough to advocate for its institution in Congress and state legislatures, who seem to often have a lot of empty seats.

———

The inefficiencies Marshall and Madison found in the Virginia government were not unusual around the new nation. Each state had its own way of doing things, and most of that was crude, chaotic, or both. The routing of the British at Yorktown to end the war itself was a celebratory moment, but then most families had to get back to their business.

The states made an attempt to align, with the Articles of Confederation and a legislature meeting in Philadelphia, but there always seemed to be a large federal bill unpaid, needs unmet, and frustration all around. The Congress could not require states to pay their share of the governmental expenses, and legislators came and went home as their needs came about. "The treasury is empty, though the country abounds in resources, and our people are far more unwilling than unable to pay taxes," wrote John Jay to John Adams in early 1787.[17] Government was disdained, if not altogether disregarded. The Shays Rebellion, the attack of a band of local men in central and eastern Massachusetts to shut down courts and perhaps stoke an armed conflict to overthrow the federal government, scared even staunch federalists like John Adams.

Finally, almost out of desperation, several of the more foresighted statesmen called for a convention to be held in Philadelphia to revamp the Articles of Confederation. As the spring presumed start date of the convention came closer, it became apparent that the convention would seek a wider path, that if the nation were going to survive intact, there needed to be something greater than a mere confederation. Thus, the Constitutional Convention met in the spring and summer of 1787, its delegates forming and signing the grand compromise document in the space of four months of largely secret deliberations.

Having stood down from the Virginia legislature for a term, attending to his law practice, Marshall became energized again as the convention was meeting in Philadelphia and was elected for the fall 1787 term to the Virginia legislature. It took some time for the Virginians to come to the point of figuring out how to deal with the new Constitution. One of its delegates to the convention, George Mason, worked on the document but then refused to sign it because, unlike the first draft of the Virginia Declaration of Rights he wrote in 1776, it did not contain a Bill of Rights.

Marshall, though, was all in for the new Constitution. He had become convinced, especially in the wake of the lack of gravity of the Articles of Confederation, that there needed to be a strong federal government—a secure attachment of the states to each other—if such a disparate nation in culture, ideology, and geography were to survive and thrive.

By the time Virginia met to see whether it would ratify the Constitution on June 2, 1788, eight states had done so, but not three of the largest—Virginia, New York, and North Carolina. Nine of the thirteen states would have to approve the document for it to go into effect. Virginia's decision would surely be pivotal, perhaps influencing the other two, as similarly split among their state delegates as Virginia was.

Patrick Henry, the nominal leader of the Virginia convention, was not in favor of ratification, and assumed the citizens of the state were with him. "Four-fifths of our inhabitants are opposed to the new scheme of government," wrote Henry to General John Lamb, a commander at Yorktown who had become New York's chief anti-Federalist, just as the proceedings had started in Richmond. "[South of Richmond] I am confident nine-tenths are opposed to it."[18]

Though New Hampshire actually ratified the Constitution before Virginia, officially making it law, there could be no real Union without the two most influential states, Virginia and New York, so the move would have made the union *de jure*, but hardly *de facto*. Many of those coming to the Convention had not even seen a copy of the Constitution. The debate in Philadelphia was kept secret by most who attended—though it could easily be that some let on at least their reasons for voting for or against to friends and allies. Some did complain that the delegates sent to the Philadelphia convention may not have been the right ones, if the thought of replacing the Articles of Confederation were known to be its purpose.

"Had the idea of a total change been started, probably no state would have appointed members to the Convention," wrote Virginia's Richard Henry Lee, the man who put forth the motion in the Second Continental Congress that proposed the Declaration of Independence, but who was not a member of the delegation at the Constitutional Convention.

"Pennsylvania appointed principally those men who are esteemed aristocratical," wrote Lee. "Other states ... chose men principally connected with commerce and the judicial department."[19]

Others complained that several states—Delaware, New Jersey, Connecticut, and Georgia, for instance—had ratified the Constitution quickly because they were small in population, so they would have greater influence given the makeup of, at least, the Senate. In Pennsylvania, some dissenters said that Philadelphians, who were presumed to be more influential in creating the document because it was done in their hometown, forced the Constitution through in their ratifying convention. The vote in Massachusetts, once the most rabid of Federalist states, at least until the Shays Rebellion, was only 187 for ratification and 168 against.

The oft-taught story line that the Constitution (and the Declaration before it) were documents of the people, the common man, the workers of the land, is false. In order to even attend the convention for four months, the delegate either had to have subsidy or inherent means. Those who were not upper class were either solidly middle class, or at least with a job or land that could provide means to transport, house, and feed themselves for what was at the moment an uncertain amount of time. The document, while not completely conservative, is certainly learned and with illiberal principles throughout—the regulations around slavery and who could vote and become president and congressmen would bear that out.

Back in Virginia, while there were plenty of legislators of that upper-middle to upper class, they were now among their constituents, many of whom lived virtually hand to mouth, not starving, but certainly with no pretense of formal education or aristocracy. Even the poorest, though, had to understand how influential Virginia was in the Union, and how it could probably exist quite well without it. Virginia had three-fourths of the South's population and, as well, had population equal to three-fourths of New England's. It was double that of the next most populous state, Pennsylvania, and three times that of New York.[20]

Each side in the debate was careful about whom it chose to come to Richmond. More than a fourth of the delegates had fought in the Revolutionary War, so that was a prominent marker. The Constitutionalists, proving their general conservativeness, valued family, public reputation, business success, and popularity, even and especially with the masses. Marshall probably owed his election to the latter. His reputation was as an honest man, and he always appeared genial in any gathering. His often disheveled dress gave him an extra smile and hearing from those who might otherwise be against his openly federal, Constitutionalist leanings.

The elections, though, were full of venom and subterfuge. Washington, as president of the national Constitutional Convention, lobbied virtually everyone who could be on the fence, reminding them of how he backed some of them in other times, and now demanding a vote in these. He complained that even his usual opponent, Henry, whom he often still complimented, chose to equivocate about the possible outcome of the debate.

"The ignorant have been told that should the proposed government obtain, their lands would be taken from them and their property disposed of," wrote Washington in a letter that made the rounds from Alexander Hamilton to Henry Knox and other future Federalist Party members. "All ranks are informed that the prohibition of the Navigation of the Mississippi (their favorite object) will be a certain consequence of the adoption of the Constitution."[21]

The Virginia convention, after the contentious election, started amicably enough. The members of both sides agreed on Edmund Pendleton, a longtime politician, as president of the convention, while George Wythe, who taught many of the lawyers in the group, was made chair of the Committee of the Whole. Both were Constitutionalists but still were respected by the other side.

A similarly esteemed man from that other side, George Mason, rose to speak first and asked that the Constitution be discussed line by line, which is just what the Constitutionalists, like Marshall, wanted. Their fear had been that the document would be debated as a whole, and that as a grand theory, it might be knocked out more summarily. Those who looked upon any government as anathema, as many in the outlying areas who viewed "liberty" as paramount, might actually like individual parts of the document, the Constitutionalists believed—and the best of the orators on the anti-Constitutionalist side, particularly Mason and Henry, were more adept at disdaining the whole, rather than its parts.

Henry perhaps knew that this would be his last battle were he to lose. Whether or not he actually said, "Give me liberty, or give me death" in his most glorious speech decades before, the truth is that "liberty" meant, to him, as much freedom from government as possible. State government was one thing. Dictatorial power from a federal authority was quite another. His first tack was to ask how the Convention had the gall to create a whole new constitution, rather than merely amend the Articles of Confederation.

Immediately, Edmund Randolph rose to answer. Randolph, along with Mason and Elbridge Gerry of Massachusetts, were the three of the forty-one delegates at the end of the Philadelphia convention who refused to sign the document. He was thought to be solidly in the anti-Constitutionalist camp, but he had been convinced otherwise, that if the Constitution did not stand, there would be no United States. The Union was clearly at stake for him and he said, forcefully, "I am a friend to the Union."

By June 13, as the debate in Virginia raged, dignitaries from other states were disembarking from their carriages in Richmond to influence votes—primarily to get the Constitutional forces going. Gouverneur Morris had made it in from New York and Robert Morris and James

Wilson from Philadelphia. Newsletter and newspaper editors and writers came from the Northeast as well.

By Monday June 16, the anti-Constitutionalists were confident. Patrick Henry and George Mason had overwhelmed the oratory the week before, after Randolph's defection from their side. Reports were that they walked arm in arm to the convention hall from the tavern where they were staying, The Swan, a new competitor to the old-line Formicola's that dominated all kinds of talk for years in Richmond.

Henry's main thrust was to get western (i.e., Kentucky, then part of Virginia) delegates aroused. He said the passing of the Constitution would cede navigation on the Mississippi to foreigners and increase taxes for all its projected improvements in government. There were volleys back and forth after that by such as Lee, James Monroe, and Randolph.

In the middle of the afternoon, though, Wythe directed his hand at a former student, the thirty-two-year-old John Marshall. Marshall had spent most of the last two weeks engaging every delegate he could on both sides. He spent what he had on Madeira, his favorite drink, and bringing them out on all their views. That he had served four years under Washington helped, other soldiers there like Lee and Monroe speaking against the Constitution.

For the first time before such a crowd, Marshall used what he would become famous for in arguments. He first sought out what the opposition most wanted, which was "liberty," and he assured them that the Constitution would be the best way of assuring that would stand. He then answered the opposition's favorite speaker, Patrick Henry, and agreed with him that justice and the public faith in it were paramount for the United States, and that, again, the Constitution would be the best way to assure them. He said he realized that the Confederation had treated his adversaries well, and that it would be hard for them to turn away from it, but its flaws were many, and the Constitution would help remedy them.

He turned to the Mississippi issue and said the Constitutionalists were on the same page there, too, but that the Articles of Confederation would doom that issue. "How shall we retain it?" Marshall asked. "By retaining that weak government which has hitherto kept it from us?" No, he said, by having a strong Union with military might.

Marshall said that the Constitution hammered out in Philadelphia was no conspiracy, but when the delegates got there, they realized a whole new plan of government was necessary, that the Articles of Confederation were a long-term slide into disunion. One state, he said, could not be counted on, like Virginia and its richness, to provide for everyone. "By national government only," he said, could these things be done. "Shall we refuse to give it power to do them?"

Marshall had become the go-to orator on the subject, the Constitution that he would, in the future, be the main interpreter of. By the next week, Marshall had apparently convinced some on the fence to come to the Constitution's side. He saw a stronger Virginia in the Union than in a confederation and alleged that he was all for the Bill of Rights that would appease Mason at the very least, and no doubt others not yet decided. He admitted that the weakest part of the new Constitution was its explanation of the judiciary, but the main thrust there was to advocate for swift and fair trials, something the Bill of Rights would help to do.

Eventually, the Constitutionalists agreed to bring as many as forty amendments to the next Congress, were the Constitution passed, though the vote was on the Constitution itself, not dependent on the Bill of Rights and other future amendments. The vote on June 25 was close: eighty-nine for, seventy-nine against, including ten of fourteen from the "west," the eventual state of Kentucky, with two abstentions. Word had come before the vote that New Hampshire had ratified, becoming the ninth state to do so. Virginia, though, was the most important, and John Marshall was said to pull it across that line.[22]

It often seems like the American Revolution was created out of a vacuum with two combatants having nothing to do but batter each other for a decade with no one watching, save maybe the French. If that were so, and it indeed was not, it was because Europe itself was in the midst of upheaval, particularly in France.

On July 14, 1789, not a year after the Constitution was officially ratified with New Hampshire taking the vital ninth spot in confirmation, the French Revolution became a true fight with the storming of the Paris prison tower, the Bastille. Months before, Marat-Sade, the writer and journalist imprisoned there, shouted out a window that prisoners were being slaughtered within. Louis XVI had already given what he thought were concessions, like promising to end feudalism, but each day from the summer of 1787 on seemed to bring either a different kind of general assembly, a new demand for the king, or someone escaping somewhere for fear of his or her life.[23]

It was not exactly quiet in the rest of Europe. Catherine the Great was pushing her Russian armies into the Muslim territories to the south, like Turkey, and to the east. Prussia was taking a middle route, trying to consolidate its bases in places like Poland and the Netherlands. Britain, having finally given up on its American colonies, was looking outward and inward at the same time, deciding what to do about slavery, and accumulating land in Africa, to possibly repatriate those slaves into a British-run colony, presumably Sierra Leone.[24]

If they were to contemplate the American Revolution, they often did so with a sardonic mind. No large democracy had survived long since those in ancient Greece, and they were large only in influence, not size. Thomas Paine's *Common Sense*, though, was a bestseller not only in the United States, but in France and to a lesser extent all over Europe. It was the last manifesto before actual fighting for the United States to become independent and be successful at some form of democracy.

Catherine did try to incorporate some sort of freedoms while her ardor for military achievement rose. At least at the beginning, the leaders of the French Revolution sought to do the same. Unlike the American Revolution, though, which only had to have the colonies separate from the kingdom, not overthrow the British government, the French Revolution met resistance at home.

The Founders, whose new Constitutional government was forming in the same year as the Bastille fell, received the French Revolution warmly, if not enthusiastically, almost as if they were proud another world power was copying their moves.

"In no part of the globe was this revolution hailed with more joy than in America," wrote Marshall in his memoirs. "The influence it would have on the affairs of the world was not then distinctly foreseen.... On this subject, therefore, but one sentiment existed."[25]

Jefferson was just leaving France to become secretary of state during the run-up to the Bastille insurrection. A Francophile all along, and thus with different foreign policy views than Marshall, agreed with him here.

"A complete revolution in this government has been effected merely by the force of public opinion," Jefferson wrote to a friend, but then wrote what would be an unfortunately ironic statement, "and this revolution has not cost a single life."[26]

The ardor for the French Revolution among the Founders soon abated, as the indiscriminate beheadings and violence toward any institution, even the Catholic Church, started.

"This country is," the first American minister to France, Gouverneur Morris, wrote to Washington in July 1789, "as near to anarchy as society can approach without dissolution."

Marshall was close to Morris and lamented his missives from Paris.

"With the eye of an intelligent, and of an unimpassioned observer, he marked all passing events and communicated them with fidelity," wrote Marshall, reflecting on the time a decade later. "He did not mistake despotism for freedom because it was exercised by those who denominated themselves the people, or because it assumed the name of liberty. Sincerely wishing happiness and a really free government to France, he could not be blind to the obvious truth that the road to those blessings had been mistaken."[27]

By this time Catherine the Great had performed a coup, replacing her husband, Peter III, who was soon assassinated, though she never approved of that. What she did approve of was having lots of lovers and finding jobs for them. Often they were in the military, leading battles to overcome mostly Muslim enemies in south or central Asia. One, though, Stanislaw August Poniatowski, she made king of Poland, or at least the large slice Russia got in partition of the country with Prussia in the 1760s. It is safe to say the American Founders were ambivalent about Russia but always had to heed the growing sense that it could devour American allies and potential allies in Europe.

With the beheading of King Louis XVI in 1793 and the ensuing "Terror," where thousands met the same fate as the king no matter what their politics, the Founders collectively became a bit scared. Would the same thing happen among the people in the new republic? In some ways, the answer came with the arrest in France of the American war hero, Marquis de Lafayette. Marshall's brother, James, was deputized by Washington, perhaps Lafayette's greatest friend in America, to go to France and plead for Lafayette's release, which happened with assistance from the king of Prussia.

If anything, the French Revolution confirmed the American miracle, and people moved toward symbolism of that. In Boston, Royal Exchange Alley became Equality Lane. In New York, Queen Street became Pearl Street and King Street was renamed Liberty Street. In the main, though, it was things like this that occupied Americans, not decapitating leaders. This time, perhaps, the stretch of ocean to the east, as with the American Revolution itself, preserved liberty, and not chaos.

CHAPTER FOUR

Marshall on the National and International Stage and a Small Cadre Make a Large Nation

THOMAS JEFFERSON RETURNED TO VIRGINIA IN EARLY 1789 AFTER FIVE years in Paris. Though he was thought of, having written the Declaration of Independence, as a premier philosopher on how the new nation should organize, he was thousands of miles away when the Constitution was written and ratified in the many contentious state conventions.

Whatever his loyal mentee James Madison may have written him about the goings-on, it took weeks, sometimes months, for Madison's bits of news and interpretations to get to Jefferson, and for Jefferson's musings or directions to appear back in Philadelphia or Virginia, so they were much more ineffectual than not.

When Jefferson came home, no real hoopla came with him. His Virginia governorship (1779–1781) was pretty much a disaster. He had to abandon Richmond in the wake of a British force's advance. The British general was Benedict Arnold, who burned Richmond and came within a wisp of arresting Jefferson at Monticello before Jefferson escaped to western Virginia. He was officially accused of malfeasance in office but was acquitted—noting that he worked with honor but just was bad at his job.[1]

Nonetheless, after a short stint in Congress, he was sent to France to hope for good trade relations and promises to keep away from American interests in the West. In Europe, Jefferson was reunited with two of his cohorts from that Declaration of Independence writing committee, John Adams and Benjamin Franklin. Franklin had been the most prominent and loved American in the eyes of the French. For even such as Jefferson to replace him would be arduous. Adams was to move on to Great Britain, the war having been won, and Franklin would soon take leave back to Philadelphia.

Some thought the "reward" of going to France was to cheer Jefferson up, his having fallen into deep depression after the death of his wife in 1782. He had taken one of the many vows he would during his lifetime to retire to Charlottesville and concentrate on his estate, Monticello, but he roused himself to go to the cultural capital and largest city in Europe. He brought one daughter with him and eventually called for his younger one, who came escorted by a teenaged slave named Sally Hemings, with whom he purportedly started his long affair while in Paris.

While there, he apparently dated or at least escorted prominent women and lunched often with the Marquis de Lafayette. He was there when the Bastille was stormed and then helped Lafayette write the Declaration of the Rights of Man and of the Citizen, perhaps the high point, spiritually, of the French Revolution, before it devolved to a drenching scourge of massacre and beheading, that had just begun when Jefferson returned to the United States. He had intended to go back to France soon, especially supposing he would have no other place in the nation's forming after the Constitution he did not write.[2]

Marshall, though, was wary of his second cousin, knowing him to be close to people on both sides of the Constitution debate. Though Marshall had become the leading voice in Virginia for the national Constitution, he realized it was not safe, especially if Jefferson came home to Virginia.

The new Virginia legislature, it turned out, meeting only three months after the convention that ratified the Constitution in the summer of 1788, was against that ratification and was determined to rescind the vote or at least undermine it.

"The old line of division was still as strongly marked as ever," Marshall eventually wrote in his memoirs. "[The other side thought] liberty could be endangered only by encroachments upon the states; and that it was the great duty of patriotism to restrain the powers of the general government within the narrowest possible limits."[3]

Madison, Jefferson's closest associate, was still a Nationalist at this point, and as such lost his bid for Senate to Richard Henry Lee and William Grayson, Patrick Henry's choices to see what Virginia could do to change the apparent goings-on in the national government. Marshall had left the legislature by then, but he tried to get the legislature to give the great thinker Madison a seat at the table.

George Washington, wanting to keep Marshall in government instead of private practice, appointed him the first US attorney for Virginia, but Marshall declined in hopes of getting back into the Virginia legislature, where he figured his Nationalist reputation would do the most good. He won in Richmond, a fervently anti-Nationalist area, but Marshall, the man, outdid his political stance. Richmond was still an insular place, and he was one of the people on the inside who could be seen as honorable.[4]

Marshall immediately signed up for as many committees as possible, and by 1790, he was appointed one of the members of the committee to revise Virginia's laws—even the anti-Nationalist majority realizing it was necessary to have its own house in order before denouncing the federal one. Helping his father, too, he worked on the special committee to grant statehood to Kentucky, where Thomas Marshall now lived. He campaigned for Virginia's US senators to do their best to have the debates in the federal Congress open to the public.

He was not, however, on the committee to greet Jefferson when he finally came to Richmond in 1789. The greeting was short, stiff, and barely polite. Earlier, the legislature sent a formal letter to Washington, with far more exuberant language and praise. Oddly, within a couple of years, the party of Washington, the Federalists, would be demonized in Virginia, while Jefferson would be adored by the masses and legislators alike.[5]

The first volley in that political statewide revolution came on November 30, 1789, when the US House of Representatives ratified what would be the Bill of Rights, much of which came from Madison and his Virginia colleagues. The problem was that Virginia had proposed about thirty more amendments, which were bypassed summarily, or not even allowed to be put on the floor. The Virginians were insulted and looked for new leadership to press the anti-Constitutionalist agenda.

It found Thomas Jefferson.

Jefferson, having had time to study both the Constitution and the political winds, chose to go with the majority of the Virginia Assembly and to contravene the Nationalists. As he was formulating what to do, Washington, who had appreciated Jefferson's work abroad, made him secretary of state, arguably the second most powerful position in the executive part of the triumvirate as seen by the Constitution: the executive, the legislative, and the judicial. It was the basis for the political parties Washington would fear. Marshall, though, sided with the then-current majority in the hopes that a stronger federal government would lead toward a more stable new nation.[6]

By the time the new US senators were to be chosen, though, Patrick Henry's influence in the legislature was supreme. Washington himself asked James Madison, then an ardent pro-Nationalist, to ask to be considered for election. Madison was swamped by the now-anti-Nationalist Virginia legislature, who chose Richard Henry Lee and William Grayson, two men under Henry's thumb. Madison did get a seat in the national House of Representatives, with Marshall working behind the scenes for both the losing and winning Madison runs.

Washington had already sought Marshall's opinion on federal judgeships and decided he needed Marshall at least on the fringes of his new administration. Marshall's friends suggested Washington make him US attorney for Virginia. Marshall appreciated the nomination but said he would rather try to thwart that new move to rescind the state's ratification of the Constitution by going back to the Virginia legislature. It might cut into his law practice, but he felt it the most important. The legislature had already endorsed a move by the New York legislature to call for a new federal Constitutional convention.

The legislature did just about whatever it could to twit the Nationalists and the federal government. It passed a law, which Marshall was particularly angry about, that taxes could be paid not just in money, but also in tobacco and hemp. His cohorts in the legislature put him on a special committee that would give statehood to the District of Kentucky. It was a thicket. The anti-Federalists thought that would give the states' rights side another state on its side, but the bugaboo was that it would have to ratify the Constitution to become a state. Marshall was, to be sure, in favor of the latter—his father had moved there permanently and would certainly be named to a prestigious position were Kentucky a state—but ardently against the former.

The first big fight on the issue of nationalization was when the first Congress, in November 1789, chose to adopt the first twelve amendments proposed in part by Virginia (two were dropped later for the time being). This, anti-Nationalist Virginians said, was an affront to the state, which had given as many as forty to consider. Randolph spoke for the majority when he wrote to Madison that he was sure the Nationalists in Congress thought the amendments were "being considered as an anodyne to the discontented,"[7] a sop to his side. This was the *Bill of Rights*, so sacred to modern Americans, but it was passed without support of even the state which originally proposed that it exist. The Founding Fathers did not necessarily act the way many today would have wanted them to do.

The next big debate actually turned out to be a win-win for Virginia. Alexander Hamilton, now the secretary of the treasury, was adamant about developing a national bank. Part of the negotiations were to have states assume debts in their treasuries, most left over from the Revolutionary War. Virginia had already done so, while other states were laggards.

Fortuitously, Hamilton ran into Madison and Jefferson on the street in New York and the three decided to meet on the topic. What came out of the secret meeting at Jefferson's dinner table was that Madison and Jefferson would get southern votes for the assumption issue, perhaps even the National Bank itself, in return for a similar northern coalition to move the capital out of the North and to a site in or near Virginia. Pennsylvanians were loath to vote for something like that; the prestige of having the capital in Philadelphia had grown over the years. So the three made a codicil granting the capital to Philadelphia until 1800. The Philadelphia-area representatives were sure no one would really want to build that new city on the Potomac and that inertia would keep the capital in their city.[8]

Marshall was enthusiastic in his approval of the assumption part of the deal. "The sudden increase of monied capital invigorated commerce and gave a new stimulus to agriculture," he wrote, but he realized that the debtor class, of which there was a lot in Virginia, would just see that the national government was subservient to the business sector, "the creation of a monied interest . . . subservient to its will." It is a disagreement that would be virile in every era of American government.[9]

Marshall had now become the voice of federalism in Virginia. He would argue it in Richmond taverns and ride the circuit for his law cases, stopping where he could to promote the federal government. He was still immensely popular, even with people like George Mason, one of his anti-Federalist competitors in the state. It was in this that Jefferson first saw Marshall as a force to disdain, but one with power and popularity. He was young and destined to be someone of import outside of Virginia. His popularity came from his personality and vigor, which people on both sides of the issue appreciated.

Jefferson and Madison had taken a trip through the North, to New York and New England, mostly talking about the future of the national government, which they hoped to move to their side. They developed a plan to eliminate Marshall from that equation—get him a seat on the Virginia State courts, prestigious, but out of the legislature and certainly out of national politics. It did not happen, nor would Marshall have consented to have a job that would take him away completely from the law practice that was really his financial base.[10]

By 1793, France and England were back at war. In the United States, the people generally sided with France, and there was an arm of the Jeffersonians who wanted to go to war on the side of that country. Washington, the general and now president, believed that he had not won the Revolutionary War to have a succession of more wars for his new country. He proposed neutrality, which Jefferson could not see upholding as secretary of state. The bill in Congress passed closely in the House and won in the Senate only because Vice President John Adams broke a tie.

Jefferson resigned from his Cabinet post, so instead of having to uphold neutrality, he was free—without a government post—to lead a new political faction, called the Republicans, against neutrality and so much more. It would not take long for Jefferson to realize he had a rising man on the other side who might equal or eclipse him.[11]

On August 26, 1795, President Washington sent a letter to Marshall:

The office of Attorney Gen. of the United States has become vacant by the death of Will Bradford, Esp. I take the earliest opportunity of asking if you will accept the appointment? The salary annexed thereto, and the prospects of lucrative practice in this city [Philadelphia]—the present seat of the Gen Government, must be as well known to you, perhaps better, than they are to me, and therefore I will say nothing concerning them.

If your answer is in the affirmative, it will readily occur to you that no unnecessary time should be lost in repairing to this place. If, on the contrary, it should be the negative (which would give me concern) it might be as well to say nothing of this offer. But in either case, I pray you to give me an answer as promptly as you can.[12]

Marshall would earn $1,500 a year as the attorney general with, despite Washington's supposition in the letter, much better prospects for law cases in Richmond, since there would be little time for any law work in a position like attorney general. Washington was curious. Washington had become dependent on Marshall pushing the Federalist cause in their home state, which was in general not on their side. Marshall, though, had heard that Patrick Henry might be Washington's second choice. While Marshall admired Henry's intellect, his support for the great orator would be that it would drive a blow to the Republicans in Virginia, for whom Henry was the most prominent state-based partisan. Charles Lee, yet another Virginian, whom Marshall would see nearly a decade later as William Marbury's lawyer at the Supreme Court, was Washington's eventual choice.[13]

Meanwhile, Marshall was trying to make some money as a lawyer when he fell into a strange trap. The election for the Virginia Assembly in 1795 was coming up and it seemed like the Federalists would lose in Richmond. Nonetheless, Marshall supported his party and was among the first to arrive at the polls in Richmond on election day.

When he got there, another early voter suggested that Marshall's name should "open a poll," what would essentially be a write-in during today's elections. Marshall was appalled and said he was sticking with his party's candidates, though he promised he would run again in the future.

Marshall had a court case to work on and left the polls for the court-house. As soon as he left, people "opened a poll" for Marshall and he was elected. He learned of it only after the polls closed that evening.

It was an honor, but a burden, that Marshall had to accept. Immediately, though, he was thrown into a monumental position because of Washington's obsession with getting the Jay Treaty with England approved. John Jay had been deputized by Washington, somewhat secretly, to establish a peace treaty with England. There had been a notable massing of troops at some of the forts Britain still had north of the Ohio River and into Canada. The United States had only the remnants of an army by then, and would have little defense if the British did attack, and there was a fear that not only would Britain want to take the Ohio territory but capture perhaps New York and New England, too.[14]

Jay came back with a treaty that was decidedly in the British favor. The United States only got to keep a few benefits it already supposedly had, like a surrender of those posts still on American soil, while the British got a passel of new things, like the freedom to trade along the Mississippi, freedom in all American ports, and the privilege of its citizens to own land in the territories. The only thing of substance, really, that the United States got was the assurance the British would not attack.

This did not sit well with a lot of the country, especially the pro-French Republican areas, of which Virginia was one of the more prominent. Virginians were vociferous and profane in their vilification of the Father of Our Country, not to mention Jay. There were even calls for Washington's impeachment. Marshall, though, was vociferous right back, leading the charge, especially in Virginia, for the treaty's albeit reluctant acceptance, which eventually did happen.[15]

During these times, Marshall was acknowledged to be the best lawyer in Richmond, though he dabbled in other things as well, much like Franklin and Jefferson. He bought land in the far reaches of Virginia, part of the old Fairfax estate, in speculation with his brother, James. He was a founder—like Franklin earlier in Pennsylvania—of one of the oldest fire insurance companies in the country when he got a charter for one in Richmond. He was one of the founders of the first successful large financial institution in his state, The Bank of Virginia.

He also founded the Quoits Club in Richmond, his favorite place to repair during the decades he lived there when not in Washington. He was a champion at quoits. He was also a card player, mostly whist, at the club or other taverns, and he invented a cocktail especially for the Quoits Club: a mix of rum, brandy, and Madeira. Marshall's rule for the club was that there could be no discussion of politics or religion—violators being fined a case of champagne to be drunk at the next club meeting.

He claimed he would have been happy just to stay in Richmond with his family and law practice, but that could hardly be. He was now in the top tier of national politics. He had supported John Adams in the 1796 election, and though it ended up with his despised second cousin, Thomas Jefferson, as vice president, he rationalized that Adams would have more say in what Marshall prized most, the unity of the country.[16]

In 1797, though, in the wake of the Jay Treaty, Adams felt he needed something of the same with France, which in the year before had seized more than three hundred American ships in the Atlantic and nearby waters. Adams decided to gather people close to him for a negotiating party. He picked the crusty Elbridge Gerry from Massachusetts, a longtime Adamsite in that state; the more convivial Charles Cotesworth Pinckney, a South Carolina Federalist; and the young lawyer from Richmond, so ardent in his affection for George Washington—Marshall.

In a sense, it was an odd crew. Marshall had never been abroad, and while he, like Pinckney, was a confirmed Federalist, Pinckney had a more laid-back manner, and both tended to favor the British over the French. Pinckney had been chosen as minister to France months earlier, but the French would not honor the choice. Gerry was ambivalent in the French and British feud and thus not always in favor with the Federalists who controlled Congress. Nonetheless, the three sailed to France in separate ships in the summer and made it to Paris by October, ready to begin negotiations.[17]

Not so fast, thought French foreign minister Charles Maurice Talleyrand-Perigord. Talleyrand was a shrewd diplomat, a Catholic priest who in 1780, at age twenty-six, became the minister of the Church in dealing with the French government. As the French Revolution got hot, factions ordering beheadings at a rapid rate, Talleyrand went to England in September 1782, allegedly to have secret peace negotiations. The National Assembly in France soon demanded his return, which he knew was not a good idea, so he came to the United States, mostly Philadelphia, and then New York, where he stayed with Aaron Burr. He made some real estate transactions which made him fairly wealthy before he went back to France and was chosen foreign minister in a slightly saner government in 1796.

He traveled through most of the top circles while in the United States, making a particular friendship with Alexander Hamilton, and knew the score for his country. The Republicans were pro-French and the Federalists were not. It was that simple. *If* he could delay real negotiations until the Republicans were in power, they would more likely be in France's favor.

Talleyrand made an initial visit with the three commissioners, but his only concession was that he accepted their passports. For the next several months, he did not appear and left any preliminaries to deputies. Those deputies said Talleyrand wanted what amounted to a bribe—a filtered payment through a loan—before he would begin negotiations. Eventually, Pinckney and Marshall tired of this and at Marshall's insistence went back to the United States in the spring of 1798, after Talleyrand refused for a month to give back their passports. Gerry, ever hopeful, stayed on, but mostly because he knew Talleyrand might deal with him as a less-anti-French negotiator. Marshall wrote an angry letter to Talleyrand, saying that America would never give up its right to stay neutral: "It requires no assurance to convince, that every real American must wish sincerely to extricate his country from the ills it suffers, and from the greater ills with which it is threatened, but all who love liberty must admit that it does not exist in a nation which cannot exercise the right of maintaining its neutrality."

Soon before their departure, Marshall's missives to Adams got to America, the first on March 4. The Republicans in Congress demanded them, presuming they would be indicting in some way of the French, which they were. When Adams finally relented, the French diplomats who had sent Talleyrand's demands for bribes were identified only as X, Y, and Z—thus the origin of the "XYZ Affair."[18]

The effect was certainly not what the Republicans wanted. Some of their members of Congress were outraged and embarrassed by what most Americans perceived as negotiations that were unfair at best, a clamor for war at worst. In many towns, where men wore the French cockade on their hats, they switched to the black one worn by American troops during the Revolutionary War. Joseph Hopkinson wrote what would be America's first popular anthem, "Hail Columbia," whose words were clearly an independent call: "Hail, Columbia! Happy land! Hail, ye Heroes! Heaven-born band! Who fought and bled in Freedom's cause. . . ."[19]

It took Marshall fifty-three days to get to New York from Bordeaux, ironically on a ship named the *Alexander Hamilton*. He hurried on to Philadelphia, arriving there on June 18, 1798. Knowing he was coming in, carriages filled with dozens of congressmen and crowds of city folk, primarily on horseback, met him at the dock six miles north of the downtown.

It was said that the procession to town was exceeded only by events surrounding George Washington. Three corps of cavalry led the parade and when the caravan reached the city, the constant ringing of church bells and setting off of cannons began. The Federalist *Gazette of the United States* wrote that even in the staunchly Republican Northern Liberties section of Philadelphia, "where the demons of anarchy and confusion are attempting to organize treason and death, repeated shouts of applause were given as the cavalcade approached and passed along."[20]

Jefferson was a bit dismayed that his second cousin was getting such a warm reception.

"M[arshall] was received here with the utmost eclat," Jefferson wrote to Madison three days after Marshall arrived in Philadelphia. "The secretary of state & many carriages, with all the city cavalry, went to Frankfort to meet him, and on his arrival here in the evening, the bells rung till late in the night, & immense crowds were collected to see & make part of the show, which was circuitously paraded through the streets before he was set down at the City Tavern . . . all this was to secure him to their views, that he might say nothing which would expose the game they have been playing. Since his arrival I can hear nothing directly from him."[21]

During the few days of Marshall's fêting, Jefferson came by to see him at O'Eller's Hotel and left a note that became a classic tale-starter. "He had the honor of calling at his lodgings twice this morning, but was so lucky as to find that he was out on both occasions. . . ." Realizing the "lucky" was just the opposite of what he meant, Jefferson then inserted an "un" right above it. For years, Marshall was able to start off a talk with the idea that having the original "lucky" in the note was the one time Jefferson told the truth.

As he was still in Philadelphia, Adams apparently offered Marshall the Supreme Court seat made vacant by Justice James Wilson's death, but Marshall again refused a good spot, saying that in his absence, he had not kept up with obligations and needed to go back to his law practice to make some money.

Nonetheless, the members of Congress, particularly the Federalists, never loath to give a party, had 120 dignitaries at a going-away party for the new hero at his hotel. The Speaker of the House, the Cabinet, the Supreme Court justices, and the most prominent clergymen and military officers were all there. Dozens of toasts were proposed, but the one that stuck, though anonymous, was "Millions for Defense but not a cent for Tribute," which became a Federalist rallying cry, noting that Marshall would approve of a boost to the American army, but never submit to a bribe for victory.

Adams himself praised Marshall earlier that day in an address whose theme was staunch negotiations with potential enemies, particularly this: "I will never send another Minister to France without assurances that he will be received, respected and honored as the representative of a great, free, powerful and independent nation."[22]

Marshall's path back to Richmond was full of more parades and tributes in Pennsylvania and Virginia towns along the way. When he got home to Richmond, his neighbors and associates, even his titular enemies, were there to greet him. He told them all of what had happened in France and how proud he was that the country agreed with what he did there.

"I rejoice that I was not mistaken in the opinion I had formed of my countrymen," he said. "I rejoice to find, though they know how to estimate, and therefore seek to avoid the horrors and dangers of war, yet they know also how to value the blessings of liberty and national independence. Peace would be purchased at too high a price by bending beneath a foreign yoke."[23]

As Congress quickly abated the original treaty agreements with France, George Washington said that he would be ready to come back and lead the troops were a war with France imminent. New York got its militia together and paraded in New York City on July 4. Jefferson, blaming Marshall, was dejected as he saw the very backbone issue of his party starting to destroy it.

Marshall came home to Richmond, and Federalist partisans asked him to run for Congress, which he refused to do, first because there were already what he perceived as good men to run, but also because he wanted to finally recoup some money to live on. He offered to campaign for whatever candidate the Federalists put up, but he would not run.

Word got to George Washington that Marshall refused the offer to run for Congress, and Washington was concerned that Republicans would run rampant in his home state. Washington then asked his nephew, Marshall's friend Bushrod Washington, and Marshall to come to Mount Vernon to see him. Even if Marshall knew what the visit was about, he could not refuse the man who was his former military commander and a national hero.

Bushrod and Marshall decided to take the trip on horseback, but put all their good clothing in one saddle bag for convenience. When they arrived at Mount Vernon two days later, they had just been through a rainstorm and immediately opened the saddle bag so they would be presentable to the former president.

When they unlocked the saddle bag, they only found a bottle of whiskey, some tobacco, a piece of cornbread, and a few worn out pants and shirts. Apparently they had picked up the wrong bag after staying at a tavern on the way. They got a good laugh but were a bit unpresentable to Washington, who actually roared with laughter when he saw them.

It was September, so the weather was warm and Washington invited them for the next four days to sit on the piazza and look out on the Potomac as they talked. Washington made clear that he wanted the two of them to run for Congress in their districts. Marshall told him of the other candidate he would back in Richmond, but Washington would not give up. Marshall later recounted the general's argument.

"He had withdrawn from office with a declaration of his determination never again, under any circumstances, to enter public life," wrote Marshall. "No man could be more sincere in making that declaration, nor could any man feel stronger motives for adhering to it. . . . Yet I saw him in opposition to his private feelings, consenting, under a sense of duty, to surrender the sweets of retirement and again to enter the most arduous and perilous station which an individual could fill. My resolution yielded to this representation."

There is a story that on one of those days, Marshall was finally upset about Washington's insistence and aimed to leave the estate as early in the morning as possible. When he was saddling his horse, the story goes, Washington appeared at the stable. Marshall, flustered, gave in and eventually ran for the seat with Washington's support, to be sure. Bushrod ended up with the Supreme Court associate justice seat from Adams that Marshall had refused earlier.[24]

The election was bitter—the first time Marshall had really had to deal with infamies and, in some cases, lies that the Republicans threw out at him. The national frenzy in favor of Federalists would have secured their victory in the mid-term elections, save that they gave the Republicans a huge present—the Alien and Sedition Acts.

In sum, the acts were an assault on free speech and free press, if nothing else. Congress had given the president the privilege of kicking out of the country any alien or visitor whom he thought "dangerous" or that he suspected would spread "treasonable or secret machination against the government." The Naturalization Act, part of the series, increased the time to wait for citizenship from five to fourteen years—mostly because new citizens tended to vote Republican.

The Sedition Act was even more heinous. It restricted speech against the government. It did not have to be untrue, just "malicious"—words that might "stir up sedition within the United States."[25]

The Adams Administration arrested several newspaper owners and writers from the Republican side and ended up convicting some, jailing and/or fining them.

It put Marshall in a bind, trying to win a seat in a Republican state. Marshall took his normal tack and went in between. Since the acts were already in place, there was nothing he could do about them. Since they had expiration dates of March 1801, however, he would choose to let them expire then.

It was a rare moderate Federalist stand, but it quelled his district. Meanwhile the Republicans in Kentucky declared they would not obey the laws, calling them void. The Virginia legislature joined with Kentucky in December 1798. It was good theater, but no secession or even nullification took place. Though the Federalists ended up with both houses of Congress in 1798, essentially the Alien and Sedition Acts were the party's death knell, leading to devastating losses in 1800.[26]

Marshall was a lightning rod during his time in Congress. He went to Kentucky to visit his ill father, but the Republicans, especially Jefferson, saw Marshall's travels there as an attempt to get the Kentucky resolve on nullification overturned. Then the French government, changing its tune, said it would allow the United States to have an official minister. The Republicans blamed Marshall and his XYZ mission as the reason the French had waited so long to do so.

Even staunch Federalists were skeptical of Marshall. Speaker of the House Theodore Sedgwick of Massachusetts said he seemed to be respected by his southern colleagues and was trying his best to do the right thing.

"In Congress, you see General Marshall is a leader. He is I think a virtuous & certainly an able man," wrote Sedgewick to another member. "But you see in him the faults of a Virginian. He thinks too much of that State & he expects the world will be governed according to the Rules of Logic. I have seen such men often become excellent legislators after experience has cured their errors. I hope it will prove so with General Marshall."[27]

Amid all the rancor of this Congress, a messenger came to Marshall on December 18, 1799, with word that George Washington had died four days before. He announced the confirmation of Washington's death to Congress with an emotional impromptu speech.

"Our Washington is no more! The hero, the sage, and the patriot of America—the man on whom in times of danger every eye was turned and all hopes were placed—lives now only in his own great actions, and in the hearts of an affectionate and afflicted people," Marshall said.

He went on for a few minutes more with this kind of supplicant praise, and then asked the House to pass three actions: that it would give its greatest condolences to the widow, that the speaker's chair be shrouded in black and the members wear mourning dress during sessions, and that the House would arrange events for all to mourn Washington, whom he said was "a citizen, first in war, first in peace and first in the hearts of his countrymen."[28]

The last words became immortal, but Marshall acknowledged that he did not make them up. Instead, he had heard General Henry Lee say them at an occasion three years before. They, though, have come down today as a eulogy on the man—and the myth—of Washington.

The new century started with the nation still embroiled in tensions with both Britain and France, the continuation of the Alien and Sedition Acts, the threat of secession from Virginia and Kentucky, and the upcoming presidential election.

By May of 1800, Adams was unsatisfied with much of his Cabinet, and sought to change it before the election, presumably with men the public trusted. After being badgered by Adams on some trivial matters, Secretary of War James McHenry resigned instead. Almost in knee-jerk fashion, Adams asked Marshall to take the post, which he declined. Adams then appointed an old friend from Massachusetts, then a senator, Samuel Dexter.

Adams also demanded that Secretary of State Thomas Pickering resign, since Pickering was an Anglophile and hated the idea of making peace with France. Pickering refused, so Adams just fired him. He turned to Marshall again. Marshall saw the Federalist Cabinet crumbling. Most Federalists now considered Hamilton to be running the party, not Adams, but Marshall, though he respected Hamilton, did not see that as a good thing, so he accepted the challenge of secretary of state. Even the Republicans did not come down too hard on the Marshall choice, since Marshall had at least had negotiations with France and knew something about foreign relations.[29]

As soon as Marshall was in the seat, Adams rushed to Massachusetts because his wife Abigail was ill. While Marshall was now not exactly head of the government, he was the highest man in the Federalist party, so he stayed in Washington for the summer just in case anything happened. There were decisions Marshall had to make, but mostly they were ones Adams would have made anyway. Most of his time in foreign affairs was spent trying to stop piracy on the high seas. Most of the known pirates, like Isaac Williams, who had been convicted of waging war against the British when he was actually doing his piracy thing under a French flag, were not particularly anti-American but just out for their own quests for largesse. They often flew under the French flag, the government there eager to intimidate the British and Americans alike.

Meanwhile, the British were still taking advantage of the Americans in the wake of the Jay Treaty. There was a commission to resolve American debts to the British, mostly land-holders who lost their property in the Revolutionary War, but the British commissioners walked out of the meetings after their excessive demands were not met. There was still some impressment of American sailors by British captors going on at sea in violation of the treaty.

Marshall huffily wrote that the United States was not some lower-echelon nation but a real place with a real government and, if need be, a real army. The United States was looking for peace and hoped to stay neutral in French and British hostilities, but it would not tolerate war-like actions against it, like piracy and impressment.

Yet Marshall saw on the horizon the breakup of his Federalist party. The Hamiltonians disliked Adams, and even Adams threatened to run for president under an "American Party," where he would not run up against the Hamiltonians supposedly on his side, but yet get not-so-sure Republicans to come to him. The election of 1800 was to be a crucial turning point in the young country.

In its early years, the US government barely functioned in the summer months. Congressmen and Cabinet members routinely went home, some to tend to their businesses, but mostly as a recess from goings-on in

Philadelphia. There was hardly a notion that things would be different when the capital moved to Washington.

In 1800, though, John Adams saw it as incumbent on him to at least tour the new capital being built on the Potomac, so on May 27, Adams, Treasury Secretary Oliver Wolcott, and a few of their staff members left Philadelphia for Washington. Marshall, keen on keeping his role as secretary of state going strong, met them there.

Adams decided he needed a little cheer along the way, so he stopped in Lancaster, Pennsylvania, and Frederick, Maryland, both with substantial Federalist populations—even twenty years later, future president James Buchanan would be elected to Congress from Lancaster as a Federalist, when the party was almost moribund elsewhere. Adams stopped quickly in other towns as well, a nod and a few words doing just as well there as the fêtes he had in the larger villages of Lancaster and Frederick, which was home then to a young man named Francis Scott Key.

When Adams and his coterie got to the District line after a week on the road, dozens met him on horseback, giving him a gunfire salute and a show of marines from Baltimore and the militia in the city. They stopped long enough to listen to Adams address them impromptu.

Abigail Adams had already decamped for Quincy, Massachusetts, the Adams's ancestral and current home, so the group of high officials all stayed at Tunnicliff's City Hotel, near the unfinished Capitol building, and worked out of their rooms there. There were, at most, a little more than a dozen of them, the entire staff of the Treasury and State Departments and Adams's small office help.

Adams did get courtesy when he was in the capital. Citizens held a big dinner for him, as did General Charles Lee, who lived in Alexandria, which had been ceded by Virginia into the new boundaries of the city. Adams even went down the Potomac a bit to visit Martha Washington at Mount Vernon, the former president having died only six months before and his widow still grieving.

By June 14, though, after two weeks in Washington, Adams had had enough. The weather was already starting into its hazy summer heat. Adams said his goodbyes and headed to Massachusetts. He told Marshall, as secretary of state, that he was now in charge of everything, including being supervisor of the building of the rest of the governmental headquarters in the city, scant few of which were inhabitable, let alone finished.[30]

That this happened would not have been so unusual on the face of it to contemporaries. The government was small and insular. People who worked in it knew one another and there were not many regulations in place yet, nor a vast judiciary to hear disputes. Most of America was incredibly rural. There were only about 5.3 million people in the country, more or less a million of that number being slaves. This was a 35 percent increase in general population over the first census in 1790, but in between, the turmoil in Europe and the opportunity to live in a "free" country caused a virtual frenzy of people who made their way to the new United States.

They did not, though, land in vast cities like London or Paris. London had more than a million people. The largest city in the first census was Philadelphia, with about forty thousand souls. There were only three "cities" with more than twenty-five thousand people in the 1800 census and only three more between ten thousand and that number. Even what we would call small towns today were virtually nonexistent then. Only thirty-three more places had two thousand five hundred or more people. Lancaster, where Adams first stopped to speak on his route from Philadelphia to Washington, was the largest inland municipality in America—with fewer than five thousand people. Richmond, where Marshall made his name, had 5,737 people in 1800, a 52.5 percent rise from ten years before, when it had only 3,761.[31]

So to be the big cheese in a town, like Marshall became in Richmond, would not have been that difficult. That Marshall "knew everyone" as is often said about him, would not have been unusual. That he had enough legal work to amass an upper-middle-class living meant there were not many lawyers in a town so small. A career in government likely would not have been much of an option forty years before under British rule, so this was a learn by doing profession, no different than farming for those who came from cities in Europe. Marshall and his contemporaries got elected, and then figured out what to do with their jobs.

Further, in 1800, only 364,000 of the slightly more than two million white males in the country were forty-five or older, making the competition at the top, after experience, pretty slim. There were few old heads, and lots of young men to get things started, whether it was in government or commerce. So once Marshall, for instance, shimmied his way to the top in Richmond, and then conveyed that to Philadelphia and then Washington, he was responsible, being nearly alone at the top, for figuring out how everything would work.[32]

While he was the boss man in Washington, Marshall moved into the upstairs quarters at the President's House—now the White House—even though it was being worked on while he was there. He looked after foreign affairs, which was a big deal since those years were fraught daily with every communique about France or England, at the very least, if not Spain and the Netherlands. He would stop by other departments to see how things were faring on a day to day basis, though only the Navy Department had a complete building.

That Navy building and its provenance showed how few people there actually were of significance in Washington. Looking for a building, Navy Secretary Benjamin Stoddert used a local with apparently some sway, a guy named William Marbury, to find him a spot. Marbury failed, but he did find himself a new home, a mansion overlooking the Potomac in Georgetown, the home of the former mayor of Georgetown, Uriah Forrest, where in 1791, there had been a dinner for George Washington after the site had been approved to be the capital. Marbury became a big advocate for Adams, especially in the 1800 election in Maryland, and was living there when he filed suit against the Jefferson Administration in 1801 to get his justice of the peace job. Stoddert eventually found grounds for a Navy Department building and got the construction started himself.

In November, the Adamses moved into the President's House, though they perceived, with the Electoral College meeting in a few weeks and news not good from the hinterlands, they would not be there long. Marshall was diligent in getting the Capitol finished as much as possible, since more people would be coming down to work there in the Congress. The President's House still had exposed pipes, unfinished stairways, and unfurnished rooms. The Adamses were said to have a sleepless night in the spooky place the first night they were there, but still, John Adams, ever the forward-thinker, wrote to Abigail about the place, "May none but honest and wise men ever rule under this roof," a line that is now inscribed on a fireplace in the mansion.

Marshall had one more duty in his overseer job. Despite building equipment all over the place, Adams insisted that the public be able to wander through at least part of the grounds around the President's House, being as it was "the people's house," with only a wood rail fence to hold them back. So many gawkers came that they made it into the house unescorted. Marshall had to figure out a security system, which would still allow the flow of onlookers. What those visitors might have seen, though, is the Adams family using a wooden privy in the back—indoor water closets had not yet been built for the presidential family, which would have to wait for the nation's citizen inventor Thomas Jefferson.[33]

Thus, Marshall was already prepared to transform the judicial branch of the government. After all, even such a respected man as John Jay had not done much there in his six years in office. It was a new thing, almost a *tabula rasa*, where one of the most supple men in government could work his trial-and-error magic, just as Fulton would revolutionize river travel with his trial-and-error steamboats, and Eli Whitney would revolutionize cotton growing with his trial-and-error cotton gin. It was an era of can-do men with vast swaths of experience, dreams, and confidence. And John Marshall was as can-do as they came.

CHAPTER FIVE

Marshall Was Almost President, So Who Else Came Close?

THE DATE WAS SERENDIPITOUS, BUT SURELY AN HISTORIAN'S DELIGHT. Seventy-six years to the day before, perhaps the most momentous American event had happened on that very spot—the vote to declare independence from England.

On this day, though, it was another signal American event—the viewing of the body of the most prominent politician of his age in his simple casket in the room where American independence had been declared.

It was something unprecedented in those initial seventy-six years of the republic. Henry Clay had been the first man whose body lay in state in the US Capitol Rotunda. After that, it went by rail through half of America so that citizens in its major cities, and some smaller towns along the way, could pay tribute to him. In early July 1852, it had come to Philadelphia's Independence Hall. No politician before, no matter how hallowed in his age, had received this honor—not George Washington nor Thomas Jefferson; not Alexander Hamilton nor Andrew Jackson; not even the local hero of the Revolutionary Era, Benjamin Franklin.

Clay, though—Clay was a unique American. Practically every major piece of federal legislation for the four decades before his death had to be filtered through him, and often was created by him. The Missouri Compromise, the Compromise of 1850, the Back-to-Africa movement: They were all Clay-inspired. He was in every debate, standing out in front, and never afraid to challenge the power of the day. The Whig Party was his idea—and he reveled in adapting the name from the British party that was opposed to the monarchy. It is not that he was contrary, but he hated entrenched power and thought the best compromise was, indeed, compromise.

Clay had run for president three times officially and tried to get a nomination at least twice more. His country may not have elected him to the top job, but he was no doubt as representative of America's post-Founding-Fathers age as anyone, even the alleged icon of the era, Jackson.[1]

He did everything right in the myth department, and then backed it up by also being a man also of substance. Clay moved West in his youth, married upscale, gambled and drank with the best, loved racing thoroughbreds, and had a standoff duel. He was the youngest person to have several offices—a US Senate seat and Speaker of the US House of Representatives among them. Then he outlasted most of his friends and pretty much all of his enemies.

He started to become mythical early. When James Buchanan was a young lawyer, he decided to go himself from Pennsylvania to Kentucky to adjudicate a land claim dispute for his father. It was 1812 and Kentucky was America's western outpost. Still, Clay's name was enough for the future president to be cowed.

"I went there full of the big impression I was to make—and whom do you suppose I met, There was Henry Clay!" wrote Buchanan in his memoirs. "Why, sire, he was a giant, and I was only a pygmy. Next day I packed my trunk and came back to Lancaster—that was big enough for me."[2]

Clay had opinions on everything and was able to rouse multitudes in his oratory passions from those, yea and nay. He could seemingly convince legislators, diplomats, and sometimes even presidents to advocate positions they naturally would disdain—and often he would change his position because that would make things come out right for what he believed the country craved: unity.

It remained, though, that he never succeeded in the one area he himself craved—that of actually being president. It is probable that no

American worked so hard at trying to become president without succeeding. There always seemed to be a proverbial banana peel to catch him on each of his quadrennial quests.

When the 1848 election eluded him, he seemed finally drained. He would be seventy-five years old the next time around, far beyond the age of any previous candidate. Still, there was a country to keep unified, and Clay engineered the Compromise of 1850, the nation's last, best hope to prevent a civil war. He was that vaunted figure—the Man of the Hour—but the hour was late and tuberculosis was settling in.

Before he acceded to take the nomination of the Republicans in 1796, Thomas Jefferson surmised that the strange thing about the office was that it was a greater honor to be considered for the presidency than actually having it.

"I have not the arrogance to say I would refuse the honorable office you mention to me, but I can say with truth that I would rather be thought worthy of it than to be appointed to it," Jefferson wrote to those who wanted him to run for president that year. "Well I know that no man will ever bring out of that office the reputation which carries him into it."[3]

Despite his own famous quote, "I had rather be right than president," Clay clearly would have loved to have dodged the brickbats Jefferson warned of and hoped to have been both right, and president.

All those who really had been president died in retirement at home, or, like William Henry Harrison and Zachary Taylor, from illness while in office. Clay, almost defiantly, met with aides, confidants, and competitors from his Washington chambers, his family back in Kentucky, maybe all of them still hoping the tuberculosis would lose and 1852 would be Clay's year.

It would not be, but that did not make Clay an unworthy presidential aspirant, yet in his time, the presidency had mutated from one where its occupant was a wide-ranging thinker and doer, to one where the president was more or less a director of the board. Clay would be among the first, and probably most prominent, of those who could have, perhaps should have, been president—America moving along, despite its ultimate leadership being more fallow than it should.

Before Clay's body made it to his plantation, Ashland, in Kentucky, for burial, it passed through Springfield, Illinois. One of the leaders of Illinois politics, Stephen T. Logan, was supposed to give the eulogy when the train stopped in the state capital. At the last minute, though, Logan's junior law partner, a circuit judge named Abraham Lincoln, got the job instead. Lincoln, beardless then and aspiring to greater office as a Whig like Clay, used the opportunity to laud Clay as "my beau ideal of a statesman" whom "all rose after, and set long before him." The speech in the summer sun pushed Lincoln, almost fortuitously because his senior partner ceded the place of honor to him, to greater prominence, and eight years later, he got that opportunity, unlike Clay to be both right—and president.[4]

Lincoln was clearly upset, maybe even flummoxed, by Clay's inability to become president. Clay was a friend of Mary Todd's, Lincoln's wife's, family, which put another sheen on him for Lincoln. In that eulogy, he said that Clay had an "enduring spell" on the American public. Clay was an eloquent speaker, Lincoln, said, not just for the effect, but "from great sincerity [and] thorough conviction." He said that Clay was always there to lead the country into compromise for the great plague of slavery, from bringing North and South together in 1820 for the Missouri Compromise and then again, when he was seventy-three, banging heads together to pass the Compromise of 1850, getting the end of the slave trade in Washington, DC, and California into the Union as a free state in return for a continuation of the Fugitive Slave Law.

As things went in the first decade of the nineteenth century, with only 5.3 million people living in the United States, nine hundred thousand of whom were slaves, there was a significant connection between Clay and John Marshall. Clay, then a young Kentucky politician and attorney, was the lead defense attorney who got Aaron Burr out of an initial grand jury indictment for treason, a case that eventually came before Chief Justice Marshall in the Virginia Circuit Court. Burr was accused, while still vice president, but after his duel with Alexander Hamilton, of planning a military expedition into Spanish territory, allegedly to have a base to form his own nation out of that territory and part of the American West. Clay was an official candidate for the presidency in 1824, as a Democrat-Republican, and then in 1836 and 1844 for the Whigs, a party he was the lead in founding, mostly in opposition to Andrew Jackson and his successors.

The early twenty-first century seemed to pit candidates from the two parties for whom the electorate seemed to believe were a ballot of lesser evils. It culminated in the election of 2016, when the ABC-*Washington Post* poll showed that on the eve of the vote, Hillary Clinton was viewed unfavorably by 56 percent of the nation's adults and Donald Trump by 63 percent, by far the highest—or actually, lowest—readings in the three-decade history of that poll.

How amazingly different that was from the beginning of the nation, though similar kinds of polling were not available then. George Washington was, more or less, elected unanimously—there were Electoral College votes for others, but they were interpreted as a race for vice president, which John Adams won handily in both of the first presidential elections. While Marshall was a possible compromise candidate in the 1800 election, it was because of a glitch in the Electoral College system, fixed by the Twelfth Amendment in 1805, which allowed presidents and vice presidents to run on a ticket, rather than opposed. The first seven presidents were either of the founding clique, a commanding general, or, in the case of Washington, both. Of the possible alternate choices in those early days besides Marshall, a host of founders like Patrick Henry and Ben Franklin were too old by the time they could have run, and Alexander Hamilton and Aaron Burr eliminated themselves by their feud, if not their duel.

After Andrew Jackson and until Abe Lincoln, the power in American politics lay in Congress. None of the presidents in between were of the first rank. Two prominent generals had the bona fides to reach the top—a commanding generalship. William Henry Harrison and Zachary

Taylor, though, were struck down by disease and served less than two years between them.

Two of those other presidents—Martin Van Buren and James Knox Polk—were actually acolytes of Jackson, almost hand-picked by the more significant seventh president. Each served only one term, Van Buren trying again and again to make a comeback, even on the fringe Free Soil Party ticket, and Polk dying soon after his term ended.

The power in the mid-nineteenth century found its way to men like Clay, Daniel Webster, John Calhoun, and Jefferson Davis, all of whom could have been president if the timing were different. Webster actually got a few electoral votes in the 1836 election as a northern Whig supported in his home state, Massachusetts, but that effectively gave the presidency to Van Buren. Webster's resume would be overwhelming if it were in modern times. He was secretary of state three times and served in both houses of Congress. He also appeared in what may be a record number of times before the Supreme Court, more than two hundred arguments, including such monumental cases as *McCullough v. Maryland*, *Gibbons v. Ogden*, and, most famously, *Dartmouth College v. Woodward*, with his four-hour speech culminating in the oft-quoted peroration to Marshall: "Sir, you may destroy this little institution; it is weak, it is in your hands. . . . It is, Sir, as I have said, a small college. And yet there are those who love it."[5]

Calhoun was vice president twice and seemed to be a shoo-in for president, but he ran afoul of Jackson and receded to being the maverick senator from South Carolina. Davis, much like Dick Cheney under George W. Bush, was often said to be the real power as the secretary of war in the Franklin Pierce administration, being Pierce's conduit to Democratic legislative votes, but then the country imploded a few years later and Davis did become president, albeit of the Confederate States of America.

Though Calhoun and Davis were not especially fond of the major legislative compromises Clay and Webster worked on most diligently, they had become resigned to them, even when they came up to the edge on slavery. Davis, of course, became the leading politician of the secessionist movement after the election of Abraham Lincoln, and Calhoun was the leader in South Carolina's threat to nullify the tariffs of 1832-33 and secede if it did not get its way.

Of the four, Clay had the best opportunity to become president—a southerner who had sufficient ties in the North—but any one of them had forceful backers and, had circumstances been different in the country, the list of presidents may have included Webster and Davis instead of Van Buren, Fillmore, and Pierce.

Davis is one of the more curious figures in American history. Born less than a hundred miles from Abraham Lincoln in Kentucky a year earlier than his later presidential rival, Davis eventually moved with his family to Mississippi, where the family developed a cotton farm. Davis returned to Kentucky to go to Transylvania University, which was more or less a prep school, and then got appointed to the US Military Academy at West Point. Davis was a sort of ne'er-do-well by the standards of West Point, once even given house arrest for filching whiskey and putting it in eggnog against academy rules. He was no star pupil either, graduating in the lower third of his class.

He gained cachet as an assistant to General Zachary Taylor in the Michigan Territory, and it was Davis whom Taylor appointed to escort Black Hawk, the Native American leader of the eponymous Black Hawk War of 1832, to prison.

Davis had fallen in love with Taylor's daughter Sarah, and in 1835 asked Taylor if he could marry her. Taylor refused because he did not want her to lead an itinerant army life. Davis agreed, and resigned his command. Unfortunately, the couple chose to take in the summer months at her sister's rural Louisiana home, away from the floodplains in Mississippi. They both contracted either malaria or yellow fever, and Sarah died, at twenty-one, after only three months of marriage. Davis was ill for months and recovered, but the incident helped foster other illnesses that plagued him the rest of his life.[6]

Instead of a military life, Davis became a politician, attending the Democratic state conventions and holding office when he could win an election. He rose to the US House of Representatives in 1845, soon after marrying Varina Howell, the granddaughter of the governor of New Jersey, when he was thirty-eight and she eighteen, an age difference both families frowned upon, yet Varina became his staunchest partisan.

He became a US senator in 1847, and influenced all legislation to have at least something to mollify the South. He was the lead legislator in trying to buy Cuba and make it one or more slave states. He even thought of a Theodore Roosevelt–like expedition to conquer the island. He resigned to run for governor and lost by fewer than a thousand votes, leaving him time to campaign for the 1852 Democratic presidential ticket of Franklin Pierce and William King. Pierce rewarded him by making him secretary of war.

Davis became the presidential whisperer of his age, much like Cheney always seemed to have President George W. Bush's ear. He kept his Cabinet post through the whole Pierce Administration—as did every member of the Cabinet, the only time this ever happened. He was the lead on what seemed to be a zillion projects.[7]

He authorized surveys to see where a transcontinental railway could go. He got Pierce to sign off on the Gadsden Purchase of Mexican land in southern Arizona as a prime spot for a railroad line. He increased the size of the standing peacetime military from eleven thousand to fifteen thousand and raised pay for all soldiers. Pierce spearheaded the building of the Washington Aqueduct in the capital and the expansion of the US Capitol, among other projects, all on Davis's recommendation.

When the party bosses thought Pierce a dead candidate in the 1856 election, Davis made himself available, but the party, on the convention's sixteenth ballot, instead gave the nomination to longtime party officeholder James Buchanan, whose ineptness, ironically enough, caused secession and the Civil War, and Davis got his top job, albeit the presidency of the Confederacy. After the Civil War, Davis strongly campaigned against thoughts of a second secession, saying the Union was worth saving—and working within for what the South would need. Had Buchanan not been so inept, perhaps the country would have seen, in 1860 or beyond, a President Davis.[8]

A confusion of parties probably thwarted William Seward's attempts to be president. He was a New York state senator in the 1830s under the Anti-Mason banner, and then ran for governor as a Whig and lost. He won the next time, serving four years, and then was elected twice as a Whig to the US Senate. He moved to the Republican Party in 1855 and probably could have gotten the party's first presidential nomination, but he saw no way to win and so stayed in the Senate while John C. Fremont lost to James Buchanan in 1856.

As things started sliding downhill quickly in the Buchanan Administration—the *Dred Scott* decision disaster, followed by a precipitous recession and then the continued mayhem in the Kansas Territory—Seward primed himself for a presidential run in 1860. As the leader of the newly energized Republicans in New York and the East, he started lining up support early.[9]

What Seward did not count on, however, was the rise of the ex-congressman from Illinois, Abraham Lincoln. As Lincoln entered his debates with Stephen Douglas for the 1858 Senate race, it was already assumed he would lose the political race. Seward, to be frank, never viewed Lincoln to be his competition. As word spread, though, about Lincoln's performance in those debates, western party bosses saw a chance to have someone on the ticket from their section of the country. No one from the old Northwest Territory had been a major presidential candidate. Further, they secured the Republican convention for Chicago and, once there, had massive pro-Lincoln rallies nearby. Seward was blindsided, and Lincoln became the nominee. To Seward's shock, though, Lincoln was solicitous of him, asking advice, and eventually naming him secretary of state. It was no false recognition, as the two met often, especially in the depths of the Civil War.

Seward's reputation has grown over the years, especially as the purchase of Alaska, which he engineered, went from "Seward's Folly" to a natural resource–laden bargain. Like Alexander Hamilton in the musical

Hamilton, Seward's character shone in the film *Lincoln*, and thus his reputation was burnished for twenty-first century audiences. There is little doubt that he would have performed well had he been elected instead of Lincoln, since the president did take a lot of his counsel. Yet having laid back in 1856 and having been outmaneuvered in 1860, he was not to have a third chance at the presidency itself.[10]

Democratic contemporaries of his would say Samuel Tilden actually was elected president and was not really a could-have-been. Tilden was a reform governor of New York, having not only eschewed help from Tammany Hall's bosses but also called for prosecution of their corrupt practices. He was for civil service reform and the gold standard to quell the Panic of 1873. The Republicans nominated another reform-minded governor, Rutherford B. Hayes of Ohio, and ran on the politics of Lincoln and Reconstruction in the South.[11]

There was, however, a schism between Tilden and the leaders in primarily Democratic states, especially in the South. Democrats loved that Tilden was successful in being elected, especially in a swing state like New York, but the southern states mostly wanted to get out of Reconstruction reforms. On election day, Tilden clearly won states, falling one shy of a majority of the electoral vote, and he also won the majority of the nation's popular vote. Four states, though, had close votes, two of which initially favored Tilden. A complex set of maneuverings tried to settle the dispute, as both sides apparently went out of their way to manipulate the returns in the four states.

Finally, just before the election would have gone to the House of Representatives, like it had when John Quincy Adams had won a half-century before, the Compromise of 1877 emerged. Essentially, the compromise allowed Hayes to take office if the Republicans acceded to the southern Democrats and dismantled Reconstruction. Hayes himself emerged rather unscathed, since he vowed to serve only one term and continued pressing for other reforms, but the nation itself stayed tense. The army mobilized in Washington and nearby to diffuse any thought of armed rebellion.[12]

Tilden, a bachelor, was favored again to be nominated for president in 1880, but he had various health issues and demurred. He made a half-hearted effort to get the 1884 nomination, but by that time another Democratic New York governor, Grover Cleveland, was ascendant and Tilden stepped aside.

Tilden is still the only presidential candidate to get the majority of popular votes (more than 50 percent) and not be elected president. (Andrew Jackson, Grover Cleveland, Al Gore, and Hillary Clinton had pluralities, not the majority.) He may well have been manipulated by national Democrats had he won, losing his reform ideals, but he would never have the chance to find out.[13]

William Jennings Bryan, like Henry Clay, got to run three times for president, all as the Democratic candidate, from what at the time was looked upon as the frontier—in Clay's case, Kentucky, and in Bryan's, Nebraska. Neither state has had a serious candidate since—Lincoln grew up in Kentucky but spent his adult life in Illinois. Each of them tried to be conciliatory and progressive for their eras. Both were said to be amazing orators, Bryan being nicknamed The Great Commoner.

Though Bryan was most well-known as the model for Fredric March's Matthew Harrison Brady in the 1960 film *Inherit the Wind*, railing against evolution in the infamous Monkey Trial in Tennessee, he did not play the fool during the decades he spent in politics, seeking reform at every crossroads.[14]

Bryan was one of the more complex men in American political history. He grew up in the small town of Salem, Illinois (not to be confused with New Salem, where Lincoln lived in his early adult years, and which was sixty miles to the west). His father was a local politician who eventually rose to be a state circuit judge. Bryan was the oldest surviving child, three older ones having died in infancy, though his mother gave birth to five more after him. She homeschooled Bryan until he was a teenager, encouraging his precocity in public speaking. He gave public speeches from the time he was four, and he also attended them, especially religious ones, and had what he called a "conversion experience" at age fourteen.

Thereafter he went to a private high school, then college nearby and to what became Northwestern University Law School.[15]

He worked in Illinois for a few years, and then in 1887, a law school buddy convinced Bryan that Nebraska was a golden land with plenty of room for growth, so Bryan moved to the capital of Lincoln and went into practice with that law school classmate, Adolphus Talbot. He also decided to get into politics and won a seat in Congress in 1890, only three years after coming to the state. He was just thirty years old. His three main campaign issues were lowering tariffs, limiting the power of big corporations and, most famously, growth in the coining of silver while getting off the gold standard, which he associated with the fat-cat corporation czars and big bankers. Bryan was only the second Democrat elected to Congress from Nebraska. In 1892, he disdained support for the Democratic presidential candidate, Grover Cleveland, because he felt Cleveland too conservative and stumped for the Populist Party candidate James B. Weaver instead. With a smidgen of local Republican support, Bryan won that election, but only by 140 votes.

Then came the Panic of 1893 and, not coincidentally, the decline of the Democratic Party. Bryan gave up his seat in the House to run for Senate, but the Republicans were ascendant and he lost.[16]

Bryan, though, did not panic. By that time, he had become editor-in-chief of the *Omaha World Herald*. He did not run the day to day operation, leaving it to real news people, but it gave him a forum for his political ideas. He went on a nationwide speaking tour, advocating free silver and attempting to push the Democratic Party to be one of reform, not conservatism.

When the 1896 Democratic Convention rolled into Chicago, free silver was having its day. As a main advocate of the issue, Bryan got a chance to speak on its behalf the day before the actual balloting. There he gave one of the grand speeches in American history, nicknamed the "Cross of Gold Speech," where he defined his people as the real people of America, as opposed to the rich plutocrats of the gold standard.

"If they dare to come out in the open field and defend the gold standard as a good thing, we shall fight them to the uttermost, having behind us the producing masses of the nation and the world," Bryan said, while seemingly raising his voice at every phrase. "Having behind us the commercial interests and the laboring interests and all the toiling masses, we shall answer their demands for a gold standard by saying to them, 'You shall not press down upon the brow of labor this crown of thorns. You shall not crucify mankind upon a cross of gold.'"[17]

The crowd shrieked its approval and demonstrated in the aisles for a half-hour. By the time the first ballot rolled around the next day, Bryan was in second place, and by the fifth ballot he had the nomination, the youngest man, at thirty-six, ever to get a presidential nomination from a major party.[18]

Since the Republicans had a huge campaign finance advantage, and a candidate, William McKinley, who represented the industrial states' growing power, Bryan and the Democrats had to invent a new presidential campaign strategy. Unlike most previous candidates, and certainly McKinley, who stayed near home and let surrogates stump around the nation, Bryan went on a national speech-making tour—seeing five million people in twenty-seven states. He was able to build a coalition of white southerners, poor farmers, and hopeful silver miners. It was not enough, as McKinley won the entire Northeast, much of the Midwest, and the Pacific coast.[19]

Bryan, though, had built up a following, and though the Gold Standard Act was passed, many in his coalition hoped he would be able to overturn it. Then President McKinley handed Bryan his next passion with the Spanish-American War. Initially Bryan supported the war, in hopes that Cuba would gain its freedom through it. But then, the administration chose to keep the Philippines. Bryan, who was given a command in the Nebraska National Guard, but did not see active duty, did not want the United States to become a colonial power.

He got the 1900 Democratic nomination unanimously on the first ballot. The party still had platforms on free silver and trust-busting, but the economy was decent and McKinley fortuitously chose Teddy Roosevelt as his running mate—nearly as young as Bryan, but also now famous as the swashbuckling leader of the charge up San Juan Hill in Cuba. Roosevelt was also, like Bryan, good at giving speeches, and this time McKinley won by an even bigger margin.[20]

Bryan sat out the 1904 presidential campaign, in which Alton Parker, the Democrat, got swamped by Teddy Roosevelt. In the meantime, Bryan published a weekly magazine, *The Commoner*, which espoused Bryan's progressive political, but also his strict religious, views. It eventually reached a circulation of 145,000. For 1908, he was ready to get back on the presidential trail and easily won the Democratic nomination, but Roosevelt's choice to succeed him, his longtime friend William Howard Taft, took on a lot of the progressive ideas that Bryan leaned on—though not women's suffrage, which was part of Bryan's later platforms—in effect neutralizing Bryan as a candidate. Taft won easily.[21]

Bryan did not recede from view, however. He crisscrossed the nation giving speech after speech on his many subjects—the need for prohibition of liquor; the moral imperative of women's suffrage; the limitation of tariffs; state-owned railroads; the ballot approach to some legislation by initiative from the states.

He became President Woodrow Wilson's secretary of state, signing treaties with twenty-nine nations, from El Salvador to the major powers of Europe, save Germany and Austria-Hungary. In 1914, Bryan tried to negotiate a swift end to what would become World War I, but failed. When Wilson sent an official rebuke to Germany in 1915, Bryan knew that he, as secretary of state, could not countenance the US entry into the war, having cleaved to the Wilson who campaigned on "He kept us out of war."[22]

After he resigned, Bryan took the part of Famous Man, doing lots of things in a somewhat scattershot manner. He went on speaking tours for some pet causes—decent minimum wage, Prohibition, women's suffrage, agricultural subsidies—and still got lots of people fired up for him to run for president again. He even got involved in the Florida land rush, moving to Miami and touting the new development of nearby Coral Gables. By 1924, he was a delegate to the Democratic National Convention, in time to have his brother, Charles, be nominated for vice president on a ticket with John W. Davis, a ticket that lost badly to Calvin Coolidge.[23]

However, what Bryan was known for at the end of his life was his speeches against the theory of evolution. He was one of the first radio preachers, and he also published several books espousing biblical literalism. Five states did vote to prohibit the teaching of evolution in the public schools, one of them being Tennessee, whose restriction was called the Butler Act. The American Civil Liberties Union, in order to protest the law, had a substitute teacher named John Scopes teach evolution in a classroom and get arrested for it.

Scopes's trial in rural Dayton, Tennessee, was attended by national press, including the sardonic columnist H. L. Mencken. The famous defense attorney, Clarence Darrow, agreed to defend Scopes for free. Since everyone agreed that Scopes broke the law, the trial itself was a forum for the debate around Darwin's theory of evolution. Darrow called Bryan as a witness to expound upon his belief in biblical literalism. Reporters, particularly Mencken, thought Bryan had embarrassed himself, but Bryan never thought that, so when he was not allowed to give a closing statement, he had it published, criticizing science as amoral and promoting the Bible's word as literally sacred. Bryan had plans to go around the country, speaking his gospel, but he died days after the trial ended in Dayton and received what amounted to a state funeral at Arlington National Cemetery.[24]

Because of the Scopes Trial, and his ignoring of Jim Crow laws, opinion about Bryan is mixed. In the movie *Inherit The Wind*, somewhat based on the Scopes Trial, he is played by Fredric March as a blowhard, solidifying that view of him. In 1934, though, Franklin Roosevelt said of Bryan: "It was [his] sincerity which made him a force for good in his own generation and kept alive many of the ancient faiths on which we are building today. We . . . can well agree that he fought the good fight, that he finished the course, and that he kept the faith."[25]

Charles Evans Hughes had a uniquely varied background before becoming the Republican candidate for President in 1916 against the incumbent Woodrow Wilson. Though he was never in Congress, he had been the governor of New York and an associate justice of the Supreme Court and, while in private practice in New York City, had been on any number of commissions and boards.[26]

Republicans had won most of the elections from the time of Lincoln through the early twentieth century, only Grover Cleveland and Wilson breaking the streak for the Democrats. Hughes had an impeccable reputation. He had gotten the highest score ever for an applicant to the New York Bar, after having graduated from Brown University and Columbia University Law School, despite being homeschooled for much of his youth.

The presidency, though, was to elude him. Despite taking many of the progressive stances that had gotten Teddy Roosevelt elected, and that he had implemented as New York's governor, he got swamped by Wilson in the South and Midwest, winning only four states west of the Mississippi or south of the Ohio. Wilson was known as a pacifist then, which went along with the isolationist views of the South and Midwest. It became ironic, then, that a year later, he signed on to World War I.[27]

Hughes might have run in 1920, but his daughter, Helen, had died that year from tuberculosis and he felt too distraught to run. He accepted Warren Harding's offer of secretary of state when Harding won in 1920, and stayed on through the first part of Calvin Coolidge's administration. Hughes was a vocal advocate for the League of Nations but finally relented on the topic in 1921, when his party in Congress became firmly against it, turning isolationist again.

He resigned and went back to private practice, taking on high-profile, mostly business cases in his Wall Street firm. When Chief Justice—and former president—William Howard Taft became severely ill, Taft resigned and asked then President Herbert Hoover to consider Hughes as his successor, which came to be.[28]

Hughes was the moderating force between ardent conservative and liberal forces on the bench during the Hoover and Roosevelt administrations. He retired again in 1941, just before World War II erupted, and went back to New York to practice until he finally retired a few years later. He died at the age of eighty-six in 1948.[29]

Though Hughes considered himself far too old at that point, Roosevelt himself was vulnerable in 1940. The Depression was not completely over and the war had started in Europe, with the nation not officially taking sides but clearly banking toward the Allied cause. Further, no president had run for a third term, with Washington setting the tone and refusing calls for him to run again after his second term ended in 1797. It was presumptuous by Roosevelt, and all signs pointed to the Republicans nominating a different kind of candidate.

They surely did in Wendell Willkie, who was a Democrat only months before the Republicans nominated him. Born in Indiana, Willkie first became a lawyer in his small hometown, Elwood, Indiana, but then rose in business in Akron and finally on Wall Street. He had somewhat unconventional views for a Wall Street lawyer. He hoped the country would get into the war in Europe, unlike most conservative isolationists. He was not so much pro-business as anti-anti-business, but he also was a big supporter of government programs to help individuals succeed. In fact, as early as 1937, when it was not yet apparent Roosevelt would seek a third term, Democratic bosses sent feelers out for Willkie to be their party's nominee.[30]

The Republicans met in Philadelphia, with Willkie's two main rivals, Robert Taft and Thomas Dewey, still espousing isolationism. While the convention was meeting, the Nazis, having steamrolled through France, announced they were making an attack imminently on Britain. Willkie won the nomination the next day.

He campaigned vigorously; the photos of him speaking always showed his tousled hair. When Secretary of the Interior Harold L. Ickes mockingly called Willkie, "a simple, barefoot Wall Street lawyer," Willkie actually liked the sound of it and had supporters use it. Willkie's first formal rally, in his ancestral town of Elwood, was reported to have one hundred fifty thousand in attendance, the most ever for a political rally.

Roosevelt took the tactic of not campaigning, saying the work around the war was too important to leave Washington. Willkie took the other tack and whistlestopped through all but the Deep South states, which would surely go to Roosevelt. Since both were interventionists, the war was effectively off the table. Since most Americans said their top issue was the war, and that Roosevelt had done a relatively decent job around it, Willkie was doomed. He did get twenty-two million votes, more than any Republican in history and more than any in the future until Eisenhower.[31]

After his defeat, he went to Roosevelt and said he would help him in any way. He even proposed forming a liberal party, made up of disaffected Democrats and Republicans, but Roosevelt was happy to stick where he was. Roosevelt dispatched Willkie to England to find out what he could. He eventually went through North Africa, the Middle East, and China for Roosevelt, and his recounting of that thirty-one-thousand-mile trip, *One World*, became a bestseller in early 1944. Willkie took more and more liberal positions, like promising to racially integrate the Army and advocating against colonialism.[32] He tried to run again in 1944, but his policies were either too far past—interventionism—or too soon—civil rights. His health was failing him, though. He suffered through multiple heart attacks, some reports said a dozen of them, in the summer and fall of 1944, finally succumbing on October 8, a month before the next election. A mercurial character on the American scene, to be sure, Willkie was eulogized by Roosevelt as having "tremendous courage." It "prompted him more than once to stand alone. . . . In this hour of grave crisis the nation loses a great citizen."[33]

Then there was Adlai Stevenson, most well-known to those who peruse historical photographs as the candidate with the hole in his soles, presumably from working so hard. A father and son (John and John Quincy Adams) and a grandfather and grandson (William Henry and Benjamin Harrison) had been presidents, but the elder outshined the latter in both cases. Grandfather Adlai Stevenson I had been vice president under Grover Cleveland and father Lewis Stevenson almost became the Democratic nominee for vice president in 1928. Adlai II, despite the handicap of growing up in an upper-class section of Bloomington, Illinois, and going to private schools, became as much a man of the working Joes and Josephines as any twentieth-century politician.[34]

He married a rich socialite, Ellen Borden, and they were the fun couple of their group, particularly apt to give costume parties. They had three children, one, Adlai III eventually becoming a US senator from Illinois in the 1970s and 1980s. Born at the turn of the new century, in 1900, Stevenson became a reformer and progressive. His first jobs in government, after working for several years in a prominent Chicago law firm, were in Roosevelt's New Deal. He then went back to practicing law in Chicago but volunteering for Democratic and progressive bodies, like the Committee to Defend America By Aiding the Allies in 1940 and 1941.[35]

During World War II, Stevenson was a speechwriter for Secretary of the Navy Frank Knox, and when Knox died near the end of the war, Stevenson worked in the State Department. Secretary of State Edward Stettinius soon made him a delegate to the commission that would form the United Nations.

So when Jacob Arvey, the head of the Chicago Democratic clubhouse, looked around for a candidate for the Illinois governorship in 1948, Stevenson was clean, experienced, and ready to hold elective office for the first time at age forty-eight.[36]

Stevenson projected what he wanted to about himself during the governorship—being an intellectual with good public speaking skills. That served him well among the Democratic leaders as a juxtaposition to the sure Republican candidate, Dwight Eisenhower. Like other worthy candidates running against a war hero—Henry Clay clearly comes to mind against Andrew Jackson—he hardly stood a chance, despite his energetic speaking and a reputation so impeccable, even Eisenhower liked him. He brought young people and serious thinkers into the Democratic Party, reviving it in a new way. He got the nomination again in 1956, but lost when Eisenhower's recent heart attack proved not to be a campaign issue.[37] Stevenson tried again in 1960, but by that time, younger Democrats like John Kennedy and Lyndon Johnson had taken the stage from him. Senator Eugene McCarthy from Minnesota put his name in nomination, with his impassioned speech asking them not to "reject the man who has made us proud to be Democrats. Do not leave this prophet without honor in his own party."[38]

Kennedy, after winning the presidency, and despite his general antipathy toward Stevenson, made him ambassador to the United Nations, and Stevenson died from a heart attack in that job when on a mission in Britain in 1965, not a prophet without honor in his party, but not its president either.[39]

CHAPTER SIX

The Necessity of the American Myth

"ON JULY 8, 1835," JEAN EDWARD SMITH WROTE AT THE END OF THE introduction of his 1996 biography, *John Marshall: Definer of a Nation*, "as Marshall's funeral cortege made its way through the city, the muffled bells of Philadelphia reverberated their mournful message. As fate would have it, July 8 marked the anniversary of that date in 1776 when Philadelphia's bells had first rung out to celebrate American independence. And then, on that day in 1835, again as if by fate, the greatest of the bells, the Liberty Bell in Independence Hall, went silent. It had cracked while tolling the death of the great chief justice. It was never to ring again."[1]

Though Smith has one hundred endnotes for that twenty-page introduction, there are none for the last three sentences above. The anecdote he describes, the ringing of the Liberty Bell, its cracking and its silence again thereafter, is not found in any other major biography of Marshall, nor in the official National Park Service history of the Liberty Bell. There is a good reason for this.

Though it had become an oft-told tale, none of it is true. The Liberty Bell did not ring that day—it was precariously hung in the rickety tower of Independence Hall, so difficult to get moving to ring. It had already had a crack, but it was rung ceremonially at functions later and taken on tour when it was named the Liberty Bell, as opposed to its long-standing association with Independence Hall as the Pennsylvania state house, and carefully rung all around the country on several excursions.

The bell also was not ringing, as legend had it, when the proclamation of the Declaration of Independence was made on July 8, 1776, or at least no newspaper mentioned it. In fact, the Liberty Bell was not named as such until it appeared on a pamphlet at the Massachusetts Anti-Slavery Fair in 1839 in Boston—and that "Liberty" part did not have anything to do with the founding of the country but was instead about the attempt to free slaves.[2]

Yet that in and of itself does not make the Marshall Bell story without value. On the contrary, its value lies in that it makes Marshall's life more of a story to be retold, for if a character is imbued with myth, and that myth's extent is heightened so that it changes important parts of history, Marshall enters that realm of what modern myth-makers call "larger than life."

Marshall himself was a large cog in the machine of myth-making around George Washington. Soon after the general died, his nephew, Bushrod Washington, a fellow Supreme Court justice and longtime friend of Marshall's, got control of Washington's papers and, deciding he would not be good for the job, offered the honor of writing George Washington's first biography to Marshall.

Bushrod Washington knew Marshall to be at least an acolyte of his uncle's, if not a sycophant. He also knew Marshall could use the money such a project would no doubt spin off. Marshall was still in debt for buying a chunk of the old Fairfax estates in Virginia, and though his chief justice's salary was enough to keep him going for normal expenses, it was not enough to unburden him of the debt of the land purchase.

So Bushrod Washington arranged to have the publisher C.P. Wayne of Philadelphia sell subscriptions to what would be a five-volume biography at $3 a volume, with the first couple of books due by 1803. It was a disaster, a year late and several dollars short. At least a quarter of the original subscribers had asked for their money back by the time the first volume—an "Introduction" of mostly a dry recounting of the country's history before Washington—came out in 1804. By the time it was all done several years later, John Adams, who adored both Washington and

Marshall, panned it as "a Mausoleum, 100 feet square at the base and 200 feet high."

Still, sanitizing and mythologizing Washington was more well done by Parson Mason Locke Weems. A year after Washington's death, in 1800, Weems was ready to pounce. Washington actually had suffered in esteem in his later years. The Federalists, of whom he was the titular head, bungled a lot of policies, both foreign and domestic, and Washington took many hits. Even Benjamin Bache, Ben Franklin's grandson, made Ben's old friend a target for his editorials in the *Aurora*, his Philadelphia newspaper.

"If ever a nation was debauched by a man," Bache wrote of Washington in December 1796, "the American nation has been by Washington." And when John Adams took over the presidency in 1797, Bache wrote, "Every heart, in unison with the freedom and happiness of the people, ought to beat high in exultation, that the name of Washington ceases from this day to give a currency to political iniquity and to legalize corruption."[3]

Yet, as Daniel Boorstin noted in his 1965 social and political history, *The Americans*, "What is most remarkable is not that Washington eventually became a demigod, Father of his Country, but that the transfiguration happened so quickly. There is no better evidence of the desperate need Americans felt for a dignified and worshipful national hero than their passionate haste in elevating Washington to sainthood. . . . To this end, many people had collaborated, but the cult could not have grown so quickly or so vigorously without the peculiar American needs and vacuums."[4]

Weems was ready for action, having started collecting biographical material on Washington during his time as an itinerant bookseller, his evangelical career as an Episcopalian minister petering out when he was thirty-four in 1793. Ironically enough, he was employed by C.P. Wayne to sell those subscriptions to Marshall's volumes. He wrote an eighty-page booklet that did not get much traction in 1800, but Weems saw that Marshall's first sales were awful and went to the publisher, Matthew Carey, and tried to convince him to drop the rest of Marshall's volumes and go with his version instead.

In 1806, a year before Marshall finally completed his opus, Weems had rewritten his book, cumbersomely titled, *Life of George Washington: With Curious Anecdotes, Equally Honourable to Himself and Exemplary to His Young Countrymen.* It did the job Marshall's dreary, if factual, volumes could not. It eventually went to twenty printings by the time Weems died in 1825, selling at least, by estimates, fifty thousand copies in the first few editions, ten times more than Marshall could muster.

For that 1806 edition, Weems added what has probably become American history's most enduring myth. George, playing with his new hatchet, chops down his father's favorite cherry tree. As Dad is wondering what happened, young George, saying he cannot face telling a lie, admits it was him. Instead of this becoming a sad story, Weems quotes Dad in almost sycophantic form himself:

"'Run to my arms, you dearest boy,' cried his father. 'Run to my arms; glad am I, George, that you killed my tree; for you have paid me for it a thousand fold. Such an act of heroism in my son, is more worth than a thousand trees, though blossomed with silver, and their fruits of purest gold.'"

George's schoolmates cry when he leaves them. George apologizes again to Dad after he eats a whole apple, not giving some to his siblings. George's mother dreams of him becoming a great leader in the eventual Revolution. An Indian warrior during the French and Indian War says, "Washington was not born to be killed by a bullet! For, I had seventeen fair fires at him with my rifle, and after all could not bring him to the ground."

Weems excuses these and other whoppers by saying his book is for "the admiring eyes of our children" and says the book should not be looked at as nonfiction but as a category he called booster literature.

"Where shall we look for Washington, the greatest among men, but in America?" Weems writes in the first chapter of his book. "So far superior to any thing of the kind in the other continents, that we may fairly conclude that great men and great deeds are designed for America."[5]

In a way, then, Weems did not just become famous and relatively well off because he perpetrated a fraud of sorts; he provided what the nation needed—a founding myth, or at least a mythical leader at its founding. Other countries had long-standing traditions, and long-ago heroes. America, being the new idea among nations, did not have time to wait centuries to prove itself. It needed a myth to count on quickly.

Washington was, indeed, the man to hang the myth on. He had his detractors. Some said his military might was merely being good at retreating. Others said he added few, if any, substantial political philosophy ideals to the formation of the Union. A large majority, though, saw his bearing and ability to organize and bridge factions as the most substantial personal trait of anyone in the Revolutionary brigade.

Washington was already a mythical figure of sorts when he was made commander of the Revolutionary forces, taking command in Boston in 1775. Most of his seventeen thousand troops there had never seen him in person, and most portraits of him that circulated were imaginary and looked nothing like him. Many of them immediately called him "Lesemo," as in "generalissimo."

When they did see him or hear of his supposed powers, they were mostly impressed. He stood more than six feet tall, which was power-forward height in the late 1700s. He looked so powerful in the saddle that some believed he could have been the premier horseman of his time. He had wide set gray eyes and high cheekbones, which made him seem aristocratic in a sea of rough-hewn soldiers.

"Dignity with ease and complacency, the gentleman and soldier look agreeably blended in him. Modesty marks every line and feature of his face," John Adams's wife Abigail told John when she met Washington. She then paraphrased John Dryden, the poet: "Mark his majestic fabric! He's a temple / Sacred by birth, and built by hands divine."[6] His men heard the wondrous tale of his service on the Monongahela during the French and Indian War—that he survived four bullets through his uniform and had two horses shot from under him, then dragged his mortally wounded commander, Major General Edward Braddock, across the river and rode sixty miles for help in staying a step ahead of the British as they retreated.

The need for the myth to become permanent was evident in the national mourning following Washington's death at Mount Vernon on December 14, 1799, conveniently coming near the end of the millennium, making Washington a grace note in the timing.

It took three days for the news to get to the capital, which almost immediately became draped in black crepe, from the State House and congressional meeting rooms to the presidential mansion to homes up and down every street and alley. Roads and communications being what they were it took several weeks for the news to disseminate, not reaching Frankfort, Kentucky, for instance, until January 9, 1800.

John Marshall, generally acknowledged to be the most prominent Washington booster in Congress, introduced a resolution to make December 26 the day of mourning in Philadelphia and to have a national period of mourning until what would have been Washington's next birthday, February 22, 1800. By that time, more than four hundred memorial services already had taken place around the new nation.

Typical was the one that took place in the capital. A memorial parade on December 26, with soldiers and congressmen at the front, wound around Philadelphia, ending at the German Lutheran Church, where one of Washington's favorite officers, Major General Henry Lee, gave a rousing eulogy.

"First in war. First in peace. And first in the hearts of his countrymen," Lee said with passion. "His example was as edifying to all around him as were the effects of that example lasting."[7]

In the eulogies, Washington was compared to kings, current and ancient, but also biblical figures, most often Moses. Napoleon declared a period of mourning of ten days in France and delivered a eulogy himself at the Temple of Mars, including these words, "He seems so little to belong to modern times that he imparts to us the same vivid impressions as the most august examples of antiquity."

Abigail Adams was more succinct: "History will not produce to us a parallel."

The alternative myth in the early American narrative was that everyone from scrubmaiden to land baron was of equal footing in the history of this new nation of alleged equality. It is difficult to see it that way, even in retrospect.

"The democratic, sentimental idea that cobblers and seamstresses are as much history makers as generals and politicians is false," writes conservative columnist George Will. "A few individuals matter much more than most. . . . No George Washington, no United States.

"The more that Americans are reminded by . . . supreme practitioners of the historians' craft that their nation was not made by flimsy people, the less likely it is to be flimsy," writes Will.[8]

Between Weems and Marshall, though, there was little flaw-mongering. Washington, in this necessary myth phase, was not dipped by his heel in the River Styx, but fully flushed in the waters of immortality. It was no better when Jared Sparks, who would become Harvard's first professor of history and then president of Harvard itself, got the rights to publish Washington's papers from Bushrod Washington, subject to the editing of any material Bushrod thought inappropriate to publish. Sparks, then the editor of the *North American Review*, a leading serious critical magazine out of Boston, would promise to publish the papers "in a form suited to the dignity of the subject, a national interest and a national feeling would be exited, and a wide and honorable patronage might be expected." Not to mention that Sparks would split the profits with Bushrod and Marshall, who would no longer have to decide whether to do the work themselves. For the better part of a decade, between 1827 and 1837, Sparks culled everything Washington kept, a monumental task and nothing that had been attempted before in America. Over the three years from 1834 to 1837, eleven volumes of selected papers and a whole new biography of Washington came from Sparks's pen.

Life and Writings of George Washington was a smash. Washington's family gave Sparks, in tribute, a cedar cane fashioned from wood from the tree next to Washington's tomb. George Bancroft, the founder of the United States Naval Academy and the first prominent scholarly American historian, said the series was "beyond my praise for its calmness, accuracy, and intense interest of authenticity." In his own *North American Review*,

Sparks commissioned the never-succinct Edward Everett (known later as the orator who spent hours talking at Gettysburg before Lincoln summed the real issues up in minutes) to "review" *Life and Writings*, which he managed to do in only sixty-three pages, concluding, "Not a single trait of indiscretion is disclosed in his work."

And therein lies the issue. The need for an American hero was still paramount a half-century after the founding of the country. Sparks's Washington was flawless. He had no blemishes, physical or in character. "His moral qualities were in perfect harmony with those of his intellect," Sparks concluded. Sparks did not leap to conclusions; he bounded over credulity. Sparks, a Unitarian minister in his early years, felt a need to establish Washington as a moral and practicing Christian. Washington was known for not taking communion, even during his rare visits to a church, many of which were ceremonial as a political and military leader. Sparks could produce no papers from Washington that expounded on his possible Christian beliefs, but neither did he find any to doubt them. Thus, Sparks's Washington was respectful and tolerant of those who might be offended by any religious writing—no truer Christian, then, lived in the nation.

Marshall was not the only "celebrity" biographer of Washington. Though in the modern era Washington was the subject of biographies, some multivolume like Marshall's by noted historians like Ron Chernow, James Thomas Flexner, Douglas Southall Freeman, and James MacGregor Burns, prior to that, lives of Washington were the province of really big names. Woodrow Wilson wrote a scholarly biography of Washington prior to his own presidency. Washington Irving wrote one, as did Henry Adams, the grandson and great-grandson of presidents himself. Owen Wister, author of the great novel *The Virginian* wrote a Washington biography, as did Henry Cabot Lodge, President Wilson's major senatorial nemesis in the president's quest for the League of Nations.

Washington, then, was the necessary man for the new republic, not only in life, but also in his mythical residue after his death.

Once established with Washington, the American myth-making machine rarely wavered. Mostly, it took a trait of the subject, however vague, and made it into a "truth" to be repeated and enhanced in as many types of media as possible over time. Ben Franklin and his kite; Davy Crockett and his glib bravado and coonskin cap; Lincoln and his rail-splitting; Civil War general Abner Doubleday inventing baseball; any number of politicians and their births in log cabins.

As the nation left its founding phase and went into one of adventurous homesteading, it needed another type of mythical figure, and Davy Crockett was ready for it. His feats were indeed legendary—killing 105 bears in 1825 and 1826; outrunning captors and ferocious animals; making peace with hostile Indians; manufacturing his own gunpowder. A lot of it lies in an 1834 autobiography that he used in one of his many US congressional runs.

When he realized the account of his alleged exploits was not just effective campaigning but good reading for the masses, Crockett went out on tour, telling his folksy stories and enhancing his legend. Such a scene had never happened in the United States, so many observers thought he was prepping himself for a presidential run.

Crockett even wrote an anti-campaign presidential biography of Andrew Jackson's chosen successor, Martin Van Buren. Crockett was back and forth on Jackson himself, supporting him in some cases during his congressional terms in the 1830s, but severing himself from Jackson's ill-treatment of the Creeks. So when Van Buren ran, Crockett penned a book with the unwieldy title *The Life of Martin Van Buren: Heir-Apparent to the "Government" and the Appointed Successor of General Andrew Jackson: Containing Every Authentic Particular by Which His Extraordinary Character Has Been Formed: With a Concise History of the Events That Have Occasioned His Unparalleled Elevation: Together With a Review of His Policy as a Statesman.*

Rather than stay around and stick it even more to the Jacksonians, though, Crockett saw a chance to continue enhancing his populist reputation in Texas. He got there in January 1836 and within weeks met his demise at The Alamo, which only made his legend grander. Many people have been in Congress for a few years, but few died in an ambush, allegedly with a dozen dead Mexicans at his feet and a much-bloodied knife buried in one of them.[9]

Crockett was the subject of books for nearly a century after his death, culminating in a three-part Walt Disney TV series starring Fess Parker doing all sorts of frontier-guy things, especially wearing a coonskin cap with a coon tail akimbo. (Author Note: I still have the coonskin cap my uncle, a furrier, made for me around the time of the 1955 series on my office shelf.)

One of those other log-cabin births belonged to James Garfield, a somewhat improbable choice to run for president in 1880. Though by the time he ran, he had been a brigadier general in the Civil War, the president of Hiram College, and a US senator from Ohio, none of that was deemed as saleable on its own as a proper myth-flaked campaign biography.

Garfield entered the convention way down the list of Ohio politicians. The incumbent president, Rutherford B. Hayes, who eventually took himself out of the running for a second term, was a former Ohio governor. Former president Ulysses S. Grant, another Ohioan, led in early balloting, and the secretary of the treasury, John Sherman, for whom Garfield entered the convention as campaign manager, had preceded Garfield as a senator.

Garfield had placed Sherman's name in nomination with a fiery speech. By the thirty-fifth ballot, Sherman, Grant, and James G. Blaine of Maine were in a hopeless deadlock. Several delegates remembered Garfield's speech and put him forth as a compromise candidate—nominating him on the very next ballot.

The campaign leaders knew they needed a way to introduce Garfield in a positive way to voters and knew just the guy to write the candidate's biography—the champion of feel-good stories, Horatio Alger Jr. Alger did not quite conjure facts, just emphasized the ones that fit his usual up-from-the-bootstraps writing—Garfield's birth in the log cabin; the death of his father when he was in his teens; the need to help support his family with menial jobs while studying by candlelight, culminating in managing mules guiding boats along the canals near Cleveland.

As fortune would have it, Garfield was felled by an assassin's bullet four months into his term, dying two months later. In process by that point was a juvenile version of Alger's biography. Garfield had become his generation's version of John F. Kennedy—a young, educated, liberal war veteran, often taking his own counsel against even his party bosses. The new book was titled *From Canal Boy to President: The Boyhood and Manhood of James A. Garfield*, this one adding in Garfield's "front porch campaign," the first of its kind, where he met with famous folks and working stiffs alike at his home east of Cleveland, espousing, Alger-like, equal opportunity and hard work.

In fact, the residue of sympathy for Garfield, presumably because of his assassination, made *Canal Boy to President* almost required reading for the nation's youth. The good vibe inspired Chester A. Arthur, Garfield's vice president, who assumed the presidency after the assassination, to do an about-face on a lifetime of machine politics in New York. That a disgruntled office-seeker, thinking Arthur would appoint him to a sinecure, killed Garfield led to Arthur's leading the charge for civil-service reform—and given that Arthur's whole political life was in positions to which the spoils system ruled, it was a radical change. Arthur became a reformer in many areas—civil rights, domestic infrastructure improvements, labor issues, and immigration, though his veto of a Chinese immigration restriction bill was overridden.[10]

Though Garfield and Arthur now are in one of those periods resolutely unstudied by all but the most rabid of American history buffs, at the time, the Garfieldian myth actually provided cover for Arthur to be respected. "No man ever entered the presidency so profoundly and widely distrusted as Chester Alan Arthur," wrote journalist Alexander McClure, "and no one ever retired ... more generally respected, alike by political friend and foe."[11]

The run of American historical mythology is deep, and actually somewhat fun. The image of Lincoln splitting rails—one of the many jobs he took when he was young—reinforces him as a man of the people. Teddy Roosevelt charging up San Juan Hill with his round spectacles and prominent facial hair makes him the unconventional leader of men. The Teddy Bear, then, softens that image to just the right fatherly place. Though seemingly making him a nonstarter for the presidency, Franklin Roosevelt's crippling polio ended up making a marvelous story—that even a rich man can be a Horatio Alger never-give-up character. John F. Kennedy's witty sayings were collected, and his reputation for "culture" brought the likes of Pablo Casals to a White House concert; even his womanizing made him seem all the more transcendent.

Save for Lincoln, though, nothing speaks to the American myth more vividly than does the founding of the country. Whenever some crisis befalls the nation, or even some minor flurry of verbal fisticuffs, the Founding Fathers are most often invoked. "This is not the nation the Founding Fathers envisioned." "The Founding Fathers are rolling over in their graves. . . ."

"The creation story of America's founding remains valid, vivid and exhilarating," wrote historian Rick Atkinson in an op-ed piece in the *New York Times* entitled "Why We Still Care About America's Founders." "At a time when national unity is elusive, when our partisan rancor seems ever more toxic, when the simple concept of truth is disputed, that story informs who we are, where we came from, what our forebears believed and—perhaps the profoundest question any people can ask themselves—what they were willing to die for."[12]

The cynics find holes in the founding myth. What was this constant referral to freedom when fully one-fifth of the population in 1776 were slaves? The ragtag army of Washington would not have won the war without French help and the decision by Britain to concentrate on its European challenges. George III, seen as an incompetent fop in our myth, was actually a shrewd man who lasted on the British throne through sixty years of primarily good times.

The Founders, too, were such an interesting lot. Franklin had his coon-skin cap in the French court, his experiments with electricity, his invention of bifocals, his common-law wife and, by another woman, his Tory illegitimate son, William, the last royal governor of New Jersey. Jefferson was the red-headed genius, full of fancy, with a Black slave mistress who bore his several children. Madison was lauded as the five-foot-tall impeccable writer with the taller beautiful wife, Dolly. Hamilton and Burr were the outliers and duelists, and what is more glamorous than a duel?

Most all of the Founders apparently knew they were going through a magical age—and that they were going to be important figures. We know this because they all kept notes and letters and polemics. They kept these things because they knew there would be someone in the future who would want to see them, to know what they thought, and to make stories about them. This was not a group that saw their fates come down just in word-of-mouth stories but also with the flair of urgent letters and notes.

"The Revolution not only brought forth a nation, afire with a sense of destiny; it also embodied aspirations of an idealistic people," wrote Atkinson in his essay. "No wonder the world was agog."[13]

Marshall himself gets his own version of the myth category. Legend had it that when he died, the bell in the tower of the Philadelphia State House, a few blocks from where Marshall's body lay, tolled several times in the next few days. That bell was not yet called the Liberty Bell—that name came from the Abolitionists—but it was an old bell with a crack. Then the legend went on to say that the Bell cracked irrevocably that day, never to ring again.

Sounds almost magical if true, but, alas, it is not. The historian of Independence National Historic Park noted that there was no mention of bells of any sort being rung for Marshall. Beveridge has no mention of it in his deeply researched biography, even as a possibility people talked about. Further, the Liberty Bell did ring for events and such long after Marshall died in 1835. The Bell had several national tours, where it may have been rung, but they stopped in 1915, when the crack became too big for the bell to travel safely.

Fortuitously, the property just kitty-corner from the Capitol was open when William Howard Taft, the former president, was chief justice after his one term in the White House. The digs were new and grand, unlike the basement hovel in the Capitol where Marshall first sat in Washington. In the present day, visitors can stroll through the first floor, where the mandatory displays of memorabilia and wallboards explaining historical thisses and thats are housed. The standard tour takes a visitor into the Supreme Court chambers in times when the justices are not hearing arguments, but it is more fun to hope for a seat while those arguments are going on.

Though he never sat in those chambers in life, Marshall is always hovering about now. His statue overlooks the visitors area, clearly the mythical figure of the American judiciary. In a case in the memorabilia display is a rather ordinary looking mahogany chair with black horsehair padding. To the justices of the Supreme Court, though, it is a reminder of the mythical near-high priest of the Court, John Marshall.

The chair was the one used by Marshall from 1819 to 1835. Though it is not certain, it was probably the work of local cabinetmaker Benjamin Belt, who got the contract to make the desks and chairs for the then-seven members of the Court. They replaced the ones lost when the British burned the Capitol, where the Court then met, in 1814.

When Marshall died in 1835, the justices got new furniture and the old pieces were sold off. The deputy clerk at the time, D. W. Middleton, bought the Marshall chair and used it for his home. It was sold once again, but bequeathed to the Court in 1936, and placed on display in the "new" Court building.

It is a piece of its time, Federal style with neoclassical tinges, with armrests curling to the front. Though the padded arm rests have been recovered, the casters are original.

Since 1972, each time there is a new justice to be sworn in, he or she gets to sit in the Marshall chair for good luck. The chair is placed facing the other justices below the clerk of court's desk and the incoming justice waits patiently in the mythical chair before being called to take the Judicial Oath.

On the centenary of Marshall's appointment to the Court, in 1901, lawmakers and scholars proclaimed John Marshall Day. As the introduction to the three volumes of speeches and declarations reads: "The suggestion by Mr. Adolph Moses of the Chicago Bar of such a day struck a sympathetic chord which vibrated throughout the land." And then there were these words seemingly sounded on high about Marshall's influence beyond his death:

"The influence of the universal celebration of the day will not cease with the occasion, but will be wide and lasting. It has taught the people at large what before was chiefly known to lawyers and special students of our history, and to these often imperfectly, that to Marshall more than to any other person is due the establishment of the principle of nationality in the Constitution of our country. This principle has profoundly affected our national life. It has determined our destiny."[14]

CHAPTER SEVEN

From XYZ to Marbury

JOHN JAY MUST HAVE AT LEAST CONSIDERED HE COULD DO SOMETHING with the Supreme Court chief justiceship when President Washington enthusiastically appointed him, and the US Senate two days later confirmed him unanimously. After all, Jay had rejected Washington's offer of secretary of state first, which Jay ceded to a presumed political enemy, Thomas Jefferson.

The big problem was that there was nothing to decide yet because the executive and legislative branches were just getting started themselves. The first few years, the six justices—yes, an even number, though there was no place in the Constitution that said any number restriction at all, and the Congress set it at that odd, even number—had little on the docket.

The first case that came up, *Van Staphorst v. Maryland*, in 1791, about a private loan given the state of Maryland, which the state wanted to welch on, was settled out of court. The first case on the docket in which the Court gave an opinion was *West v. Barnes*, the same year. William West had been a Revolutionary War militia general from Rhode Island who also had a farm there. Due to a bad business deal, he owed a mortgage on his farm. For twenty years, from 1765 through 1785, he paid the mortgage to the Jenckes family, and then, running short, he asked Rhode Island to let him run a lottery to pay off the rest. The state allowed him to do that, it said, because of his military service. Since it was a lottery, many folks paid West in paper currency, not silver or gold. David Barnes, a noted attorney, represented the Jenckes family and said the whole thing should have been paid in silver or gold, and sued West to get the rest of the settlement. The lower courts sided with Barnes—West, impoverished, represented himself, but when West appealed to the Supreme Court, he hired Pennsylvania's attorney general to argue in Philadelphia, to which he could not travel due to his dwindling finances. The justices decided for Barnes, but not because of the payments. Barnes discovered that only the Rhode Island courts had signed the writ that brought the case to the Court, not the Supreme Court clerk, so the Jenckes won the decision and West lost his farm.

The Justices all rode the circuit, though, hearing similar cases to *West*, things not trivial to the combatants, but certainly not the kind of thing Supreme Court justices, or even lower court panels, hear today. Jay spent his off time doing political work, especially doing Washington's bidding, including promoting the Federalist view of the nation and the idea of neutrality when he went to the small courts on the circuit. He did reject Hamilton's request for an endorsement of a bill he was proposing to have the national government assume state debts. In fact, Washington sent Jay to Britain for what became the infamous Jay Treaty while he was still on the Court, something that would be amazing today. Jay said the Court could not comment publicly on the work of the other branches, save in lawsuits, an important precedent.[1]

Finally, Jay stepped down to run for governor of New York. Washington then nominated John Rutledge, an original Court associate justice, who had resigned to become the head of South Carolina's courts, a post he felt was more prestigious. The Senate, where Rutledge had many Federalist enemies because he so hated the Jay Treaty, rejected his nomination. He still might have been confirmed, but before the confirmation hearings, he gave a speech denouncing Washington, the hero, and the Jay Treaty itself again. A few days later, unhinged, Rutledge tried to commit suicide by throwing himself into Charleston Harbor. Two slaves dived in to save him. Embarrassed, and probably mentally ill, Rutledge retired from public life.[2]

Adams then went with a safe choice, the long loved Oliver Ellsworth from Connecticut. Ellsworth was confirmed unanimously, but his term was undistinguished and, like Jay, he crossed over to the executive while still on the court, becoming a negotiator in France to reach a settlement in what was called the Quasi-War, the one where the French subsidized pirates in the Atlantic and other nearby waters.

While still in France in 1799, Ellsworth came down with a severe internal illness and his doctors there advised against going to sea for several months. Ellsworth sent, instead, his letter of resignation by way of the final ship out of France for the winter in December 1800. The resignation letter came just in time for Adams to appoint one last justice—he had already lost the presidential election to Jefferson, and the Senate would change from Federalist to Republican majority in March 1801 as well.

Adams again looked to Jay, who had been elected to a second term as governor of New York. Jay was not to be moved yet again. He liked being the boss in New York and dreaded the circuit rides to capitals far from Washington—the northern states were difficult enough coming from Philadelphia. Further, he said, the Court lacked "the energy, weight, and dignity which are essential to its affording due support to the national government."[3]

Adams was a bit desperate when he got Jay's note. He was reading it with Marshall, his secretary of state, in his office. Marshall started going through possible names of successors to Ellsworth, pushing mostly William Paterson from New Jersey, but Adams stopped him.

"I believe I must nominate you," Adams said. It was another case of Marshall being in the right place at the right time. Marshall had rejected other things with almost a mere shrug, but here, finally, was his calling.[4]

The 1800 presidential election was a mess. Because there was no provision to separate the electoral votes between the presumed presidential candidate and his vice presidential running mate, each was usually given the same vote from each elector. Thus, Jefferson and Burr each got seventy-three electoral votes; Adams had sixty-five and Pinckney, who some Federalists would rather have had as president, got sixty-four, the Federalist electors doing the "right" thing by withholding at least one vote so the proper presidential candidate got the most. The Republicans, unfortunately, did not.

Burr would not drop out, so as the Constitution mandated, the tie balloting went to the House of Representatives, where each state, big or small, had one vote. Ironically, as sitting vice president and, thus, president of the Senate, Jefferson presided over the vote. Of the sixteen states, when the new Congress met in February 1801 to decide the election, eight were controlled by Republicans, and six of the other eight controlled by Federalists chose Burr. The lone Congressman in Georgia, a Federalist, voted for Jefferson, the Vermont delegation was split, and a Maryland switcher made its state split as well. Eight to six was not good enough. A candidate had to win nine, a majority.

It was at that point there came a squeak of support to nominate Marshall, the well-liked secretary of state, a man of many talents and much experience, as acting president. The idea, on the Federalist side, was to keep stalling the vote and have Marshall there long enough to establish his credentials, and maybe either move the next election forward in time, or have the ruse long enough to have Marshall run on his own in 1804. That hardly sat well with the Republicans. Some would have voted for an acting president, but with a deadline. Marshall would be fine for a few months, but they were hardly going to accept him when they had won both houses of Congress and, they presumed, the presidency.

Finally, Alexander Hamilton entered the fray. He disliked Jefferson's views but had respect for him as a man. Burr was an anathema, a schemer and, maybe, a scoundrel, "the Cataline of America," according to Hamilton. Hamilton wanted the mess over and perhaps could get something out of the resolution of the case with the Jeffersonians.

Initially, Hamilton went to Marshall, hoping he would use his influence to get the stalling Federalists to vote for Jefferson, but the best Marshall could offer him was that he would stay on the sidelines, not having the Supreme Court do anything one way or the other.

"Your representation of Mr. Burr, with whom I am totally unacquainted, shows that from him still greater danger than even from Mr.

Jefferson may be apprehended. Such a man as you describe is one to be feared, and may do more immediate, if not greater mischief," Marshall wrote Hamilton on January 1, 1801. "Believing that you know him well, and are impartial, my preference would certainly not be for him, but I can take no part in this business. I cannot bring myself to aid Mr. Jefferson. Perhaps respect for myself should, in my present situation, deter me from using any influence (if, indeed, I possessed any) in support of either gentleman."[5]

Hamilton then went to James Bayard, the lone US representative from Delaware, and a Federalist. He got Jefferson to promise not to have a wholesale firing of Federalist officeholders and to give Bayard's father-in-law, the governor of Delaware Richard Bassett, one of those federal judgeships.

On February 17, just two weeks before Inauguration Day, Bayard put Jefferson over the top, and three other states changed their votes in unison as an almost-acclamation. Burr, now left with disgruntlement and the vice presidency, renewed his hatred for Hamilton, three years later bringing disastrous consequences.[6]

Meanwhile, Marshall had continued in his dual posts of secretary of state and Supreme Court chief justice, something he would have thought an anathema when he was a more savvy Supreme Court justice by itself. Finally, he was ready to abandon his law practice. The salary for secretary of state was then $3,500, but he would get a bump up as chief justice to $4,000. The only officials who would make more than him were the vice president ($5,000) and the president ($25,000).[7]

There was going to be one more job, an important and history-changing one, that Marshall would have to perform as secretary of state, however. For most of the time of the republic, the party in power got to fill vacancies in the federal court system, and it was often a party advocacy in presidential campaigns that it will do so. By 1800, though, there were no Republicans at all in the federal court system, Washington and Adams having carte blanche to fill any opening since theirs were the only presidencies up to that point.

Marshall wrote Adams's address to Congress at the end of its term on December 3, 1800—what is now called the State of the Union address—noting that a law that would expand the national court system was "indispensably necessary" for the Federalists to have sway after its demise in the Congress was official on March 4, 1801. If so, states' rights claims could at least be delayed and nationalism would stay its course.

Soon after the Congress reconvened, what became the Judiciary Act of 1801 was quickly passed by the Federalists, still in the majority. The Supreme Court was reduced to five judges from six, technically not until a justice resigned or died, so the Republican president, if Jefferson or Burr were to win, would not have a chance to replace a justice when an opening came up there. At the same time, Supreme Court justices would no longer have to ride the circuit—at least as much—because three new Circuit Court judges for each circuit would have those duties. Then there would be a host of district court judges, and magistrates of even lesser courts, to make the federal judiciary decidedly Federalist.[8]

By this time, Marshall had been confirmed as chief justice, but since he was also still secretary of state, he was responsible for sending the commissions for all those new judgeships out in time. In one case, Marshall's lack of focus at the final moment caused a monumental dust-up—William Marbury's failure to get his commission, in the District of Columbia no less, which would later become perhaps the most important Supreme Court decision ever, two years later, in *Marbury v. Madison*.

The Judiciary Act of 1801 became known as the "midnight judges" bill. The origin of the phrase, which remained well-known for a long time, was uncertain. One legend had Levi Lincoln, the incoming Republican attorney general, going, with Jefferson's watch, to Marshall's room at midnight and seeing Marshall still signing and sealing commissions. Lincoln supposedly pointed to the watch, showing it to be past midnight on March 4, and Lincoln told Marshall to lay down his pen. In this version of the phrase's origin, Marshall got up from the desk and left.[9]

Jefferson, though he hated Marshall, gave all the credit to Adams for the midnight judges. Jefferson even did not stomp on ceremony and had Marshall give him the oath of office the next day. Jefferson probably thought Marshall was up and away where he should be—in a pretty powerless judiciary, one scorned even by such a patriot as Jay. Mostly, the Federalists also thought that, as demonstrated by Jay's disdain for the post. Both sides would end up being quite surprised.

The city of Washington was hardly a Valhalla when the Jefferson Administration, and the concurrent Marshall Supreme Court, started at the beginning of 1801. The census the year before put the population at 3,210, of which more than 30 percent were black, the much larger number of them being slaves.[10]

There were two "neighborhoods." One was a little bigger and centered around the "eastern hill," where the massive Capitol-to-be was partially built. There were a little more than a dozen freestanding wooden houses, and half of them were boardinghouses. Most of the rest of the buildings, also wooden, were poorly constructed. One was a tailor shop, another a shoemaker, yet another was a printer—and then there were a dry goods shop, a washer woman, a grocery, and, of all things, an oyster shop.

A mile away, with a clearing through the swamp in between, lay what would become known as the White House, even then painted in that color. There was a roadway between the two villages, but it was full of stumps and what became mud holes in rainy weather. There was a small stream to be forded in the middle, rain or shine. The half-dozen larger structures, which held businesses and warehouses, near the White House were brick and there were a few small houses nearby, brick as well.

Paris, or even Philadelphia, this was not.

The weather, even in September, was malarial, especially given the swampy environs. Government virtually ceased in the summer, with even the southern members, presumably used to this kind of weather, looking for reprieve from the heat.[11]

Two or three congressmen to a room inhabited the boardinghouses, which went for about $15 a week, with maybe another dollar or two for boarding, whiskey and other alcohol usually thrown in for free. Jefferson boarded at Conrad and McMunn's until the day he was inaugurated. Thirty men would sit at one long table there, Jefferson being left with the lowest, and often then the coldest, seat since he was the tallest.

Once Jefferson moved into the President's House, he made sure there were no more outdoor privies, at least for the president's quarters, ordering indoor plumbing immediately. John Adams was so loath to see his successor come to actual power that he left town in a public carriage with two of his aides to Massachusetts at four in the morning. He lived another quarter of a century, but he never saw Washington again.

Jefferson awoke at dawn on his inauguration day and had the breakfast he usually had when he was at Monticello—corn cakes with cold ham—but still on the lowest seat at the big table at Conrad and McMunn's.

Marshall had a rented room at the Washington City Hotel on the other side of the Capitol. Marshall had already been planning his biography of George Washington, so he had with him a footlocker full of papers and letters that Martha Washington had given him to get started. That morning, he wrote a letter to his friend, the recent Federalist vice presidential candidate Charles Cotesworth Pinckney.[12]

"Today the new political year commences. The new order of things begins," he wrote Pinckney. He was wary of Jefferson becoming an erratic leader, and if he did, "it is not difficult to foresee that much calamity is in store for our country."[13]

Marshall and Jefferson suspended their usual war of words and deeds for the inauguration. Jefferson had derided at the time both Washington's and Adams's inaugural prelims. Both former presidents had dressed in almost monarchical garb and rode to the Capitol in grand carriages. Jefferson toned it down, wearing just a plain suit and no powdered wig, his red locks flowing for all to see. He also walked to the capital with only a few US marshals and militiamen from Alexandria to guard him.

Jefferson gave a rather humble address in his somewhat squeaky voice before about a thousand people in the Senate chambers. Marshall sat on one side of Jefferson when on the dais, and Vice President Aaron Burr on the other—Jefferson seated between his two worst enemies must have been a sight for the visitors. After giving the oath, Marshall went back to his room and finished the letter to Pinckney, being himself more subdued, calling the address "in general well judged and conciliatory."[14]

—⁓—

Jefferson, seemingly, had two kinds of political philosophy—one for when he was in office and one for when he was not. He was an ardent foe, for instance, of executive power when he was challenging the Federalists, but once he was president, he felt above the rabble in Congress, and certainly was disdainful of the judiciary. It was said that not even the smallest piece of congressional legislation got introduced without his approval and nothing that he ever opposed would become law.

Despite some passing notes in *The Federalist Papers* mentioning that the courts, especially the Supreme Court in its appellate mode, could block a law, even overturn it, Jefferson, and even Madison, who wrote some of that language, primarily thought that the federal court system should be of little influence.

Though it was probably not solely because of Marshall, but more because the courts were almost wholly Federalist, Jefferson launched an assault on the judiciary, seeking to blunt its possible influence, but certainly to lessen its size. He immediately limited the number of new justices of the peace in Washington to thirty, instead of the forty Adams had appointed. Proposed legislation would shrink the lower courts just expanded, and there were secret meetings on how to impeach Federalist judges, and which ones to go after first.[15]

Meanwhile, Marshall started going about setting up his own fiefdom in the dusky city. His initial Court session as chief justice started the first week in August 1801. It had been decided by that time that the Court would meet twice a year in Washington, once in August and then again in December.

Marshall knew that little would be accomplished were the members of the Court dispersed, as they had often been under Jay, who himself went abroad to negotiate his treaty, and Ellsworth, who also went on a diplomatic mission to France while chief justice. This was not going to be the Marshall way. It is uncertain whether Marshall came into office intending to be an activist, but he certainly was going to be active.

Marshall had spent the late spring and early summer at home in Richmond, mostly working on his George Washington biography. When he arrived in Washington, he changed his quarters to the fancier Conrad and McMunn's boardinghouse on the other side of the Capitol. He liked the idea that it was essentially the Republican headquarters. He wanted to be in the flow of things, and also to hear gossip and news from the "other side." He had gotten rooms for the other justices there, though with no space for their wives. The point was to be collegial, to see each other in work hours and at play.

The justices came from all parts of the country. Alfred Moore came up the coast from North Carolina. Marshall rode his horse from Richmond. Samuel Chase had the shortest carriage ride—from Baltimore. William Cushing, the oldest justice, rode a carriage almost a week from Massachusetts and William Paterson, who often had bad luck in transit, regularly encountering accidents, was the last to arrive, also by carriage, from New Jersey.

Marshall, more like Franklin than Jefferson as a party—not the political type—man, was never formal and always ready to raise a glass. A later justice, Joseph Story—who would become Marshall's greatest friend, despite being originally a Republican—after Bushrod Washington's death said the constant contact, even when the Court terms were short, made the Supreme Court run efficiently and jovially.

"We take our dinners together, and discuss at the table the questions which are argued before us. We are great ascetics, and even deny ourselves wine, except in wet weather," wrote Story. The last line was, indeed, a joke. Marshall would often ask Story to go over to a window and see what the weather was. When it was sunny, Story reported that. But Marshall would always then say that the jurisdiction of the Court was so extensive in geography that it must be raining somewhere, and ordered drinks for everyone. Story said that Marshall was "brought up on Federalism and Madeira, and he was not a man to outgrow his early prejudices."[16]

Marshall also hoped that all decisions of his Court would be similarly convivial and unanimous, or at least assented to. Marshall believed the Court's deliberation was important, and minority voices would always be heard, but once a decision was reached, that was the decision for all. As members of the Court, they might be in the majority in one case and not in the next, but they were members of a serious, educated body, and answering every call as one was important for the dignity of the Court. It did not happen always—there were some dissents, especially in Marshall's later years, when Republicans took all the rest of the seats. But for the most part, Marshall could confidently write the majority opinion, as he did most often, knowing that even the minority in any case were believers in his system.

That first Marshall Court's official headquarters, though, was ignominious. It was a rather restricted and remote committee room in the lower level of the Capitol—a room that community churches often would lease out for Sunday services even in the seasons the Court was in session. Marshall made one significant change, however, and that was to have all the justices in academic robes, while he wore a black robe. For Justice Cushing, this was a real change, since he had worn British Court–style ermine robes and even had a white powdered wig during his first Supreme Court session—which was also the first ever, in 1790.[17]

The Court heard only one case in that first session, and then went home, arriving back in the city in early December, this time being there at the same time as Congress, filling the boardinghouses with more whispering and, to be sure, lots of flowing Madeira. Though the city was far more crowded, Marshall convinced the justices again to stay together

By the time a quorum of justices were there, it was December 8, and after convening early in the morning, the group recessed at 11:00 a.m. to go up to the Senate chambers to hear Jefferson's first State of the Union address. To no one's surprise, Jefferson did not deliver it in person—though quite erudite, Jefferson had a high voice and did not project the way his predecessors did. The clerk of the House read it instead, and it followed Jeffersonian principles.[18]

Since the most recent tense event had been the war with the Barbary pirates in Tripoli, Jefferson led off with a rather glorious note of how the Navy was about to defeat them, something even Federalists could get on board with.

Then his address turned political. He intended to shrink the federal government to the point of cutting taxes almost to nothing, farming out most of its functions to the states. Most vividly, he assailed the courts and their bloated hierarchies. The new judges the Judiciary Act of 1801 had put in place, he implied, were unnecessary.

Within a few days, though, the wheels would be turning toward a different confrontation. On December 16, a dreary Wednesday in the new capital, Marshall's old friend from the Adams Cabinet, former attorney general Charles Lee, came to the Court with a request. Four men had come to him who had been appointed justices of the peace in the last few days of the Adams Administration and had not had their commissions delivered, so they were being prevented by the Republicans from taking office. Three were to be seated in Alexandria and one, William Marbury from Maryland, was to take office in the District of Columbia itself.[19]

They were all well-known characters. Dennis Ramsey was a former mayor of Alexandria and an honorary pallbearer at George Washington's funeral. Colonel William Harper was the commander of an artillery unit at that funeral, having known Washington since Valley Forge. Socially, Harper was known in the capital for having fathered twenty-nine children. Robert Hooe was a real estate developer and the former sheriff of nearby Fairfax County.

Marbury, though, was the most well-known, a longtime active Federalist and a businessman first in Georgetown and then in Annapolis. He was a member of the Board of Directors of the Bank of Columbia in the capital and the naval agent of the Port of Georgetown, a job he got because he had helped out Adams's secretary of the navy, Benjamin Stoddert, when he was in financial difficulty. When Jefferson took office, the new secretary of war, Henry Dearborn, let Marbury go. So not only had he lost his Navy job, he was now in jeopardy of losing the justice of the peace appointment because of a late commission delivery. The one job he still had was as the organizer of the Federalists' dance assemblies, fewer also in number as the Republicans were taking over the city.

Lee had tried to get Madison to deliver the commissions and then went to the Senate in hopes of that body making Madison deliver them, a futile gesture now that the Senate was Republican. Lee was going to try his shot, then, to have the Supreme Court deliver a writ of mandamus, a judicial order to make Madison concede on the appointments. Lee then argued his case the next day in the cold and subterranean Committee Room Two. Though Lee never mentioned it, the five justices present—Alfred Moore was sick and actually never attended any arguments in the December session—were quite aware that the man sitting in the middle, Chief Justice Marshall, was the secretary of state who fumbled getting the commissions out in time.

Madison had stayed far from the proceedings, but he sent Levi Lincoln, who happened to be Lee's successor as attorney general. Lincoln said he had no instructions on what to do, so he told Marshall the Court could rule without a reply from the current secretary of state. Justice Samuel Chase, known for his temper, said he wanted to rule right away, but Marshall calmed him and said the Court would take the matter under advisement and scheduled oral arguments for the next term, in June 1802. There were some rumblings and reporting in the partisan press, but mostly Jefferson wanted to resolve the Barbary wars and his secret planning for his secretary, Meriwether Lewis, and his exploration of the American West.[20]

Still, the idea that the Supreme Court and most of the lesser ones were filled with Federalists made President Jefferson keen on reversing its power. When a few Federalist senators were not yet in Washington for the January 1802 session of Congress, Republicans jammed through a bill repealing the Judiciary Act of 1801, which had set up the many courts housing Federalist judges. It passed as closely as possible, with Vice President Burr breaking the tie vote. In its place, the Judiciary Act of 1802 reorganized the courts into six circuits where each Supreme Court justice was paired with a district judge to hear cases on the circuit—meaning out of Washington in state capitals—twice a year. Marshall, for instance, would have to traipse to Richmond and Raleigh, North Carolina, two times a year to hear whatever cases were bouncing around in the lower courts.

The more devious and current part of the bill was that it changed the Supreme Court's schedule. No longer would there be June and December terms for the Supreme Court. Those terms were cancelled and replaced with February and August terms, but there would be no meetings of the highest court in America until February 1803—a complete shutdown of the Supreme Court for more than a year. Mostly, this was around two probable cases—a challenge to the repeal of the Judiciary Act of 1801, and the hearing of *Marbury v. Madison*.[21]

Marshall did his best to be sanguine about the new Judiciary Act. He was not all that enthusiastic about riding the circuit, but at least half of the sessions would be in his hometown of Richmond. *Marbury* was not yet its famous self, and Marshall had not yet devised his monumental decision. It did, however, show how weak the federal judiciary was, able to be manhandled at every turn.

Marshall was hardly sanguine about that. It is hard to say that his decision in *Marbury* was personal retribution, but there lingers an idea that it might be so. Marshall never really believed, as Court purists would like to believe now, that politics were completely eliminated in Court proceedings. After all, politicians argued the cases—Daniel Webster, a longtime US senator who also ran for president as a Whig and was secretary of state as well, argued more cases in front of the Court than any other man, for instance, political at every turn.

In April, Marshall rode into Alexandria from Richmond, just to keep tabs on the political winds. He met with Delaware congressman James Bayard, a confidante even though Bayard was the one who cast the final vote in the 1800 presidential election for his nemesis, Jefferson, in the dilemma with Aaron Burr's challenge.

They met at Gadsby's Tavern, the place in the hamlet where the hob-
nobbers and the political and social elite did their public drinking and
schmoozing. It was said that on his last birthday ever, George Washington danced with Martha at Gadsby's.

It was there that Marshall was rumored to have raised the possibility with Bayard—perhaps after several rounds of Madeira—that the
Supreme Court might really have the power to declare an act of Congress or the executive invalid if it contradicted parts of the Constitution.
Bayard, a committed Federalist and the son-in-law of one of the midnight judges, former Delaware governor Richard Bassett, was enthusiastic
about the idea—also perhaps after a few more Madeiras.[22]

Back in Richmond, though, Marshall turned to his biography of
Washington, which no doubt bugged Jefferson. Marshall had Washington's papers, and who knew what was in there about Jefferson? If there was
some dirt or derogation, Marshall, thought Jefferson, would be enthusiastic to use it, and Marshall, no doubt, would always put himself in the best
light, vis-à-vis Washington.

Jefferson went to Madison and asked his secretary of state and closest Republican ally to find someone who would write another history
of Washington, which he might bankroll, or at least give him his own
sources, from himself, Madison, and other Revolutionary friends. Jefferson figured Marshall was only writing his biography with eyes on the
1804 elections, to run himself or at least to promote the Federalist cause.
Eventually, Jefferson got a poet who studied at Yale and later had gotten
into foreign affairs, Joel Barlow, who was then living in France. Jefferson
wrote to Barlow proposing a "history of the United States, from the close
of the war downwards." Jefferson, too, hoped it would be out in time for
1804.[23]

Meanwhile, as Jefferson was resting on his two-month hiatus at
Monticello, a Federalist newspaper, *The Gazette of the United States*, wrote
about allegations that Jefferson, when he was twenty-five, "offered love"
to the wife of his neighbor, John Walker. Jefferson had acknowledged to
friends that he was enamored of her then but never carried out an affair.

Still, that was far in the past. What James Callender, a former Republican ally, who had been put in jail by President Adams under the Sedition Act for writing anti-Federalist diatribes, had to write now was more salacious. Jefferson had denied Callender a decent job in the administration after suffering for the Republican cause, so Callender changed his allegiance. In his new newspaper, *Recorder*, published in Richmond, he wrote something that has been debated now for two centuries, that Jefferson "keeps, and for many years past has kept, as his concubine, his own slave … by which the woman and our president had such children." Nothing much transpired politically about this at the time—Jefferson won overwhelmingly in 1804—and though the publication of it irked him, he hardly stopped seeing Sally Hemings, the woman Callender alluded to.[24]

Marshall strategically missed the presidential levee—Washington, DC's most extravagant party to date—at the White House on New Year's Day 1803. The French ambassador wore gold lace and the Tunisian ambassador had full mufti—a turban, red jacket, and silk slippers. Native Americans had their silk moccasins and hair feathers. The president's two daughters, who had spent seven weeks in Washington away from their husbands, who were worried about their father spending time alone in the still-unfinished White House, were nonetheless the stars of the party—everyone wanted to meet them.

Marshall, though, was in Raleigh, a three-day, 165-mile trip from his home in Richmond. It was circuit riding time for him, though he always loved a good party, but just not one that would glorify his rival Jefferson. Washington may not have been much of a place back in 1803, but Raleigh was only barely there. Despite being the state capital, it had perhaps as many as seven hundred residents, and no real hotel, so Marshall stayed in Henry Cook's boardinghouse, which he ended up using for the next thirty-four years of riding circuit.[25]

Polly Marshall was almost a recluse by this point, having lost children early, no doubt causing depression. Marshall still was faithful to her. He was said to maybe have had an affair when in France during the XYZ negotiations, but even if so, that time was long gone. He knew he would have to keep his wife a part of his life's journeys by mail. The note he wrote her from Raleigh recounted a foible of his: forgetfulness. On the way to Raleigh, he lost $15 from his coat pocket and, when he unpacked his saddle bag, he found he had only day-to-day clothes, not formal judge wear. There were no tailors available to remedy the situation in tiny Raleigh, so he had to go déclassé for the circuit term.[26]

Those who think the modern-day tweet storms are disturbing and even vicious would be wise to consult history. Just a couple of days before the wonderful party at the White House, Congress got back into session and renewed its animosities. Republican senator Christopher Ellery of Rhode Island had accused Federalist senator John Rutledge Jr. of South Carolina of writing anonymous letters critical, maybe even defamatory, of Jefferson. Rutledge, the son of the former Washington nominee to be the second Supreme Court chief justice, was none too pleased. Rutledge came up to Ellery and started clubbing him with his cane and pulling his nose and ears.

It was reminiscent of an altercation a few years earlier when the capital was in Philadelphia. Congressman Matthew Lyon of Vermont, who was to be the first person charged in the Sedition Act in 1798, was indeed loud and critical as a Republican against the Federalists, whom he considered pompous monarchists. The year before, Connecticut congressman Roger Griswold mocked Lyon on the House floor, most specifically because of what he alleged was Lyon's cowardice during the Revolutionary War. Lyon then went across the House floor and spat in Griswold's face. Two weeks later, while Lyon was sitting alone at his desk, Griswold came over to him and beat him with his hickory cane. Stumbling in pain, Lyon grabbed some fireplace tongs and started swinging them wildly. House members started cheering the two as if at a bullfight but finally had them separated.[27]

Marshall was seeking nothing of the kind when the Court finally got back after its forced fourteen-month recess on February 7, 1803. The problem was that only Marshall and Justice Paterson from New Jersey were there. By the next week, Samuel Chase and Bushrod Washington had showed up, making a quorum—four of six. William Cushing would never make the February term due to illness, and Alfred Moore finally made it from North Carolina by mid-February. *Marbury v. Madison* was first on the docket.

As described elsewhere in this volume in the chapter on Marshall's significant cases, the court scene was pure theater. Former attorney general Charles Lee, a longtime friend of Marshall's, took on the case of Marbury and his fellow petitioners. Marbury was a known striver in Washington, even though perhaps undeserving of the post he was seeking. The current attorney general, Levi Lincoln, mostly watched the case. Secretary of State James Madison was never going to appear in the case bearing his name, the Jefferson government trying not to do anything to make the case seem legitimate. Lincoln was called to the stand but would only answer questions tangential to the case.

After the couple of days of argument, it seemed clear the case would go Marbury's way. After all, not just the majority, but all of the justices were appointed by Federalist presidents. As Marshall was deliberating what to say, an unusual Court session emerged. Justice Chase was plagued with a severe case of gout and could not leave his room at Stelle's Hotel, where all the justices were staying, as per Marshall's wont.

For two days, Chase agonized, as the Court could not meet without a quorum. But Marshall had a Mohammed to the mountain idea. He moved the entire Court to the parlor at Stelle's and Chase managed to get out of his room there. Court cases were held during the daytime, and at night, the social dances of Washington used the same parlor. Spare as the stage of the current Supreme Court chambers are, it is unlikely a deejay will be on call there any time soon.[28]

Finally, on January 24, 1803, starting at 10:00 a.m., Marshall was to change the balance of power in the nascent nation forever. He read a nine thousand, four hundred word decision, more or less the length of fifty pages of this book, denying Marbury his right to petition Madison for his commission but allowing the Court to decide whether he could do so. It essentially invalidated previous judiciary acts, for the first time having the Court overturn a law. To this day, in the Supreme Court back offices, portraits of William Marbury and James Madison sit on the same wall, reminding justices every day how important the Marshall decision was, and is.

The Court that John Jay said had no real mission and that the Jeffersonians scorned would now be elevated by the wiles of one man, Marshall, who might have saved the Union. Without a Court to level the field, partisan Congresses and presidents could fashion laws that would perhaps cause rebellion, a split of the country that nobody could cement together. Ironically the next law to be invalidated would be the Compromise of 1820, by Taney's *Dred Scott* opinion in 1857, which essentially led to the Civil War four years later.

CHAPTER EIGHT

The Worst Supreme Court Decisions, the Worst Justices, and the Best Dissent

IN NOVEMBER 2018, WHEN MATTHEW WHITAKER WAS INTERIM US attorney general, an old question-and-answer type profile from the website Caffeinated Thoughts four years before resurfaced. It was a seemingly innocuous piece, with twenty questions, as Whitaker was preparing for the Republican primary race for US Senate from Iowa.

Among the answers Whitaker, a conservative Republican, gave were assurances that he was not a climate change denier, that his favorite historical politicians were Presidents George Washington, James Madison, and Ronald Reagan, and that he believed life began at conception. None of these views would have been much of a shocker.

Then, just before the last question about his favorite politicians, the interviewer asked Whitaker, "What's the role of the courts and what is or what are some of the worst decisions in the Supreme Court's history?"

Whitaker alleged that the "courts are supposed to be the inferior branch of our three branches of government," a challenge to the constitutional ideal that all three branches are supposed to be co-equal, but that still was not much of a head-turner. A few sentences later, though, he said, "There are so many [bad rulings]. I would start with the idea of *Marbury v. Madison*. That's probably a good place to start and the way it's looked at the Supreme Court as the final arbiter of constructional issues."[1]

Though the quote probably was not the primary reason Whitaker lost the Senate nomination four years before, it certainly stirred up the political opinion-arati—particularly those who remembered their teachers who put *Marbury v. Madison* on the top of the winner's perch when it came to the best of Supreme Court decisions. How could the top US Justice Department official, interim or no, take the name of *Marbury v. Madison* in vain?

Professor Laurence H. Tribe, the premier constitutional law scholar at Harvard University, called Whitaker's view "ignorant."

"He seems to think much of the fabric of federal law that is part of our ordinary lives violates the Constitution of the United States to which he is evidently going to take an oath," Tribe said in a column in the *New York Times* by Charlie Savage.[2]

Ruth Marcus, the deputy editor of the *Washington Post* editorial page, called Whitaker a "crackpot."

"Reasonable people can differ over the constitutionality of the Affordable Care Act. Maybe there's some space to debate the New Deal era cases that cemented the authority of the regulatory state," wrote Marcus. 'But *Marbury?* This is lunacy. For any lawyer—certainly one now at the helm of the Justice Department—to disagree with *Marbury* is like a physicist denouncing the laws of gravity."[3]

It would have seemed that after more than two centuries *Marbury v. Madison* would have long passed *stare decisis*, literally from the Latin "to stand by things decided," but in general judicial practice meaning the decision referred to has firm legal precedence. Yet it is clear, even if Whitaker represents a limited-government minority, there have long been people who do not like the idea that the Supreme Court, or any court, could nullify a law that it deems does not reach constitutional scrutiny.

Certainly, when Marshall presented the opinion, a whole slew of people, primarily Jeffersonian Republicans, were hardly happy about it. Without *Marbury*, though, the Supreme Court itself would have been a completely different kind of body. Without judicial review, as Whitaker perhaps slyly intimates, the judiciary is the lesser of the three branches of government laid down in the Constitution. There would be little point to go on with a listing of good or bad decisions without it, since all other decisions would be minor, or at least not effective at all.

Trying to make a case for *Marbury v. Madison* being a bad decision, then, requires a suspension of the basis of American judicial history. At least the Jeffersonians who objected were most likely going on the courts as they had been seeing them—settling certain small kinds of disputes and dealing otherwise with conflicts between the states. The idea of what might now be called an "activist" Supreme Court starts with *Marbury* and has been the way of the judiciary ever since.

Marbury was the first Supreme Court case to overturn a law—in this case a portion of the Judiciary Act of 1789, but even with Marshall as chief justice for nearly the next quarter-century, with judicial review well in place, the justices did not overturn another law. It took yet another generation, and extraordinary circumstances, to have that happen again. In that case, it was the 1857 decision, written by Chief Justice Roger Brooke Taney in *Dred Scott v. Sandford*.[4]

Dred Scott was a slave who claimed he was owed his freedom, having traveled with an owner to what is now Minnesota, but then a part of the Wisconsin Territory, when the owner was a military surgeon there. The case bubbled up through the system for nearly a decade before Taney took it on to settle the question of slavery that had haunted the nation since its inception. Taney ruled that, as a Black man, Scott was not a citizen and, thus, had no standing to sue the government, and as a former slave was liable always to be returned to his owner. The decision effectively nullified the Missouri Compromise, which had barred slavery in any new state north of Missouri's southern boundary. Congress should not have passed that law, Taney ruled, because the Constitution had never given Congress the power to prevent or allow slavery in the coming territories, and so the Fugitive Slave Law had to be enforced.

Dred Scott was a huge shock to the nation's nervous system. There were many opinions about slavery, but Taney's was perhaps the most radical one to be written down. Its application brought financial chaos—those expanding industry or movement throughout the country on the railroads just stopped all activity, not knowing where a slave-worker factory or business might spring up, and within months large businesses, particularly railroads, declared bankruptcy, ending a twenty-year boom in the economy and causing the Panic of 1857, the worst precipitous economic slide in American history. While many in the anti-slavery camp were silent before, the decision brought out their most formidable opposition yet to the perfidy. With perhaps the most ineffective president of all, James Buchanan, in office, it cleared the path to southern secession and Civil War.[5]

It was not the last racist decision the Court handed down. Two other prominent ones were *Plessy v. Ferguson*, which reaffirmed the separate, but equal, standard in 1896, and *Korematsu v. United States*, which, in 1944, allowed the internment of Japanese Americans during World War II. Even with these heinous decisions, though, there is a ranking.

"*Korematsu* is bad, but not as bad as *Plessy v. Ferguson*," said University of Pennsylvania constitutional law scholar Kermit Roosevelt III, President Theodore Roosevelt's great-grandson, who himself wrote a novel based on the Japanese internment, *Allegiance*. "But *Plessy* is not even close to being as bad a decision as *Dred Scott*. That is by far the worst decision ever to come out of the Supreme Court, and I believe just about every scholar would tell you that."[6]

Among these three cases, only *Plessy v. Ferguson* has been directly overturned—in this case by *Brown v. Board of Education* in two trials in the 1950s. *Dred Scott*'s pronouncement on slavery was solved by the Thirteenth Amendment to the Constitution, so no other case was necessary. Numerous politicians and justice officials have apologized for *Korematsu*, and it would seem far-fetched now to have a similar internment proposition, but it is not certain that if one would come about that the Court would strike it down.

Perhaps the most influential Supreme Court decision for the Progressive Era—similar to the reaction to *Dred Scott*—was the 1905 decision in *Lochner v. New York*.

Joseph Lochner owned Lochner's Home Bakery in Utica, New York. In 1895, the New York state legislature had passed the Bakeshop Act, ostensibly to improve safety for bakery workers by limiting their work hours to ten per day and no more than sixty per week. In 1899, Lochner was indicted for allowing a employee to work more than sixty hours in a week. He paid a fine of $25. Two years later, Lochner was fined $50 in the Oneida County Court for another violation of the Bakeshop Act but decided to appeal that one. It was upheld in two state courts up the ladder, and he finally appealed to the Supreme Court.

As critics note, the strange thing about the Lochner suit is that the law was designed to keep employees safe by limiting their hours, but the eventual decision said even alleging that, the state law prohibited workers from earning as much money as they could. The Lochner defense was based on the "due process" clause of the Fourteenth Amendment, more fully, "nor shall any State deprive any person of life, liberty, or property, without due process of law."[7]

In some earlier cases, the Supreme Court allowed work restrictions. In *Holden v. Hardy* in 1896, the Court allowed a Utah law that set an eight-hour work day for a miner, as Justice Henry Brown wrote in his decision, though "the police power cannot be put forward as an excuse for oppressive and unjust legislation, it may be lawfully resorted to for the purpose of preserving the public health, safety, or morals." So for the Court, the decision in Lochner rested on whether the state's "police power" was valid in the Bakeshop Act. The five to four decision said the Bakeshop Act was not that proper use of police power.

Two master dissenters had at the case. Justice John Harlan, the only dissenter in *Plessy v. Ferguson* and whose dissent there was later used to help decide *Brown v. Board of Education*, said the majority had it all wrong. There was enough evidence in the oral argument that bakery employees could contract respiratory disease by being around the ingredients and fuel used by bakeries, so the state's police power was justified, even if it abridged the workers' rights to make more money.[8]

Justice Oliver Wendell Holmes blamed the majority for being "activist," but its activism was that the business of America was all business, which is not how the citizenry in general felt. Further, there had been restrictions in business that had little to do with health, particularly Sunday blue laws, which prohibited work on "the Lord's Day." He noted, finally, that the Constitution subscribed to no particular economic theory, save that each person was to enjoy equal rights to life and liberty.[9]

Lochner v. New York stood as precedent for several decades. State laws, especially when it came to similar types of labor issues, were overturned regularly or never got to the Supreme Court because of *Lochner.* The principle was never overturned, but eventually, in the "liberal" Warren court, it withered and lost its precedent overview. While never on the level of *Dred Scott*, the case today is looked upon as, at best, a mistake in judgment whose influence lasted far too long.[10]

There was probably no thornier, or potentially politically motivated, case to reach the Supreme Court than *Bush v. Gore*, the appeal of the 2000 presidential vote in Florida by George W. Bush, ostensibly because one more recount in four counties, which were primarily Democratic, would result in "irreparable harm" to Bush.

Al Gore got more popular votes than George W. Bush in the 2000 election, but he needed one more state's electoral votes to become president. He did not win some states he was expected to win, including his home state of Tennessee, so all depended on Florida, with its twenty-five electoral votes. Were Bush to gain those electoral votes, he would win the election by the slimmest of margins, 271 to 269 in the Electoral College.

There were a series of recounts, which gave some back and forth results. On November 10, Bush's vote total was larger than Gore's, which the Florida secretary of state, Republican Katherine Harris, wanted to certify. The margin, though, was close enough for Gore to ask for manual recounts, which he did in Palm Beach, Volusia, Broward, and Miami-Dade Counties, all presumed Democratic strongholds and more likely than not to have mistakes to add to Gore's total.

While the recount started, Bush sued to stop it, which was denied by the two highest Florida courts. On December 9, the Supreme Court voted five to four in favor of Bush, along party lines of who was a Republican before nomination and who was a Democrat, to take the case. The Electoral College was to meet December 18, and both sides wanted a decision before then, so oral arguments were held on December 11.[11]

Each side, to be sure, had a powerful lead attorney. The Republicans chose Theodore Olson, from Washington, DC, and the Democrats had David Boies of New York City. Each had and would argue cases from both the conservative and liberal side. In fact, they teamed up to win the case that overturned the ban on same sex marriage.

Because of the extraordinary nature of the case, the Court delivered its opinion the next day, December 12.

Few doubted what it would be. In fact, law clerks later said that the four judges in the eventual minority (John Paul Stevens, Ruth Bader Ginsburg, David Souter, and Stephen Breyer) started writing their dissents even before oral arguments started.

Technically, the decision, five to four along the same "party" lines as expected, remanded the case back to the Florida courts to see if they would assent to a further recount. Gore ended up dropping the case, both because he was not confident that the Florida courts would rule for him, but also because he felt the nation was being held hostage by the political nature of what he felt should have been a judicial hearing. He also felt that even if he had won in Florida, the Republicans would have taken the result back to the Supreme Court, which would probably rule in Bush's favor completely that time around.[12]

One thing that, in its aftermath, the Gore forces brought up was what they thought were conflicts of interest. Olson, the Bush attorney, was made solicitor general in the Bush Administration. Both William Rehnquist and Sandra Day O'Connor had made pronouncements that they wanted to retire under a Republican administration, so that their successors would be of their ideology. Clarence Thomas's wife was a Bush advisor and, at the time of the decision, was working on lists of possible Bush appointees were he to win the election. Antonin Scalia's son was working for Olson's firm, though no one accused him of working on the case.[13]

The aftermath, to be sure, was that a Republican administration replaced the Clinton presidency, in an era when the Republicans were moving farther to the right while the Democrats under Gore would probably have been farther to the left of Clinton. Compromise was going to be shorter, so the outcome was severe.

John Paul Stevens, in his dissent, noted, perhaps prophetically when it came to the Trump Administration choice of Brett Kavanaugh and its divisive hearings, that *Bush v. Gore* may have changed how the Supreme Court would be viewed.

"It is confidence in the men and women who administer the judicial system that is the true backbone of the rule of law," wrote Stevens, whom Breyer and Ginsburg joined in the dissent. "Time will one day heal the wound to that confidence that will be inflicted by today's decision. One thing, however, is certain. Although we may never know with complete certainty the identity of the winner of this year's Presidential election, the identity of the loser is perfectly clear. It is the Nation's confidence in the judge as an impartial guardian of the rule of law."[14]

For much of the last generation, well before and after *Bush v. Gore*, there has been a virtual litmus test for Supreme Court justices over where they would stand on *Roe v. Wade*, the 1974 case that effectively approved abortion based primarily on privacy issues. Thus, on the anti-abortion side, there is a critique that coincides with that feeling, essentially seeking to negate that privacy proposition.

"*Roe* is one of the most embarrassing decisions the Supreme Court has ever issued since *Dred Scott*," Clarke Forsythe, senior counsel at Americans United for Life said in a National Constitution Center podcast in 2019. "*Roe* lacks any support in precedent. [It] has to ignore history to get to its result. . . . It does not justify the Court being the National Abortion Control Board."[15]

Jeffrey Toobin, the writer on judicial subjects for the *New Yorker* and an analyst of same for CNN, has been an advocate of the idea that almost every focus on the Supreme Court in the last several decades comes down to *Roe v. Wade*. This may not be fair, since there have been plenty of cases, even significant cases, decided in that time, but neither *Bush v. Gore* nor *Citizens United* nor even the rulings on the Affordable Care Act, otherwise known as Obamacare, or those on gay marriage equality would have been the proverbial litmus tests for elevation to the Supreme Court. That alone makes it an historic case, and that it has ceased to have been agreed upon a half-century after the decision may mean it is the most blood-pressure-heightening case in American judicial history, perhaps one without conclusion.

Under the court of Chief Justice John Roberts, there have been threats, particularly from Justice Clarence Thomas, to suspend the idea of *stare decisis* completely—the idea being that a bad decision is not valid just because it has swayed law for a reasonably long time. Thomas and his allies in this fight would argue that a court decision really reflects the thoughts of the majority at the time, that no decision is "right" or "wrong," just constitutional, or what the current Court believes to be so.[16]

Thus, *Roe v. Wade* is as ripe for overturning as any minor case. In fact, that could have been the case had the court found differently in *Planned Parenthood v. Casey* in 1992. Instead, in a narrow vote, the Court in a sense modified *Roe* with different restrictions on abortion and implying the states could pass their own laws, so long as certain standards were maintained. The next Court case on abortion, then, could bypass trying to overturn *Roe*, and instead modify when and where abortions could take place in such a way as to virtually outlaw them, or allow states to outlaw them, or something in between, or even something less restrictive, were the Court to lean left by the time that a case wound its way up the ladder.

The final word will not come soon on *Roe v. Wade*, then. There is some feeling that Chief Justice John Roberts would like never to hear a case that would overturn it completely. More than congressmen, Supreme Court justices, especially chief justices, feel strongly about their legacies. More than half of Americans feel there should at least be some room for abortion, if not quite on demand, then at least early in pregnancy.[17]

David Cole, a Georgetown Law Center professor and the national legal director of the American Civil Liberties Union, made the point in his essay on a biography of John Roberts in the *New York Review of Books* that Supreme Court justices are more conscious of elite opinions than popular ones.

"First, the justices are themselves part of the elite; [as of 2019] they all attended either Harvard or Yale Law Schools, for example," he wrote. "Second, they care deeply about their reputations, which are largely determined by their elite peers. Third, the general public does not follow the Court's decisions closely, if at all; the legal and media elites, by contrast, pay close and sustained attention."[18]

To be left with the legacy of making abortion completely illegal in the United States is a position, then, that could only please the doctrinaire, and perhaps only Clarence Thomas, if even he would fall under that category in the 2020 Supreme Court.

Having written *Worst. President. Ever.*, excoriating James Buchanan for his frets, foibles, and failures during his presidency, I have grown accustomed to the idea that failure is as important to study, especially historically, as success. We lived in Palo Alto, ground zero, so to speak, for the Silicon Valley revolution, especially in the late 1990s, when we were there. The mantra at the time was that no one trusted anyone who had not failed. The learning curve, especially for leaders, was hooked to the idea that having failed, the leader would know what pitfalls might come and would be prepared if they did.

I hesitate to call each of the Supreme Court justices to follow as "the worst," but they are all good, if variable, examples of justices whom I deem both insufficient and deleterious to the challenge of the workings of the Supreme Court. The memoirs of former and current Supreme Court justices rarely delve into who was bad, either among their contemporaries or in the past. They will allege ideological differences but often temper those comments with some "but"—"But he was

John Marshall House, Fauquier County. Oak Hill was an early home of John
Marshall, the great chief justice. The wood-frame dwelling, completed in 1773
when John Marshall was seventeen, is a classic example of Virginia's colonial
vernacular. John Marshall became the owner of Oak Hill in 1785 when his father,
Thomas Marshall, moved to Kentucky. Although John Marshall lived mostly in
Richmond and Washington during his adult life, he kept and used his Fauquier
County property, making improvements and using it as a retreat. In 1819 he
built an attached Classical Revival house as a residence for his son, Thomas.
In 1835 Oak Hill was inherited by Thomas Marshall's son, John Marshall II,
whose "overindulgence in hospitality" forced him to sell Oak Hill to his brother,
Thomas. The property left the family after Thomas Marshall Jr.'s death during
the Civil War. Oak Hill can be seen from Interstate 66 and is located north of the
highway just east of the exit for Route 17 near Delaplane. It is a private residence and is not open to the public.

Marshall delivering oath to Andrew Jackson on East Portico of Capitol, March 4, 1829, the first time a presidential oath of office was delivered there ALLYN COX, ARCHITECT OF THE CAPITOL, COURTESY OF THE LIBRARY OF CONGRESS, PRINTS AND PHOTOGRAPHS

John Marshall Home, Richmond. Marshall built his home in Richmond's historic Court End neighborhood in 1790 and lived there for forty-five years until his death. It is a Federal-style brick building that originally included several outbuildings, including his law office.

James Fagan's etching of John Marshall
COURTESY OF THE LIBRARY OF CONGRESS

Marshall, print by J. H. E. Whitney after St.
Mamin COURTESY OF THE LIBRARY OF CONGRESS

John Marshall Harlan. Named after the chief justice, Harlan, a southerner brought up in a slaveholding family, wrote perhaps the most influential dissent in Court history in *Plessy v. Ferguson*. More than a half-century later, it was the basis for the plaintiffs' argument in *Brown v. Board of Education*, the case that overturned the principle of "separate but equal" laid down in *Plessy*.
COURTESY OF THE LIBRARY OF CONGRESS

James C. McReynolds was one of the worst of Supreme Court justices. Woodrow Wilson grew to dislike him as attorney general and was said to have appointed him to the Court to get him out of his administration. McReynolds was openly anti-Semitic, most of the time walking out of the room when Justice Benjamin Cardozo spoke. He also would not listen to arguments from women attorneys. COURTESY OF THE LIBRARY OF CONGRESS

Adlai Stevenson. Perhaps the losing presidential candidate most endeared to his public, defeated twice by an even more-endeared man, Dwight Eisenhower. COURTESY OF THE LIBRARY OF CONGRESS

Roger Taney, Marshall's successor as Supreme Court chief justice, rendered many opinions over his nearly thirty years on the bench, none so infamous as the one in the *Dred Scott* case, which went a long way to causing the Civil War. COURTESY OF LIBRARY OF CONGRESS

Dred Scott. A slave who claimed his freedom because, he said, his late master took him for a time to free territory in present-day Minnesota before returning to slave Missouri. Scott lost his case, but that loss emboldened Abolitionists, leading in four years to the Civil War. LIBRARY OF CONGRESS

John Marshall portrait

John Marshall statue outside Supreme Court Building

Wendell Willkie. The "bare-foot boy from Wall Street," a businessman who lost as the Republican nominee to Franklin Roosevelt in 1940, then immediately offered his services to Roosevelt in trying to unite the American people in the face of war. COURTESY OF THE LIBRARY OF CONGRESS

Supreme Court Building

John Jay. The first Supreme Court chief justice, Jay hated the job so much he disdained it to run for governor of New York. COURTESY OF THE LIBRARY OF CONGRESS

First six presidents print LITHOGRAPH BY ANTOINE MAURIN

Henry Clay. "I had rather be right than president," Clay said, even though he desperately wanted to have the high office, having run for it three times. At his death, he was still a hero to many and was the first politician to lie in state in the Capitol building. COURTESY OF THE LIBRARY OF CONGRESS

erudite and intelligent . . ." "But he was amenable in social and intellectual settings. . . ."

Still, the below had to vex their contemporaries, and surely historians. Since history commands us to view what is past, not present, there is no place in this list for justices who, at this writing in early 2020, are still on the bench. There might be someone who is a disaster at first, but then recoups, or someone who is roundly respected, but then falters disastrously, as one on this list, William O. Douglas, did. To those who are frustrated by the current Court and some justices in particular, it will be good to think of these past justices who veered way off the mark:

JAMES CLARK MCREYNOLDS

Given their collective exclusive status, the members of the Supreme Court appear to be among the most collegial folks in government. Ruth Bader Ginsburg, perhaps the most liberal member of the Roberts Court, and Antonin Scalia, perhaps the most conservative (Clarence Thomas would have been close), were said to be the fastest of friends, bonding particularly over opera, but also keeping their families close to one another.

So it may be surprising that when James Clark McReynolds, who was on the court for nearly twenty-seven years, having been appointed by Woodrow Wilson and resigned under Franklin Roosevelt, died, not a single justice, former or then-current, attended his funeral.[19]

This was not a well-regarded man.

William Howard Taft, who arrived as chief justice in 1920, after McReynolds had been on the court for seven years, was said to be one of the more congenial presidents, always deferring and supportive. McReynolds, though, was clearly not one of his favorites.

"[McReynolds was] fuller of prejudice than any man I have ever known," said Taft, "one who delights in making others uncomfortable. He has no sense of duty.

"[He] has a continual grouch, and is always offended because the court is doing something that he regards as undignified," Taft said. "In the absence of McReynolds, everything went smoothly."[20]

Though McReynolds was happy to do the hard work of writing opinions, averaging nineteen a term, 157 of them were dissents, and an astounding ninety-three of them were against New Deal legislation. He wrote against the Tennessee Valley Authority, the Agricultural Adjustment Act, the National Industrial Recovery Act, and, famously, Social Security.

"I can not find any authority in the Constitution for making the Federal Government the great almoner of public charity throughout the United States," he wrote of the Social Security Act.[21]

McReynolds was the most virulent and outspoken anti-Semite to become a justice. When the first Jew to be made a justice, Louis Brandeis, came to the court, McReynolds did not speak to him for three years and often left the conference room when Brandeis spoke. When the next Jew, Benjamin Cardozo, was appointed, McReynolds read a newspaper at his swearing in and would hold something over his face when Cardozo read opinions at the Court. A former law clerk said McReynolds never spoke to Cardozo during their time together on the Court. He did not sign the farewell letters given as a custom to retirees, for either man.[22]

Having grown up in the Jim Crow South, McReynolds was no more charitable to African Americans, his black servants nicknaming him "Pussywillow."

Still, he had his good side. He hated smoking and put "No Smoking" signs all over the courts well before that might have been popular.[23]

His credentials were magnificent; he was valedictorian at Vanderbilt University, completing his courses in three years, and then the same at the University of Virginia Law School, running through the curriculum in only fourteen months.[24]

Though he was said to be a gracious date, he would leave the bench if a woman attorney was speaking.

His reputation was hardly unknown before he got to the Court. When Wilson appointed him, he was already Wilson's attorney general. Commentaries at the time said that McReynolds was so loathed in the office that Wilson gave him the appointment just to get him out of his administration.[25]

ROGER BROOKE TANEY

As the second son of a rich family in Maryland, Taney early on knew that the first-born was always likely to inherit the estate, so Taney chose to go into the law after he graduated in 1796 from Dickinson College, then known as a proper finishing school for mid-Atlantic elites.

Taney climbed the political ladder intermittently, winning and losing elections, then going back into a lucrative law practice in between. Though he started as a Federalist, he became disenchanted with the party during the War of 1812 (where his brother-in-law Francis Scott Key became rather famous) and was particularly enchanted by Andrew Jackson, whose election campaign he chaired in Maryland in 1828.[26]

Three years later, Jackson fired most of his Cabinet in the "Petticoat Affair," an internal administration scuffle originally surrounding wives of other Cabinet members not respecting the wife of another. Attorney general was open and Taney stepped in. He was the primary voice in declaring the Second Bank of the United States unconstitutional, and Jackson, who hated the national bank and its Philadelphia operator Nicholas Biddle, loved him for that. When Treasury Secretary William J. Duane would not remove federal funds from the bank, Jackson gave a recess appointment to Taney. When he came up for a vote when Congress resumed, Taney was not approved, the first Cabinet nominee in history to be rejected.

Still, Jackson liked him, so when John Marshall died, Taney became Supreme Court chief justice. It was a complete turn of events from the long Marshall era, Taney being an advocate of states' rights over federalism. Presaging his worst decision, indeed the worst decision ever written by a justice, Taney led the Court to decisions restricting African-American rights at nearly every turn. Though he freed his own slaves and gave pensions to many, Taney had written that even free Blacks were not protected by the Constitution, and that slaves who voluntarily returned to their home slave state from a free one were still slaves.[27]

The coup de grace, of course, was his ruling in the *Dred Scott* case, which would consign him to among the worst justices on its own. No Black person, Taney wrote in his opinion, had ever been a citizen, according to his interpretation of the Constitution. Since the Constitution was written he said, Black people had been "regarded as beings of an inferior order altogether unfit to associate with the white race," and just to be clear, he wrote they were "so far inferior, that they had no rights which the white man was bound to respect."[28]

Thus the Compromise of 1850 and the Missouri Compromise of 1820, the pieces of legislation that held the warring sides of slavery and their opponents together, were invalid, while the dreaded Fugitive Slave Law, requiring the return of any slaves back to their owner anywhere in the United States, was whole. The case was a wake-up call to Abolitionists, who were almost a fringe group before but gained credence opposing the decision. It is not a stretch to say Taney's writing here was the precipitating cause of the Civil War.

He was not done during the war either. A Confederate sympathizer, Taney nonetheless stayed in his job. In the case of *Ex Party Merriman*, where a Maryland legislator, John Merryman, was held after accusations that he destroyed Union infrastructure in his state, Taney ruled that only Congress, not Lincoln as the executive, could suspend *habeas corpus*, allowing the Army to arrest and hold such as Merryman. Lincoln ignored the ruling but asked Congress to pass a law, the Habeas Corpus Suspension Act of 1863, to allow him that executive privilege.[29]

"I think Roger Taney was religiously in the brightness of his own cause. He was devoted to the Southern mentality. He thought the country would not change. He was out of date for his own time," said Supreme Court historian Lyle Denniston. "I am sure he was proud of his constitutional legacy. In fact, there may have been no one as significant to the law itself than Roger Taney."[30]

Taney died in 1864, having served twenty-eight years as chief justice, the longest term besides Marshall's. Lincoln made no comment on his death, and only Attorney General Edward Bates, among the Cabinet, attended his funeral in nearby Frederick, Maryland.[31]

HENRY BILLINGS BROWN

Like Chief Justice Taney, Brown is most remembered for writing one of the most heinous decisions in Supreme Court history, in Brown's case *Plessy v. Ferguson*, the 1896 decision that confirmed the theory of separate but equal public facilities for blacks and whites, thus legitimizing the Jim Crow laws aborning in the South.

Though Brown was a northerner, from the home of slavery abolition, Massachusetts, he became the symbol of segregation, with his somewhat convoluted decision, bending over backwards to keep white supremacy in its worst form afloat.[32]

It is not as if Brown would have had to survey the amendments to the Constitution, like the Thirteenth and Fourteenth, designed to make the Black man equal in opportunity to the white. Nor would he have had to do anything but read the headlines and see that in the 1890s, the decade in which he was writing, there were more than fourteen hundred lynchings of Black men in the South, more or less three per week. If this was separate but equal, then there was still a long way to go.[33]

Brown's decision in *Plessy v. Ferguson* would only make things more separate and less equal. The case came up out of a Louisiana law requiring Blacks and whites to be in separate train cars when traveling to a destination within the state's borders. Homer Plessy, a light-skinned Black man, was set up in the case by civil rights groups hoping to eliminate the law. Plessy took a seat in the white car, admitted to a conductor he was Black, and was fined. The case eventually worked its way to the Supreme Court.[34]

The Plessy defense was somewhat convoluted, too, saying that one thing Plessy was deprived of was "the most precious of all inheritances . . . the reputation of being white," that reputation being what counted for a lot in the South. Brown instantly negated that argument saying that Plessy could not be deprived of something he never had in the first place.[35]

Instead, Brown produced the thought that the Black man's feeling of being second-class came not from the law, but from his own mind.

"We consider the underlying fallacy of the plaintiff's argument to consist in the assumption that the enforced separation of the two races stamps the colored race with a badge of inferiority," wrote Brown. "If this be so, it is not by reason of anything found in the act, but solely because the colored race chooses to put that construction upon it."[36]

If that were not blind enough, then Brown alleged it was up to the Black community to change it themselves.

"The argument necessarily assumes ... that social prejudices may be overcome by legislation, and that equal rights cannot be secured to the negro except by an enforced commingling of the two races," he went on. "We cannot accept this proposition. If the two races are to meet upon terms of social equality, it must be the result of natural affinities, a mutual appreciation of each other's merits, and a voluntary consent of individuals."[37]

Brown had ascended to the bench after a long term as a judge in Massachusetts, put there by the one-term president, Benjamin Harrison, who actually lost the popular vote in his election. Brown, financially secure himself, married into a wealthy family and, thus, he said, could endure the low pay of being a federal judge. He went to law school at both Yale and Harvard, and dropped out of both. According to Steve Luxenberg, who wrote a 2019 book on the case, *Separate: The Story of Plessy v. Ferguson and America's Journey from Slavery to Segregation*, in life Brown was worried only about "ascent, dignity, money [and] stature." Richard Klugar, who wrote about the case that upended *Plessy*, *Brown v. Board of Education*, in his book *Simple Justice*, called Brown "one of the Court's dimmer lights."[38]

Brown usually sided with business over government regulation, but never again wrote a significant opinion, though it took a half-century for his dismal one in *Plessy* to be fortunately overturned in *Brown v. Board of Education*. But the legacy of the opinion wore on the country, not just the South, for those generations unable to escape the racist terror in daily life.

WILLIAM O. DOUGLAS

In 1966, Associate Justice William O. Douglas, then sixty-eight years old, married Cathleen Hefferman, a waitress in her early twenties, at a mountain lodge where he visited that summer in his beloved home state of Washington.

That might seem unusual, especially for a man who had served on the Supreme Court for twenty-seven years at that point. Douglas, though, had already been there. Three years before, Douglas had divorced his second wife, and married his third, Joan Martin, a twenty-three-year-old Allegheny College graduate who, in 1961, he started pursuing when she was writing her thesis on him. Douglas had married that second wife, Mercedes Hester Davidson, only a few years before, in 1954, after a three-year open affair that ended his first marriage in 1953. Douglas did not know immediately of his first wife's death in 1969 because his two children from that marriage had stopped speaking to him.[39]

Douglas's marital peccadillos, though, came well after his initial splash positively into the Court. He and Hugo Black, for two decades almost twins in their liberalism until the 1960s, were Franklin Roosevelt appointees who effectively stopped the Supreme Court's opposition to much of the New Deal in the late 1930s. Black was more the academic and judicial theorist; Douglas, the more practical and populist doer, rather than thinker.

Douglas was said to be always working when he was in Washington. The joke was that he could write an opinion on a cocktail napkin, and that he could write someone else's opinion and his own dissent before the other justice could even get started.

One of Douglas's biggest stumbling blocks was that what he really wanted to be was president, and he made few attempts to hide that desire. Some critics claim he was obsequious in his early Court alignments toward the New Deal and other Roosevelt Administration legislation, including the Japanese-American internment in the *Korematsu* case during World War II, in hopes that he would be Roosevelt's choice as a vice presidential running mate in 1944. Democratic bosses, though, pressured

Roosevelt to choose Harry Truman instead, doubting that a Supreme Court justice had much popular following.[40]

Truman apparently offered Douglas the vice presidential spot in the 1948 race, but, as scholar Jeffrey Rosen noted in his 2006 study of the Court's more famous characters, *The Supreme Court: The Personalities and Rivalries That Defined America*, "Douglas turned it down, apparently on the grounds that he didn't want to be a number two man to a number two man." He fumbled a chance at the presidential nomination in 1952, by speaking out that the United States should recognize Communist China, the kind of grandstanding not in keeping with the Supreme Court's mission. In 1960, still going on in this vein in his third decade on the bench, he hoped to be Lyndon Johnson's vice presidential pick had Johnson won the nomination, which never materialized.[41]

In addition, as time went on, Douglas became overshadowed on the Court by two men who were somewhat conservative as they were appointed, and trended more liberal later, but also had personalities that led later justices to both revere and follow them—Black and William Brennan.[42]

After that, Douglas's work and life became sloppy. His opinions and discussions had less reference to the Constitution and precedent and more use of flowery, not legal or practical, language. His drinking became more pronounced and he would leave earlier and earlier at the end of a term to camp in his favorite Washington State wilderness. Black, as Rosen notes, lamented about his former close friend: "What a waste. The guy has the best mind on the Court. He could have been the greatest justice ever. It's a shame. Bill is so lazy. [If he] worked harder, we'd be in better shape."[43]

After Black died in 1971, Douglas was given mostly to polemics—often in freelance journal articles—about the environment and against the Vietnam War, in all its phases. He detested Richard Nixon ("This attitude toward 'enemies,' this use of 'threats' marked the essence of Nixon's *Mein Kampf*," Douglas wrote in his memoirs. "I personally thought his ascendancy to power marked the inquest of the Free Society which had been our boast since Jefferson and Madison"), but gave another flowery concurrence in his joy to see *Roe v. Wade* decided as it was.[44]

His demise, though, disappointed even his adversaries. He had to be helped to the bench in a wheelchair, and his mind would wander during arguments, suggesting that dementia had set in. He resigned in 1975, after thirty-six years on the bench, the longest serving justice to that time. He did write his memoirs and his fourth wife, in fact, stayed with him until his death in 1980. He would always wave his hand at detractors, knowing that he wanted to get to a result in his decisions, rather than bend to theory. "For those who liked the result," he told a journalist late in life, "It was scholarship."[45]

It is not hard to think that John Marshall Harlan had a walk through his own personal Gethsemane before writing his dissent in the case of *Plessy v. Ferguson.*

The case was a prominent one in the Supreme Court's docket in 1896, but its resolution was hardly in doubt. The principle of "separate but equal" had been accepted both *de jure* and *de facto* in the South, where it had been enshrined since soon after the Civil War, and in the North, where civil rights had been pushed back from most people's minds in the rush toward the Industrial Revolution, the economy thought of as a way to equalize things a bit.

Harlan had grown up in a prominent slaveholding family in Kentucky, one of the border states before and during the Civil War. In fact, though he was born in Boyle County, nearby Harlan County was named after his great-uncle, a Revolutionary War hero. His father was a lawyer and served two terms in Congress in the 1830s. He no doubt saw great things for his son, born in 1833, naming him after the sitting Supreme Court chief justice.

There being no public schools in Kentucky, Harlan went to a private academy and then Centre College and Transylvania University Law School, one of the few law schools in the country, most lawyers still apprenticing in order to enter the bar. His father was a Whig, a friend of the Kentucky Whig hero, Henry Clay, so he became one, too—for a little bit. The Whigs disintegrated soon after he joined his father's firm, but then he became a Conservative Unionist, a Know-Nothing, and a Union Democrat before finally settling in as a Republican in 1868.[46]

All throughout that time, though he was adamant that Kentucky should stay in the Union, he saw abolition as a violation of property rights. He did not see the Civil War as a crusade against slavery and even though he was a colonel who had decisive victories over Confederate forces, said he would quit the army if Lincoln signed the Emancipation Proclamation, calling it "unconstitutional and null and void." His time in the Know-Nothing Party would not be a recommendation for tolerance either—since its main tenet was anti-immigration, particularly Catholics from Ireland and Germany.

Harlan, though, did not resign his commission, returned home to his post as Kentucky attorney general, and freed his slaves only after the ratification of the Thirteenth Amendment required him to do so in December 1865, calling the amendment a "flagrant invasion of the right of self-government which deprived the states of the right to make their own policies."[47]

Yet not a few years later, now a Republican, Harlan shifted his views on slavery and even discrimination against African Americans.

"I have lived long enough to feel and declare that . . . the most perfect despotism that ever existed on this earth was the institution of African slavery," Harlan said in 1871, noting his change of heart to be genuine. "Let it be said that I am right rather than consistent."[48]

Some said Harlan's change on the issue was political expedience— that being a Republican with any thought of being elected meant being on the side of equal rights. More likely, though, he never viewed violence against African Americans, slave or no, to be desired. He was also appalled at the rise of the Ku Klux Klan and its hangings, arson, and general mayhem. Though Kentucky turned Democratic in his time and he lost two tries at becoming governor, he kept advocating prosecuting Ku Kluxers, a tough position in the South.

Harlan was Rutherford B. Hayes's point man in Kentucky during his successful 1876 presidential run, and Hayes rewarded him with a Supreme Court appointment the next year. He continued speaking out against discrimination and in 1883, wrote a dissent, however mild, of the Supreme Court's decision to find the Civil Rights Act of 1875 unconstitutional.[49]

He saved his iconoclasm for *Plessy v. Ferguson*, though. There was no question the Court was going to find the law valid, but the majority opinion even blamed African Americans for the idea that separate but equal was a bad thing. It was "a badge of inferiority [only if] the colored race chooses to put that construction upon it."[50]

The vote was going to be all-in, but Harlan searched his conscience, writing what is often considered the greatest of all Supreme Court dissents, a courageous move that was reviled in his native former slaveholding states.

"In the eye of the law, there is in this country no superior, dominant, ruling class of citizens. There is no caste here. Our constitution is color blind, and neither knows nor tolerates classes among citizens," Harlan wrote. "In respect of civil rights, all citizens are equal before the law. The humblest is the peer of the most powerful.

"The arbitrary separation of citizens on the basis of race, while they are on a public highway, is a badge of servitude wholly inconsistent with the civil freedom and the equality before the law established by the Constitution. It cannot be justified upon any legal grounds," he said. Harlan was a man of his time, however, and did think Blacks to be inferior in culture and intelligence, which would seem to confuse his dissent, but his words were passionate and aggressive. "What can more certainly arouse race hate, what more certainly create and perpetuate a feeling of distrust between these races, than state enactments, which, in fact, proceed on the ground that colored citizens are so inferior and degraded that they cannot be allowed to sit in public coaches occupied by white citizens? That, as all will admit, is the real meaning of such legislation."[51]

Harlan might have imagined he was a loner, out of the mainstream of judicial thought when he was writing his dissent. Most dissents reach that fate and for decades, Harlan's did as well. Thurgood Marshall, though, was a constitutional scholar, and his favorite quote was "our constitution is color blind," from Harlan's *Plessy* dissent. When Marshall was feeling down during his time as lead attorney for *Brown v. Board of Education of Topeka, et al.*, he read from Harlan's dissent to gain confidence. He cited it in his case work and, thus, enshrined it as a blessed turn-around in constitutional law.[52]

Ironically, Harlan's grandson, John Marshall Harlan II, was appointed an associate justice by President Eisenhower only months after the decision on *Brown v. Board* was rendered. He replaced Justice Robert Jackson, who was originally scheduled to write the opinion but had a heart attack a few weeks before. He recovered enough to be there in court on May 17 to hear Chief Justice Earl Warren's decision but suffered another attack and died in October.

Several justices may have wanted to file a dissent in *Brown*, but they were thwarted by Warren making the Marshall-like move of insisting on a unanimous decision. In fact, Jackson's law clerk, future chief justice William H. Rehnquist, had written a memorandum arguing in favor of upholding *Plessy v. Ferguson* in the *Brown* case, but when it was first being heard under Chief Justice Fred Vinson.[53]

Dissents are often just screeds from the opposition, but sometimes, as in the elder Harlan's, they whisper for ages and eventually are the most important products of a case.

CHAPTER NINE

Marshall's Landmark Decisions and When Did the Founding of America End?

THOUGH JOHN MARSHALL'S LIFE HAD MORE FACETS THAN JUST THE decisions he orchestrated from the Supreme Court bench, it is those decisions that bring order to his biography. The major ones achieve either mythic, or clichéd, status for constitutional scholars and introductory Constitutional Law students alike.

They did not, though, come like the tablets to Mount Sinai. Their backgrounds are often obscure, when compared to the principles they came to represent. Sometimes, those backgrounds—the cases themselves—have details that are at the least entertaining and, at times, worthy of a quizmaster's mind.

The following are a sample of Marshall's major decisions, starting with the seminal *Marbury v. Madison*, which essentially gave the Supreme Court its purpose and stands as the foundation of the United States's judicial branch, making it unique, or at least unusual, among the nations.

MARBURY V. MADISON (1803)

William Marbury was a man of substance in Maryland politics. His grandfather had made a fortune in tobacco before finally depleting the soil. Still Marbury grew up among the bluer bloods in the state. That led him to his cache of patronage jobs, particularly tax collector for the state of Maryland and agent for the state in business circles. All these seemingly lower-level jobs in the early times of the republic came with possibilities to make money, either directly through tolls and taxes, or secondarily in establishing business relationships.

Marbury chose the Federalist side not initially because of a fealty to the party's principles, but because most of his clients in the agency business were Federalists. By 1791, as the federal government under Washington was making its struggling first steps, Marbury chose that brand. Many operatives like Marbury who either were part of the government or had to have contact with it through their businesses were fluid in the political partisanships, mostly being able to accommodate both. At the time of the founding of Washington, DC, though, Marbury was a committed Federalist. He became friendly with John Adams and Alexander Hamilton and settled into the good life by the Chesapeake and Potomac.[1]

In the 1800 election, the Federalists suffered a fatal defeat, losing the presidency and both houses of Congress. Adams, concluding that the party's legacy could come only through the judicial system, following the rules of the Judiciary Act of 1789, appointed forty-two men for judicial posts on March 2, 1801, and the Senate approved them on March 3, the day before Thomas Jefferson and the Republicans would take office. Marbury's commission was for justice of the peace in Washington, DC, the new capital.

That was a busy time for Marshall. He had been appointed chief justice by Adams, a bit before the "Midnight Judges" of March 3, but he was also still secretary of state. It was not so rare in those days to cross between government sectors. In fact, Marbury's two predecessors as Supreme Court chief justice, John Jay and Oliver Ellsworth, served as European envoys as they were sitting on the Court. As secretary of state, it was Marshall's duty to supervise the delivery of official appointments to the potential officeholders like Marbury, and it was especially important to get those made on the last day of Adams's term. Marshall asked his brother, James, to help him out in the deliveries, but Marbury's slipped their notice.[2]

Marbury, ever the striver, thought that justiceship could get him more money through fees and contacts in Washington, so he petitioned the Supreme Court to have the new secretary of state, James Madison, get him his commission.

Because it was a case dealing with an office appointed by the federal government, it went right to the Supreme Court, bypassing lower jurisdictions. During Marshall's thirty-four years as chief justice, about only 1 percent of the cases heard were in the original jurisdiction of the Supreme Court.[3]

This one, though, did not move swiftly. By the time Marbury filed it—there were three other men in his situation—the new Republican Congress repealed the Federalists' 1801 update of the Judiciary Act, and replaced it with their own, the Judiciary Act of 1802. Part of that act was to postpone the next session of the Supreme Court to February 1803, mostly so the Republicans could debate how to handle a Supreme Court still in Federalist hands.

When the case actually came to the Court, it was clear that it was going to be the biggest one—or at least the most star-studded one—in the somewhat fallow first two decades of the Court. Charles Lee, the former attorney general under Adams, was there to represent Marbury. Though Madison did not come to the Court, it was clear that he and Jefferson were interested—more politically than constitutionally. After all, these were forty-two Federalist jobs the two believed their opponents stole from them at the last minute. It was no secret, as well, that Marshall and Jefferson, though related by blood and marriage, were antagonists not only politically, but with personal animus.

Marshall had decided that there was no winning in merely making the decision in a political manner—like *Bush v. Gore* about the 2000 presidential election two centuries later. He wanted a political outcome, to be sure, but it would have to be couched as a constitutional decision.[4]

Ironically, of course, it was because of Marshall's lack of oversight that Marbury's suit came up at all. Had he been careful and delivered Marbury's commission on time, the new justice of the peace would have been satisfied. Marshall, were it not for the complex decision he was about to make, should have recused himself from the case.

Still, there it was, the first chance for Marshall to make something out of the poor third sister of the branches of government the Constitution was supposedly built upon.

To many, especially those introductory Constitutional Law class neophytes, the decision is unusually complex, but it is also like a tale whose curving trails eventually lead to an Oz of a decision.

Marshall gave the first volley to the Republicans, saying that at least part of the Judiciary Act of 1789 was unconstitutional because it violated Article III of the Constitution, which prohibited Congress from expanding what the Supreme Court could do.[5]

Then he gave the Federalists—or at least the remaining ones now in the federal courts—their piece, and in doing so, a far-reaching seeming nuance that finally led to making the Court a real co-equal branch of government.

Marshall wrote that the Constitution was the fundamental law of the land, and that all acts of Congress were subordinate to it. The final arbiter of whether those congressional acts could be law was the Supreme Court. The Court would not interfere in the workings of Congress or the executive branch—it would not enter into how the secretary of state actually did his job or how many advisors the president could have. It was only concerned with what could become law, specifically through acts of Congress.

Thus, the Supreme Court, as per Marshall's unanimous decision, could not force Madison to give Marbury his originally appointed post, but the Court could, and did, rule the Judiciary Act of 1789 unconstitutional.

Though it would take another half-century to have a congressional act overturned—Roger Taney's 1857 *Dred Scott* decision nullifying the Missouri Compromise—the principle had been affirmed. The Court could review the acts of the other branches. It was not just the administrative agency Washington might have deemed it, ready to confirm pensions and hear arbitrary cases.

In his first major decision, Marshall had confirmed not only his power, but his vision for the country. Jefferson and Madison may not have liked it, but they realized it was now how they would have to rule, through compromise often, but with foresight always.[6]

For those who see connections everywhere as karma, there is at least one of those connections in *Marbury v. Madison* decades after it was decided in the Supreme Court. On October 6, 1857, a few months after the *Dred Scott* decision written by Chief Justice Roger Taney, Marshall's successor, negating the first federal law since *Marbury v. Madison*, Fendall Marbury, a descendant of William Marbury, married Kate Marshall, John Marshall's great niece.

Since Thomas Jefferson and John Marshall were second cousins, the three main families involved in the most important case in early Supreme Court history were then related. While it is true that many political families, especially in Washington—the later Marburys were married in Alexandria, Virginia, just across the DC border—would certainly come into close contact with one another, it does make some sense of Jefferson's pronouncement on the cusp of the original *Marbury* decision that "We are all republicans, we are all federalists."[7]

FLETCHER V. PECK (1810)

Robert Fletcher and John Peck were hardly innocents in this 1810 case. In fact, they were in collusion even as Fletcher technically brought suit against Peck. The case had its start back in the previous century, in 1795, when the state of Georgia put what was known as the Yazoo Lands up for sale.

The Yazoo Lands were fifty-four thousand square miles of land of Indian territory west of the state that Georgia claimed it owned. They would become the states of Alabama and Mississippi. While it might have been dubious at best whether Georgia actually owned the territory, its legislature did pass the Yazoo Land Act of 1795, which divided the territory into four tracts, which the legislature then sold to four different land developers at $500,000 each. That worked out to about a penny an acre, even at rates of the 1790s, quite a bargain.

A lot of other money changed hands, though, in bribes to almost every legislator who voted for the act. When the Georgia electorate found out about this, it voted out the legislature and the new one repealed the act and tried to void the sales from it. Even though the new legislature believed not a whiff of it, it claimed that the state did not own the property, but Native Americans did.

Fletcher had bought some of the land from Peck in 1795 under the original act, but then sued when the new legislation came about, saying that Peck did not, because of it, have clear title to the land when he sold it. The two were in cahoots, though, because if the Court ruled the way they wanted—that the Native Americans did not have title to the land—their transaction would have been valid.[8]

Once again, though, Marshall came up with an ingenious way of avoiding a political decision by make it constitutional. The legislature's repeal of the Yazoo Land Act was unconstitutional, Marshall wrote in a unanimous opinion. The sale of the land, both to Peck and then onward to Fletcher, was a contract, and thus binding, according to Article I, Section 10 of the Constitution, even if it is illegally contrived later.

The case became the first in which the Supreme Court would invalidate a state law as inimical to the Constitution, one of the building blocks of American legal jurisprudence that Marshall, fortuitously, brought to the law.[9]

Martin v. Hunter's Lessee (1816)

Though the population of the United States had doubled from the first census in 1790 to the third one in 1810, there were still fewer than seven million non-slaves in the country then, a smaller population than today's New York City.

It is hardly coincidental, then, that someone in government and social prominence as long as Marshall had been by that point might have some conflicts, even in major cases. There are critics who still say he should have recused himself in what might be his most prominent decision, *Marbury v. Madison*, because he was the secretary of state who caused the problem in the first place, not having delivered Marbury's commission for justice of the peace in Washington on time, thus Marbury's appeal to have the next secretary of state, Madison, deliver it.[10]

Perhaps the country is better off for Marshall waiving recusal, but in 1816, he had a similar dilemma in *Martin v. Hunter's Lessee*. The British Lord Fairfax, who owned thousands of square miles of Virginia land under the Crown, was a mentor of Marshall's father, Thomas. Over the succeeding years, Marshall himself, and his brothers, purchased some of that land from Lord Fairfax's heir, Denny Martin. In 1797, the brothers worked out a deal with the Virginia legislature to get full title to the lands there that Lord Fairfax had for his personal use, and the state would assume title to the rest of the proprietary grant. The case turned on whether the 739-acre segment David Hunter bought was part of the Marshalls' property, now solely owned by his brother, James, or was part of the state of Virginia's.

The case took its time in the Virginia courts, but in 1810, the court of appeals narrowly found in Hunter's favor. Marshall then instructed his brother to appeal the state court's ruling to the Supreme Court, which would certainly be odd in the current day, but in the early nineteenth century, it was not unusual for a judge to sit on a case where he had such involvement.

When the case came before the Court, however, Marshall did initially recuse himself. His closest friend on the bench, Associate Justice Joseph Story, took the opinion in hand and reversed the Virginia appeals court's ruling. He wrote that treaties with Britain in effect nullified the state's attempts to confiscate the land. Since Virginia did not hold title to the land, it could not have sold it to Hunter. The Court issued a *writ of mandamus*, ordering the Virginia court to resolve the case in Martin's favor.

Then the conundrum came up. Not only did the Virginia court of appeals say it would not reverse its finding, but it also challenged the Supreme Court's authority even to hear the appeal. "The appellate power of the Supreme Court does not extend to this Court," read the verdict.[11]

Judge Spencer Roane of the court of appeals wrote a searing states' rights screed in response to Story. Roane said no matter what the Constitution said, the United States was still a confederation of states, and that the federal government had only a few functions, which were expressly written down. The Supreme Court had some jurisdiction in cases, but it only ran parallel to the state court of appeals—neither having power over the other.

Marshall had had enough. He decided to drop his feeling that he had a conflict of interest, because it was not the sale of a few acres of land that concerned him, but constitutional issues. Marshall immediately put the case back on the docket for the winter 1816 term. Though he had always recused himself before when Fairfax cases came before either the Supreme Court or his circuit court in Richmond, he was conflicted here, but eventually, he did the same, and let Story write the opinion again.

Story turned Roane's arguments back on him. The Constitution, he said, was formed not by the states but by "the people of the United States." The people, not the states, gave the Supreme Court appellate power in cases involving treaties and federal laws, and thus it was to have jurisdiction here, since it involved a treaty. Instead of remanding the case back to the court of appeals, Story's decision gave the judgment directly to James Marshall.

The decision, then, was in a series of those that emphasized the rule of the national government over the local ones. The people not only created the Constitution, they created the lesser power of the states within it, the Marshall Court would confirm here, and in different nuances, but all forcefully, in *McCulloch v. Maryland*, *Cohens v. Virginia*, and *Gibbons v. Ogden*.[12]

DARTMOUTH COLLEGE V. WOODWARD (1819)

Though the *Dartmouth* case became vastly significant in the way corporations, and thus business itself, in the United States were viewed, it is perhaps the only major case before the Marshall Court where the oral argument became more famous than the ruling.

Daniel Webster, though he is remembered as one of the most significant congressmen of the nineteenth century, a secretary of state, and a man always on the cusp of the presidency, was also probably the most prolific lawyer in oral arguments before the Supreme Court, handling more than two hundred cases before the body in his long career.

In the winter of 1819, Webster took his place in the newly refurbished Supreme Court chambers and delivered an impassioned four-hour speech that served as his oral argument for his alma mater, Dartmouth College, in this contracts case.

Once again, as Marshall would often have it, *Dartmouth College v. Woodward* had both a political and a constitutional bearing on the outcome—and Marshall again tried to weave through it like a football running back breaking out in the secondary.

Dartmouth, in rural New Hampshire, far from any urban area, was founded under a charter granted by King George III of England in 1769. British laws for such charters were simplistic. The legislature, in this case Parliament, would allow the monarch to grant a private charter to do certain economic activity, because the corporation formed was doing a public good, in Dartmouth's case providing education to mostly New Hampshire men.

In 1816, more than forty years onward and several decades after the kings no longer ruled the United States, the New Hampshire legislature wanted to alter the college's governance and economic structure by giving the governor power to appoint and fire members of the board of trustees and, further, having a "state board of visitors" able to veto any trustees' decision in any case.

In point of fact, however, all of this was because the current Dartmouth board was primarily Federalists, who were the early students there, and the Republicans, as they had earlier elsewhere, finally took control of the New Hampshire legislature and wanted more control over its most prominent educational institution.[13]

The trustees then hired a Federalist—and Dartmouth alumnus—Webster, to argue their case. The state supreme court found unanimously against Webster's argument that the Constitution's contracts clause made the original grant superior. The state court said that would be fine if it were a private corporation, but that public service corporations could be regulated by the state.

Marshall, though, agreed with Webster. The Dartmouth trustees were not a state agency but a private corporation doing a public, and charitable, service, in this case education. Further, Marshall would note, the framers of the Constitution left no doubt that the right to private property was paramount. In fact, that is one of the ways they got around the issue of slavery. Slaves were private property, and involuntarily freeing them would be taking private property, violating the owners' rights.

Since it came as a series of states' rights claims being truncated by federally given rights, *Dartmouth College v. Woodward* might have dropped into the second rank of Marshall Court decisions, were it not for the climax of Webster's oral argument. It was said that there was not a dry eye left, perhaps even Marshall's, when Webster finished his peroration.[14]

This, Sir, is my case. It is the case not merely of that humble institution, it is the case of every college in our land. It is more. It is the case of every eleemosynary institution throughout our country—of all those great charities founded by the piety of our ancestors to alleviate human misery, and scatter blessings along the pathway of life. It is more. It is, in some sense, the case of every man among us who has property of which he may be stripped, for the question is simply this: Shall our State Legislatures be allowed to take that which is not their own, to turn it from its original use, and apply it to such ends and purposes as they in their direction shall see fit.

Sir, you may destroy this little institution. It is weak. It is in your hands. I know it is one of the lesser lights in the literary horizon of our country. You may put it out. But if you do so, you must carry through your work. You must extinguish, one after another, all those great lights of science which for more than a century have thrown their radiance over our land. It is, Sir, as I have said, a small college. And yet there are those who love it . . .

Sir, I know not how others may feel, but for myself, when I see my Alma Mater surrounded, like Caesar in the senate house, by those who are reiterating stab upon stab, I would not for this right hand have her say to me, "Et tu quoque, mi fili [And you also, my son]?"[15]

The result of the case was, however, that business investment burgeoned in the United States over the next two decades. Though most businesses were still partnerships, the corporation—now if chartered federally, thus immune to state interference—expanded what became America's national businesses of the mid-nineteenth century: banks, insurance companies, and transportation firms.[16]

McCULLOCH V. MARYLAND (1819)

There was perhaps no issue debated more virulently during the early years of the George Washington presidency than the need for a national bank. It was the time when the demons on Washington's left and right shoulders, Thomas Jefferson and Alexander Hamilton, had the Great Man's ear. It is not that Washington agreed with them initially, or even was always bent one way or the other, but he respected that Jefferson and Hamilton were thinkers, and more often than not presented elucidating advocacy for their particular side of an issue.

In the case of the national bank, Washington eventually swung to Hamilton's side. Hamilton's argument essentially came down to the idea that there needed to be a central federal authority to hold national deposits and issue national currency. Jefferson saw it not just as a means to charter a bank but to usurp power from the states in, eventually, all areas.

In 1791, Congress, then dominated by Federalists, though the party did not yet exist as an entity, chartered what became the First Bank of the United States for a twenty-year term. The controversy did not die with the passage of the legislation, and by the time it came up for renewal,

Hamilton was dead, the Federalists were all but eliminated from government, and James Madison, Jefferson's successor, was president.

The charter for the bank, under those circumstances, was not renewed, but then came the War of 1812, which, while eventually won by the Americans, devastated the country's finances. In 1816, despite reservations, the Republican-dominated Congress passed a charter for the Second Bank of the United States. The federal government had only a 20 percent equity in the bank, but it still rankled some state governments, which were especially upset when the bank called in loans it had made to them.[17]

Some states tried to hinder the Second Bank's operation with various regulations, but Maryland went a bit farther—in 1818 calling for a $15,000 annual tax on any bank operating in the state not under a state charter. The only institution that fit the description was the Second Bank of the United States. Maryland became the aggressor when it brought suit against James William McCulloch, the cashier of the Baltimore branch of the Second Bank, for not paying the tax. The federal government employed that Supreme Court oral argument mainstay, Daniel Webster. The lawsuit itself was filed by an "informer" named John James, who sought to collect half the fine, as the state statute would allow.

Maryland won up to its court of appeals, saying that the Constitution did not have anything to say on banks, but the bank appealed to the Supreme Court. Marshall, as was his wont, used a creative argument to have federal power subsume state actions where those state actions might otherwise eventually subvert the Union he held so dearly.

Marshall invoked what has become known as the "necessary and proper clause," a name given to it by Associate Justice Louis Brandeis in his 1926 majority decision in *Lambert v. Yellowley*, which upheld a ban on the medicinal use of alcohol as "necessary and proper" to support the Eighteenth Amendment, the one that instituted Prohibition.

In *McCulloch*, Marshall had to decide that the establishment of the Second Bank by the federal government was constitutional. He went back to Hamilton's arguments from the *Federalist Papers* onward on how a national bank would help the government to exercise the powers it was already expressly given. The establishment of a national bank was not one of those expressly given powers, but some powers, he said, are "elastic," as the clause was familiarly known. "The Congress shall have Power," the clause in Article I, Section 8 of the Constitution reads, "to make all Laws which shall be necessary and proper for carrying into Execution the foregoing Powers, and all other Powers vested by this Constitution in the Government of the United States, or in any Department or Officer thereof."[18]

The key sentence in Marshall's decision is this: "Let the end be legitimate ... let it be within the scope of the constitution; and all means which are appropriate, which are plainly adapted to that end, which are not prohibited, but consist with the letter and spirit of the constitution, are constitutional."

Further, Marshall wrote, if the Maryland tax were allowed, it would open every federal law to a kaleidoscope of state laws, essentially negating such federal laws. He wrote later to Justice Story, "If the principles which have been advanced on this occasion were to prevail, the Constitution would be converted into the old confederation."[19]

While the decisions by Marshall over his long tenure may seem like a series merely conjured up by the chief justice, more simply, they are a consistent effort to keep what Marshall believed the Founders intended for the nation. Madison himself, in his portion of the *Federalist Papers*, advocated that there would be powers for the federal government that would come about with time, that the "necessary and proper" clause was, indeed, necessary and proper to see though a governmental structure that would last over time.

Marshall's rulings became the connective tissue that brought the nation through the hardships and trials of its first decades.[20]

COHENS V. VIRGINIA (1821)

Like Jewish families down through the ages, the Cohen family that emigrated from Bavaria to Baltimore assumed the oldest of the six sons of Judith and Israel Cohen would set the tone for the future of the family. In

1812, nine years after the family came to that Promised Land of America, Jacob Cohen, the eldest son, founded the Cohens Lottery and Exchange Office of Baltimore.

Though Jews were not able to hold public office until 1826, the Cohen family business, to which each younger brother was added when he became of age, thrived mostly on conducting lotteries or selling tickets for them, mostly from governments themselves. This was no marginal business, like lotteries might be today. With no income taxes and precious few fees, states and even the federal government used lotteries to raise funds for major government expenses. In 1802, while the new Washington federal district was slowly fitting itself out in buildings and roads, Congress established a lottery to help fund those projects.[21]

In 1820, though, the Virginia legislature passed a law prohibiting the sale of out of state lottery tickets, presumably to help the state's own lottery. By that time, the Cohens' business had established offices in New York, Charleston, Philadelphia, and Norfolk, where younger brothers Philip and Mendes Cohen ran operations. The Cohen firm was well regarded, said never to welch on a bet and often to pay off the same day.

So it was big news when on June 1, 1820, Philip and Mendes were arrested, charged with selling tickets to the National Lottery, violating the law. They were fined $100, not a significant amount even then, but something that would bring attention. The Cohens, though, appealed the fine directly to the Supreme Court, saying that a National Lottery, just like a national bank adjudicated in *McCulloch v. Maryland*, was a federal entity and, thus, not able to be countermanded by a state law.[22]

It was again one of those issues for the Marshall Court, where the decision had to have a constitutional basis, even if there was clearly a political issue involved. In this case, the political was a states' rights issue—did Virginia have the power to shut down a competitive lottery in its state so that the state could reap more funds from its own lottery sales? The constitutional issue was whether, in fact, the Supreme Court had even an appellate jurisdiction over what state courts would do about a state criminal law.

This case also had the background of Marshall versus the Republican Virginia establishment. Jefferson may have been out of office, but his sidekick Madison was now president and had the Junto in Richmond, the Republicans who essentially ran the Virginia government, to please.

Marshall took the long view, which he invoked in his decision: "A Constitution is framed for ages to come, and is designed to approach immortality as nearly as human institutions can approach it. Its course is not always tranquil. It is exposed to storms and tempest, and its framers must be unwise statesmen indeed, if they have not provided it, as far as nature will permit, with the means of self-preservation from the perils it may be destined to encounter."[23]

The decision came down in two parts—in the last week of the Madison Administration in March 1821. The Supreme Court, Marshall wrote, had jurisdiction because Article III of the Constitution allowed an appeal no matter what kind of federal issue was involved. This time, it was a state law contravening an act of Congress. If Virginia were allowed to write a law that preempted a federal regulation, it "would prostrate ... the government and its laws at the feet of every State of the Union," Marshall wrote.

Two days later, on March 5, Marshall delivered the "political" decision, that since Congress had not specifically had an interstate lottery, which it could easily have done, Virginia could actually restrict the tickets of what was essentially another local lottery in the state. Presumably, Congress would be more careful with its lottery statutes from then on, but the point was less for Marshall to win the $100 fine issue and more to win the constitutional one, which would now forever subject state laws to constitutional review, supporting again the rule in *McCulloch v. Maryland*.

The Cohens did not suffer in this battle. When the ban against Jewish officeholders in Maryland was repealed in 1826, Jacob Cohen was elected to Baltimore's City Council. He became one of the city's more prominent businessmen, among other things becoming a director of the Baltimore and Ohio Railroad. Mendes Cohen also became a member of the B & O board and was a Maryland legislator. Philip Cohen became postmaster of

Norfolk. Two other brothers, Benjamin and David Cohen, founded the Baltimore Stock Exchange.[24]

Marshall had actually postponed the *Cohens v. Virginia* case, knowing it was going to be politically charged, until the end of the term. Associate Justice Bushrod Washington was ill and was clearly going to be missing the early part of the term. As it turned out, he could not make it out of his bed at Mount Vernon, and Marshall had to have the case argued with only six justices. It was, as usual, though, a unanimous decision.

Since March 4 was falling on a Sunday, the newly elected president, James Monroe, a boyhood schoolmate of Marshall's, asked the chief justice how the inauguration, usually held that day, should proceed. Marshall made a quick decision and said no one would object if it was the next day, March 5.

Even nearly a half-century into the republic, government was close and sparse. Marshall delivered his final opinion on *Cohens v. Virginia* in the morning on March 5, then went upstairs in the Capitol to the renovated House chambers—it was rainy and the inauguration was moved inside—to give the oath of office to Monroe. Monroe gave a short optimistic speech and left the chambers to the tune of "Yankee Doodle" played by the Marine band. Never one to miss a good party, despite having basically saved the Union from fragmenting with ultra-states' rights, Marshall had quite a bunch of energy for the inaugural ball that night at the Brown's Indian Queen Hotel.[25]

GIBBONS V. OGDEN (1824)

Racking up the achievements of Robert R. Livingston, perhaps the only man with as many varied interests among the Founding Fathers as Benjamin Franklin, makes one wonder why he is not more revered. Like Franklin, Livingston was on the Committee of Five enjoined by their fellow members of the Continental Congress to write the Declaration of Independence.

Under the British rule in New York, Livingston had been given some smaller offices, but he renounced them in 1773, when he became what he called a "Whig" but was clearly a budding revolutionary. His family had money and position, but he took to the opposition nonetheless. In 1777, he became the first chancellor of New York, the highest office in the state judiciary, in the still aborning republic, and, while holding down that job, became the secretary of foreign affairs, equivalent to secretary of state, from 1781 to 1783 under the Articles of Confederation. He administered the first presidential oath of office to George Washington—because of his judiciary supremacy in New York, the first capital under Washington. Soon, though, he turned away from Washington and his former New York allies John Jay and Alexander Hamilton to become a Jeffersonian Republican. He lost the governorship of New York to Jay in 1798, but held onto the chancellorship until 1801, when Jefferson made him US envoy to France. It was Livingston who, under Jefferson's secret orders, negotiated the Louisiana Purchase in 1803.[26]

While in France, Livingston met a young painter and inventor originally from Pennsylvania, Robert Fulton. Fulton had studied art in Philadelphia and while in Paris studied with the American expatriate Benjamin West, but he also became fascinated with the steam engine, a new invention, and what it might be able to do. Livingston, being an amateur scientist himself, made plans with Fulton to make a steamboat that could ply the River Seine. In the meantime, Fulton, more scientist than partisan, invented the first military submarine, the Nautilus, for Napoleon Bonaparte in France, then turned around and developed the torpedo for Napoleon's enemy, the British army.

When Livingston went home to his mansion, Clermont, along the Hudson River in New York, he encouraged Fulton to come back and try their steamboat idea, but this time on the Hudson. In 1807, the North River Steamboat—later to be renamed the *Clermont*, after Livingston's estate—plied trips back and forth to New York City, 150 miles in only thirty-two hours.

In 1808, the New York state legislature gave Fulton and Livingston exclusive rights for thirty years to travel New York waters with their steamboats. They tried to get other rights from other states but were unsuccessful. They then sold franchises to would-be competitors, one of whom was former New Jersey governor Aaron Ogden, who had tried to thwart the Fulton-Livingston potential monopoly, but in the end threw in with it. Ogden then partnered with businessman Thomas Gibbons from Georgia, but the partnership foundered when Gibbons started running his own steamboat, licensed by Congress under a federal coastal trade statute, between Elizabeth, New Jersey, and New York, one of the routes Ogden was using under his franchise rights.[27]

Ogden sued Gibbons in the New York courts saying that states routinely passed laws in interstate matters and the state laws should run parallel to federal laws of the same sort.

Ogden won in the New York Chancery court. Gibbons, though, employed Daniel Webster, a regular at the Supreme Court, and one of the best legal minds of any age. Webster argued that Article I, Section 8, Clause 3, otherwise known as the Commerce Clause, gave Congress supremacy in interstate commerce regulations over any state charter or law. Further, Webster said, if each state were able to regulate interstate commerce, a chaos of laws, many no doubt contradictory, would result.

Marshall's opinion did not go as far as Webster's argument, but it did give Gibbons the victory. Marshall once again went back to his consistent dictum that once the states signed onto the Constitution, they gave up some individual rights to form that more perfect union. One of them was interstate commerce, as per the Commerce Clause, which said that Congress had the power "to regulate Commerce with foreign Nations, and among the several States, and with the Indian Tribes." Since Gibbons's route was granted from a federal statute, it superseded Ogden's franchise, granted by the State of New York.

The conclusion looks fairly obvious to a modern observer, but in the early nineteenth century, there was still not the assurance about, first, what the federal government could control and, second, whether the Supreme Court had the right to rule on the limits and powers of the states versus the federal government.

Marshall, still the politician even while on the bench, often tried to throw a bone to the states' rights side. In this case, he wrote that the states could act where Congress had not, for instance to pass regulation on health and safety or building a dam along a waterway for ease of commerce, a circumstance which later came to the court in *Wilson v. Black Bird Creek Marsh Company* in 1829.

Marshall's step-by-step move toward consolidating both the Supreme Court's power to review state and local cases, and the supremacy of the federal government over many supposed states' rights, continued apace with this case. It is probably worth noting, though, that while the case was in the courts, Gibbons hired a young boat captain named Cornelius Vanderbilt. Eventually Vanderbilt would scramble through the thorns of legal regulations and loopholes to become the American baron of interstate commerce, on the rivers, the canals, and the railways.[28]

In the main exhibit room of the National Archives Museum on the National Mall in Washington, the line usually snakes forward and stops in front of one of three documents—the Declaration of Independence, the Constitution, or the Bill of Rights.

Those are The Big Three when it comes to the founding of the United States. Surely there are other important documents—the Emancipation Proclamation, the Civil Rights acts, any of the other constitutional amendments after the first ten in the Bill of Rights, even negative documents like Chief Justice Roger Taney's decision in the *Dred Scott v. Sandford* case.

There is little doubt that the beginning of the founding of the United States came with the Declaration of Independence, though some still might counter with the battles at Lexington and Concord or some pre-Declaration event like the Boston Tea Party or the Continental Congresses meeting. Usually, though, the Declaration gets the nod as the time when it was, in modern parlance, put up or shut up.[29]

When, though, did the Founding end? Was it one and the same as the Founding's beginning, with the Declaration of Independence? Or was it some other event or passage? It is a fun parlor game to examine some of the possibilities, for that will require a somewhat more nuanced view of how the United States really came to be.

The Declaration of Independence

It is often some comfort to the people, if not historians, to wrap up an event quickly, to think in simplistic terms. The Declaration must have been an outsized, somewhat traumatic, event. John Adams pushed Thomas Jefferson to be the main author, in some part because he was from Virginia, the largest state, and would be able to pull some weight on its adoption. The rest of the small group of five working on the document—Benjamin Franklin of Pennsylvania, Robert R. Livingston of New York, and Roger Sherman of Connecticut, all northerners—could not match that branding.

Jefferson worked on the draft for only a few days, and then was quite miffed when not only his original committee members like Adams and Benjamin Franklin did some edits, but then the Congress assembled deleted this and that and added other things. The listing of the calumnies by King George III in the document are hardly written with a flourish, but the introduction is pure Jeffersonian. Whatever complaints politicians had with him later, they could hardly have faulted him for "When in the course of human events . . ." and its following early paragraphs.

To say, though, that the country was founded that week in Philadelphia and there was no turning back is to really oversimplify. Most of the signers knew this was a beginning, not an end point. Many of them did not sign for weeks. Though, despite its enumeration of King George III's flawed maneuvers, the Declaration was no mere petition; no one doubts its significance, but it is not nearly the thing that ended the Founding era.

It is, though, unlike the Constitution, a mostly unflawed document. It is a plea, a demand and, as it is titled, a declaration all at once. Even its words are with obvious meaning, unlike main sections of the Constitution, which, in truth, was meant at times to be vague. Those who stop the Founding with the Declaration do, then, have somewhat of a case.

THE BATTLE OF YORKTOWN

It would be reasonable to choose the surrender of Lord Charles Cornwallis to Washington, effectively ending the Revolutionary War in 1781, as the end of the beginning of America. The former colonies were all pretty much aligned with independence at this point, but there were still factions in most every state ready to use Washington's victory as a reason to declare their states independent.

There had been a Continental Congress throughout the War, trying its best to fund whatever Washington or his fellow distant generals needed, but mostly that came from individual states, which were a bit more solvent than the nascent national government.

Virginia particularly was full of influential folks unsure that a United States was the way to go. Whether or not Patrick Henry actually said, long before, "Give me liberty or give me death," he was unsure that a large entity like a United States could assure his liberty or that of his fellow Virginians. The Articles of Confederation had been in effect for only six months, but the idea of no longer having to finance a war, happy though most were about winning, caused some of those influential people back in the states to become more or less xenophobic.

Many of those elected to the Continental Congress, at least after the Declaration of Independence was passed, did not think much of their appointments. Several showed up in Philadelphia intermittently if at all. Most of those men thought being in their own states was more valuable to their future. Marshall was indeed one of them, thinking he could influence politics more in the Virginia legislature than the national one, Nationalist though he was.[30]

The Articles of Confederation took as a principle the independence and sovereignty of the states. All thirteen states signed on, giving the Congress a few powers. It could declare war and sign treaties. It could decide disputes between states. It could issue money, but it could not levy taxes. Mostly the treasury, overseen by Robert Morris, had to go out and get grants and loans, mostly the latter. Morris had been a rather rich entrepreneur. He donated a home in Philadelphia to be the pre–White

House, where Washington and John Adams lived when they were president. But Morris liked to speculate and by the late 1790s lost all his money in land speculation, ending up in debtors' prison. So when he was the prime financier, he honed his speculations in his treasurer's job.

Morris founded the Bank of North America, the first bank in the country, mostly to pay off the Revolutionary War. Much of its deposit money was from the French government, which would profit if the United States became a powerful friend. There was a lot of inflation to come, so Morris just printed more hard money.

Thus, the end of the war was hardly the congealing of a nation. If it could barely generate funding and had an idea that any state could leave the precarious Union, the victory in the war was also just a way station in the Founding era.

THE ADOPTION OF THE CONSTITUTION

Sports fans rage at the thought of a "moral victory." Losing nine to eight, to most, is no different than twenty to two. Vince Lombardi, the football coach whose desire to win became legendary, allegedly said, "I never lost. Time just ran out."

So many of the votes that ratified the Constitution in state conventions were awfully close. The debates were rabid and confrontational. The Constitution seemed to be tailor-made for Massachusetts, yet the vote there was 187 to 168 to ratify. The convention took place in Philadelphia, yet the partisans there could only get it passed 46 to 23. Rhode Island put it to a general referendum which got clobbered 2,708 against to 237 for, and even in 1790, when it became the last colony to pass the Constitution, it won only by thirty-four to thirty-two in its legislature. In Virginia and New York, the two largest and most influential states, it won eighty-nine to seventy-nine and thirty to twenty-seven.[31]

Then even after passage, in some states, it caused legislative changes, and, like in Virginia, a call to overturn the positive vote. It seemed to endure, though, because important people pressed it onward—Washington, Hamilton, and, in Virginia, Marshall. Yet there were still protests and flaws. Even as the new government started in 1789, North Carolina and Rhode Island still had not passed ratification, and popular sentiment in those far-separated places was clearly against the new document.

Washington, especially, forged onward, and sought unity. Clearly, though, the Founding had not ended yet.

TRANSFER OF POWER PEACEFULLY FROM ADAMS TO JEFFERSON

Today, when a country declares that it is going to adopt "democracy," there is a collective skepticism that the next elections would be valid. Commissions are formed and poll-watchers of the status of former president Jimmy Carter are recruited to supervise it.

Carter surely would have been on the case during the 1800 Jefferson/ Adams election. During the constitutional convention, there was clearly a different conception of the vice presidency than we think of today. The way the Constitution has it, it is primarily a second prize in the election. The only job given to the vice president is to preside over the Senate and break a tie vote. It is not clear that the vice president would be the permanent successor to a dead or disabled president, something John Tyler settled much later.

Adams as the first vice president proved a successful fit. He was subservient to Washington just enough, but one who supported most of his views. Jefferson as Adams's vice president, though, was perhaps the worst fit in our history. Still, they made it through until 1800, which almost became America's worst presidential election disaster. Aaron Burr, clearly supposed to be Jefferson's vice president as a running mate, ended up being his rival in the Electoral College. Because the Constitution did not clearly say electoral votes went only to the presidential candidate, Burr and Jefferson got the same number. Burr decided to challenge Jefferson— the election now went to the House of Representatives, where each state got one vote—and it was not until February that Delaware congressman James Bayard, the lone one from that state, decided to abstain, giving Jefferson the election.

Bayard, only thirty-two years old at the time, had the crucial swing vote. He hated the ideals of Jefferson, but he saw a constitutional crisis if March 4, the presidential transition date, came without a decision. He had worked a deal with Jefferson that Jefferson would endorse some of the Federalists' tenets, particularly in banking, and that was enough for him.

Adams, for the most part, stayed out of the fray. He wanted to be president again, but he could not do what other Federalists had done—support Burr in this fight—because he at least respected Jefferson's sincerity and not Burr's duplicity. Strangely, if the Constitution had not had its clause that slaves counted as three-fifths of a person in the census, Adams would have won the electoral vote sixty-three to sixty-one.[32]

Nonetheless, when the transition to Jeffersonian Republicanism from Adams's Federalism occurred on March 4, 1801, while Adams had left for Massachusetts, there was no violence and Jefferson took the oath of office in peace. It is no doubt how the Founders, many of whom were still alive, would have wanted it, and it is a plausible answer to "When did the Founding of the United States end?" Not my favorite, but plausible.

THE JOHN QUINCY ADAMS THEORY

While I tout Marshall as the last of the Founding Fathers still working when he died—Madison and Burr were still alive but long retired—James Traub tries to make the case that the last Founder was really John Quincy Adams. Traub's 2016 book *John Quincy Adams: Militant Spirit* supports the idea that Adams, having learned at his father's side during the early years of the republic—he was born in 1767—was at least a scion Founder.[33]

After being chosen by the Federalist legislature in Massachusetts to be a US senator in 1802, he was rarely out of politics until the end of his life in 1848. He had already served as ambassador to several European countries by that point, but he was eager to come home to be in the middle of the political discourse.

Adams's principles were steady, favoring peaceful expansion of the country's territory, avoiding war with European powers and, later, being the first high-level public official to declaim slavery and say it could be what would splinter the country. He served, at least in theory if not in actual membership, in the Federalist, the Republican, and the Whig Parties, though only because of what those parties represented, not his views, which were steady throughout.

Traub said in an interview that his "puckish" answer to the end of the Founding is February 23, 1848, when Adams died two days after having a brain hemorrhage while speaking on the House floor—he had gone back to being a representative from Massachusetts after his presidency. The less puckish one, he said, was Adams's loss to Andrew Jackson in the 1828 presidential election.

"Until then, all of the presidents were Founders or bore the biological and spiritual foundation of the Founders," Traub said. "Nothing matters more than the union to them. Without that thought, this 'thing' we call the United States could not have lasted."

There is a point to this, but I think the country was well established by then, though Jackson certainly had views counter to his predecessors.

NOT YET?

A stretch of the Jeffersonian ideal might be that a nation grows until it withers, that change is inevitable and welcome.

Historian David O. Stewart, whose 2015 book *Madison's Gift: Five Partnerships That Built America*, attempts to ply the mind of Jefferson's closest confidant.

"Though it sounds grandiose, I might say that Founding has never ended," said Stewart in an interview. "I think something can be said for that. When was the country solid? Or the government solid? I could point to Washington's leaving office and demonstrating that there was no pretension to monarchy.

"But I guess I am skeptical because by the 1790s, people were at each other's throats, and those were Founders who knew each other," said Stewart. "I would rather look at moments and the Founding was an extraordinary moment. They thought they were doing something amazing and that made them more responsible . . . and maybe those things just couldn't happen today.

"We can only hope that in our attempts to improve what they started, we are continuing their experiment," he said.

I like the theory here, but somehow, I want an end point.[34]

MARSHALL'S OPINION IN *MARBURY V. MADISON*

This one is my offering for the end of the Founding. The Constitution asked that there be three co-equal branches of government—the executive, the legislative, and the judiciary.

In its beginnings, the larger luster went to the executive—not just the president, but his Cabinet—and the legislature, which served to promote the best executive policies and thwart its worst.

It really had to be that way. The United States was lucky to have in Washington a relatively modest man ready to be president. In the "buck stops here" theory, he was ready to make decisions, whether he had consulted with others or not, when necessary. He also wanted not only the best people in his Cabinet but also those who often disagreed. While Lincoln also employed that same idea, it was rare in other presidencies.

Then there needed to be in place a Congress from all parts of the country, just to know how those people could compromise and, on the other hand, express the views of their states. This was a diverse population—other than being all white men—from a vast land. Besides Russia, which had its own issues, no previous attempt at democracy, or at least with vague pretensions of it, had ever been tried on such a wide swath of land.

So the weak and underworked federal judicial system was fated to be the last one with power and prestige. Though John Jay's early presence lent some sort of gravitas to the original Supreme Court, Jay was not able to assert any meaningful station for the Court.

As historian Stuart M. Speiser writes in his book, *The Founding Lawyers and America's Quest for Justice,* "the Supreme Court lacked the opportunity to become an important force in constitutional government, because it could not simply start making landmark decisions on its own. As a court of law, it had to await the arrival of litigated controversies on its docket...."[35]

Marshall was ready when his time came, though. He saw that there needed to be a brake, particularly on the executive but also on the legislative branch. The decision in *Marbury v. Madison* is rather convoluted, but it is just right for the times, which had been contentious between Federalists and Republicans, in one area, and the states and the federal government in the other.

It is true that it was not a given power in the Constitution for the Supreme Court to negate laws, but Alexander Hamilton, as "Publius" in *Federalist Paper* number 78, discussed the notion:

"It is far more rational to suppose that the courts were designed to be an intermediate body between the people and the legislature, in order, among other things, to keep the latter within the limits assigned to their authority. The interpretation of the laws is the proper and peculiar province of the courts. A Constitution is in fact—and must be regarded by the judges as—a fundamental law. It therefore belongs to [the judges] to ascertain its meaning, as well as the meaning of any particular act proceeding from the legislative body"[36]

Marshall's decision, though it was supposed to just be about delivering Marbury's commission, laid down this precept. "It is emphatically the province and duty of the Judicial Department to say what the law is," Marshall wrote in his opinion. "Those who apply the rule to particular cases, must of necessity expound and interpret that rule. If two laws conflict with each other, the courts must decide on the operation of each."[37]

Alexis de Tocqueville, the Frenchman who made an historic trip around America not too much later, noted that this judicial distinction was unusual in world government, but seemed so right. "The power vested in the American courts of justice of pronouncing a statute to be unconstitutional forms one of the most powerful barriers that have ever been devised against the tyranny of political assemblies," wrote de Tocqueville.[38]

And Archibald Cox, later the special prosecutor in the Watergate scandal, said that the decision was what held the new republic together at its crucial time. "The whole plan of government might well have failed," Cox wrote, "destroyed by conflict among the many parts into which the power of government was divided."[39]

If there is a time that the nation was finally in its proper form—the end of the Founding—it was when Marshall's courage made what would seem a trivial case about a few probably unnecessary jobs into something that would transform democracy throughout the world. By asserting that there was a judiciary that could negate unfair or nonconstitutional laws, the decision brought the federal courts to the equality they had to wait for after the initial phases of the Founding. Once it was there, with the Marshall decision, the Founding could be said to be over, and the rest, as the ancient Jewish dictum goes, "is commentary."

CHAPTER TEN

Transitional Courts and How Clerks Have Changed the Court

ONE DAY, WHILE A FRIEND AND I WERE IDLING, NO DOUBT ARGUING about some miniscule roster change on one of our favorite Philadelphia teams, he stopped, pivoting intellectually. He asked me whether, having written a book about James Buchanan, from whom Abe Lincoln became a transitional figure in American history, did I think Donald Trump would be the same type of person—someone who takes the run of history from one type of stage to something other.

Putting on my historian's vest and penny loafers, I told him that there has not been the right amount of time to judge a current presidency. Certainly, for something to be dubbed transformational, it by definition would have to last beyond the term of the potential transformation figure.

Clearly observers, especially those who do not consider the past in their decision making, suffer from the fallacy of immediacy. To many, perhaps most, people considering something happening in the present, that situation often gets to be the best or worst of times when, if a little remembrance of times past is consulted, it falls well short of that evaluation.

The Trump presidency aside, it is always fun for presidential or Supreme Court historians to do rankings. There have been few enough presidents, and surely few enough Supreme Court chief justices, to do all sorts of rankings and judgments.

Since this is not a book about the presidency, I will dispatch the transformational question quickly.

George Washington's style set the tone for the next five presidents, all considered Founders, and all on good terms with our first president. They were not particularly acolytes, but they tended to follow Washington's lead if at a loss for their own stamp. That Washington easily transferred the office to John Adams, and Adams, despite his reservations about the Jeffersonian passions, let the presidency peacefully go to his opponent, reinforces that view.

Andrew Jackson, however, showed a different, populist way of handling the office. He served in the US House of Representatives in the late 1700s in Philadelphia, so he had the opportunity to meet the first six Founders Era presidents.

After a post-Jacksonian period—two of the next presidents, Martin Van Buren and James Knox Polk, were essentially Jackson's choices and, thus, acolytes of his—the slide down from Millard Fillmore to Franklin Pierce to James Buchanan brings about the next transformational president, Abraham Lincoln. Though he does not finish out his term and get to have sway over what Reconstruction could be, he is followed by primarily Republican presidents who remember the Civil War as a training ground and Lincoln as their political ideal. Teddy Roosevelt brings in a hands-on progressive mode, which William Howard Taft and Woodrow Wilson make decent attempts at, and Hoover, though he fails, also tries to do. Franklin Roosevelt brings another transformation, not because he is so different from cousin Teddy, but because he is in office so long and through two horrific crises, the Great Depression and World War II.

Franklin Roosevelt's shadow hangs over both the next two presidents, until John F. Kennedy announces at his inauguration that things will be different with a generation "born in the twentieth century"[1] while the balding, seemingly aging by the second Dwight Eisenhower looks on, but his time is really not transformational. Lyndon Johnson claims Roosevelt as a major influence and continues that kind of progressive agenda, despite the war in Vietnam. Nixon, even with his Watergate scandal, follows along those lines, too, with moves like creating the Environmental Protection Agency and establishing trade with China.

The remainder of the line of presidents emanates from trying to copy or refute Ronald Reagan. Mostly it is about the attempt to rein in government. Even Democrats do things like making people work when on welfare, and letting states take over lots of functions, or at least budgets, that the federal government traditionally handled.

If Trump changes that Reaganesque movement, it would probably be less on substance than on style. As above, though, Kennedy's style was certainly not Eisenhower's or Harry Truman's, but the kinds of things he wanted to accomplish, and the way he tried to accomplish them, was pretty much the same. At this point, Trump's personal accomplishments are few. His big tax overhaul was really a congressional work. Any Republican president would have appointed three conservative Supreme Court justices. It certainly remains to be seen what the outcome of his foreign policy will be even a few years hence.

For the Supreme Court, rating transformational moments is a little harder, mostly because of the barriers of time and the constant changes in justices. To take the obvious, the Court of John Marshall was clearly different in the beginning of his decades in politics, and later because of the rules and practices of the Court in his time.

The Supreme Court did not even really exist for the first couple of years after the Constitution was signed. All the Constitution says about the possible court is that the "judicial Power of the United States" should be vested in "one Supreme Court, and in such inferior Courts as the Congress may from time to time ordain and establish."[2]

From those words, some inferred that Congress could appoint justices as need be, perhaps even for just one particular case, especially "from time to time" in "inferior" courts. It appeared, though, that there had to be a Supreme Court, but it came without rules—maybe intentionally, so that Congress could always change whatever rules there were. It says nothing about the Court being a co-equal branch with the Congress and the president, just that it had the "judicial Power of the United States."[3]

That seems to be what the first chief justices, and many of the lesser justices, thought. In the Judiciary Act of 1789, the Congress granted that the number of justices would be six.[4] Washington's first chief justice would be John Jay, of New York, one of the authors—with James Madison and Alexander Hamilton—of *The Federalist Papers*. For associate justices, Washington chose men from different parts of the country: John Rutledge of South Carolina, James Wilson of Pennsylvania, William Cushing of Massachusetts, Robert H. Harrison of Maryland, and John Blair of Virginia. Two days after that, the Senate approved all of them.[5]

The Court was to meet for terms in February and August, but during the first four terms, from February 1790 to August 1791, there were no cases at all to hear. Attendance was rather fluid. In fact, Justice Harrison was ill early on and resigned even before the first session. Justice Rutledge, living far away in South Carolina, did not attend the first few sessions. He had made an effort to get to the August 1790 session, but when he got to New York, which was where the capital was then, he was riddled with gout and could not work.[6]

Jay did not think the chief justiceship to be a really good position. Though they were in his home state of New York, the first sessions only served to swear in clerks and lawyers who might be advocates in the Supreme Court.

A big impediment to enjoying being a Supreme Court justice was what came to be known as "riding circuit." Each justice had his geographic area where he had to serve on lower courts when the main work of the Court was not in session. None of this was easy riding; on most roads the justices could travel only a few dozen miles a day. If a circuit was, say, Virginia and North Carolina, there might be a set of cases along the Atlantic coast, and then something over around Richmond or Charlottesville.[7]

By 1795, John Jay had had it. He actually had done some diplomacy abroad during his term—imagine Chief Justice John Roberts off in Israel looking to negotiate a Middle East treaty—but then came back and found his friends had nominated him to be governor of New York and had already gotten him elected.

When Jay resigned and left for New York—the capital had moved to Philadelphia by that time—Washington nominated Rutledge to replace him as chief justice, Rutledge having been his first choice to begin with. Rutledge had already left the court in 1791 to be the chief justice of the South Carolina Court of Common Pleas—something akin to Tom Brady deciding to quit the National Football League to play for Philadelphia, say, in the Arena Football League, the NFL defensive linemen being too big for him.

Rutledge was a hard sell to the Senate, which had to confirm him. He had been vocally against Jay's Treaty with England, which Washington and the congressional Federalists were hanging their reputations on. Then the Jeffersonians spread a rumor that Rutledge, a hothead, was actually insane. He lost in the Senate, fourteen to ten.[8]

Cushing was Washington's next choice, but though he was confirmed by the Senate, his health had suffered, and he left the office in a week. He went next to Oliver Ellsworth, who was confirmed post-haste, but he also abandoned the job within four years to become a commissioner to France to renegotiate a treaty it had with the United States.[9]

Now it was up to Adams, and the Court would have to go to Washington, where its quarters were to be in the basement of the unfinished Capitol building. Adams turned to the now aging Jay. The Senate confirmed the longtime patriot, but within a few months, he already had had enough. He said his health would not allow him to ride the circuit, and anyway, he was happy in his native New York. He also was a naysayer on the Court as well, saying it had no "energy, weight, and dignity." Riding circuit had already claimed Justice Thomas Johnson, whom Washington had appointed in 1793, but who quit six months later. "I cannot resolve to spend six Months in the Year of the few I may have left away from my Family," Johnson wrote Washington, "on Roads at Taverns chiefly and often in Situations where the most moderate Desires are disappointed."[10]

If there was any governmental entity that needed a transformation, it was the Supreme Court in 1801. Twenty-five years had gone by, a full quarter-century of freedom and nationhood. Yet the schism that George Washington feared had erupted. Two main political parties had formed, not the consensus or merely conflicting viewpoints that Washington had hoped for. The Alien and Sedition Acts passed by Adams and the Federalists in Congress were almost the beginnings of martial law, or, worse, dictatorship. Saying anything critical of the government in power could lead to prison. Trials had begun for allegedly treasonous acts. A full press on the acts would surely pull the country apart.

Jefferson's election had cooled things down in that corner, but there was no question the split into parties was on. The 1800 election was taken to Congress because the Constitution had made no distinction in votes for president and vice president. The Electoral College was tied between Jefferson and his vice presidential candidate, Aaron Burr. It was nearly time to inaugurate a new president. Compromise names were bandied about, including Marshall's. Could there be a caretaker president, until a new election could be held?

Finally, an elector relented and Jefferson was chosen, but a few weeks remained for Adams and the Federalist Congress, which would turn Republican on March 4, Inauguration Day. Adams appointed as many people as he could, particularly in the judiciary, and there was no bigger appointment than his secretary of state, John Marshall, to be chief justice. Marshall did not resign the most important job in the Cabinet after his confirmation as chief justice, something that would hardly be allowed today.[11]

Few would have cared enough, since Marshall's predecessors were practically workless, save for riding circuit, where there were always court cases to adjudicate. Jefferson, his disdaining Republican cousin, may have blanched a bit, but he probably would have assumed that Marshall would get some governmental job, if not in Washington, then probably senator from Virginia, or some equivalent. Perhaps wasting him on what seemed only a ceremonial position, the chief justiceship, would get him off to the sidelines in a Jeffersonian administration.

That did not happen. The transformation of the judicial system in the United States, particularly with the Supreme Court, would be focused and monumental. Marshall would be a transformational character in Supreme Court history, and his thirty-five years' worth of associate justices would be in that orbit.

Roger Taney succeeded Marshall, and he was looked upon as a political appointee of President Andrew Jackson, who had clashed with Marshall for several years before. Taney was the attorney general of Maryland after having a successful law office there. Like Marshall, he was a slaveholder and did not foresee any cases that would take that privilege away from him. He had been secretary of war, secretary of the treasury, and attorney general under Jackson, just as Marshall had served in John Adams's Cabinet.[12]

While Washington's Court choices were to be high-minded intellectuals, Marshall and Taney seemed to come from a mere political camp. All that was expected of them was to follow the party line, wherever it curved. If they were not hacks, they certainly seemed just arms of the executive.

How wrong their critics were.

While Marshall was friendly with Adams, and generally approved of his moves as president, he was not the acolyte Taney was of Jackson. For one thing, Marshall, as a southerner, had differing views of rural life, agriculture versus manufacturing and, to be sure, slavery than Adams. As a Maryland native facing south, Taney was all in with Jackson, particularly on his views of individualism and states' rights.

When the Marshall court in 1832 ordered that the federal government had to protect Native Americans from unconstitutional state laws in *Worcester v. Georgia*, Jackson allegedly said, "John Marshall has made his decision, now let him enforce it."[13] He would say nothing of the kind to his chosen Chief Justice Taney.

In her book, *Out of Order*, a casual history of the Supreme Court, former associate justice Sandra Day O'Connor writes, "Taney was widely regarded as an excellent Chief Justice, though he and the Supreme Court have been criticized for handing down the worst opinion in the Court's history—the *Dred Scott* decision of 1857."[14]

Unfortunately, *Dred Scott* was not a pebble on a super-expressway. It epitomized where the Court had transformed after Marshall's long Federalist run. As more southern, or states' rights–leaning northerners reached the Court, federalized power got pretty well stomped on. The two Whigs elected president during that time, William Henry Harrison and Zachary Taylor, died in office—Harrison within a month of his inauguration—and appointed no justices. Jackson, in his two terms, appointed five justices besides Taney, all cleaving to his will.

While Taney's Court was not always consistent—in nullification cases, it came down on the side of the federal judiciary. But observers were circumspect, because in the two greatest cases, *Prigg v. Pennsylvania* (1842) and *Abelman v. Booth* (1859), the outcome was the upholding of the Fugitive Slave Law, a federal statute Pennsylvania, in the earlier case, and Wisconsin, in the latter, wanted to eliminate, at least in their states. It was Taney's southern-leaning, and thus slave-defending Court—slavery meaning more than judicial ideology—which found that way.[15]

In succeeding Supreme Court formations, there was a sameness. It would be back and forth, with conservative and then progressive majorities, with dissents and majority opinions balancing out in their importance. Most often, the Court was a little bit behind the times, as it was designed to be. The justices are appointed for life, which usually goes on past an era of practical politics and social change. In a way, the Supreme Court, in normal times, is like the watchful parent, ready to say, "You have gone far enough," and then reining back the Congress or the president on those occasions.

The last particularly transformational Court came under the aegis of Earl Warren. Warren was a conservative politician from California, the man who, as state attorney general, supervised the internment of Japanese Americans in virtual prison camps during World War II.[16]

Yet the first significant case he had to deal with when he became chief justice was, fortuitously, *Brown v. Board of Education*. Whether he wanted to make a splash in his new job or felt in his heart segregation was one of America's greatest evils, Warren acted decisively. He knew that a bare win in the case would not have been effective. He asked the Court to cleave to the Marshall precedent, that the decision was one of the Court together, collaborative. Even if the justices did not agree, Warren convinced them that this was the right way to go, and that a unanimous decision would make the words of *Brown* stick further than some other loose decisions.

That the Warren Court also backed up freedom of the press, freedom of speech in general, and protections for the poor and less educated may have been significant, but its real transformational element was from decades of stodgy elitism to a progressive stance moving the postwar progressive nature of the country forward.[17]

Despite being a distinguished professor at Yale Law School, Amy Chua is probably better known for her book, *Battle Hymn of the Tiger Mother*. Chua, the daughter of Chinese immigrants, wrote it as a treatise on the Asian way of parenting, a no-nonsense, restrictive, and even harsh way of bringing up children. Even by her own account in the book, her two daughters had few allowed dates, forced piano lessons, and the threat of her throwing out their toys if a piano piece was not perfect.

Chua, though, was also on the Clerkship Committee of Yale Law School, trying to match students serving clerkships with judges, and, in some cases, with the ultimate judges, those justices on the Supreme Court.

In the July 12, 2018 edition of the *Wall Street Journal*, Chua had an opinion piece praising an alumnus of Yale Law who had just been nominated to the Supreme Court, Brett Kavanaugh.

"Judge Brett Kavanaugh's jurisprudence will appropriately be dissected in the months ahead," wrote Chua. "I'd like to speak to a less well-known side of the Supreme Court nominee: his role as a mentor for young lawyers, particularly women. The qualities he exhibits with his clerks may provide important evidence about the kind of justice he would be."

Kavanaugh had a rough confirmation process, being accused of improper sexual behavior by several women, but he was eventually confirmed and, to the surprise of some critics, his first four clerks were all women. A year later, he hired another female clerk—Professor Chua's daughter, Sophia, confirming the subhead of the *Journal* opinion piece, "I can't think of a better judge for my own daughter's clerkship."

Kavanaugh himself was a Supreme Court clerk coming out of Yale Law School. That year, 1993-94, there was another ambitious young fellow, this one from Harvard Law, clerking for Justice Anthony Kennedy—the man whom Kavanaugh replaced on the Court—named Neil M. Gorsuch, who was confirmed not too long before in his own Supreme Court Senate hearings and in less contentious circumstances, as the successor to the late Antonin Scalia.

In fact, eight Supreme Court clerks have gone on to be justices as well. Byron White clerked for Fred Vinson in 1946-47; John Paul Stevens, for Wiley Rutledge in 1947-48; William H. Rehnquist, for Robert M. Jackson in 1951-52; Stephen Breyer, for Arthur Goldberg in 1963-64; John G. Roberts for Rehnquist, and then Gorsuch, Kavanaugh, and Amy Barrett, a clerk for Scalia. Especially in the Jackson to Rehnquist to Kavanaugh triple play, there is even an old boy network to that first step in the chain, a Supreme Court clerkship.[18]

It was Rehnquist who created the greatest stir among Supreme Court law clerks. During his clerkship term the case of *Brown vs. Board of Education* was pending for its first hearing, while Fred Vinson was still chief justice. Unlike its second hearing, when Vinson's successor Earl Warren was pushing for a unanimous opinion, it was apparent the Vinson Court would never have done that.

Rehnquist's boss, Justice Robert Jackson, was a man whom it was thought might be a swing vote, possibly upholding segregation. Rehnquist thought, as a clerk, he should be giving Jackson what later would be called "talking points" on the case. He wrote Jackson a memo headed, "A Random Thought on the Segregation Cases." In part, the draft read, "I realize that it is an unpopular and unhumanitarian position, for which I have been excoriated by 'liberal' colleagues, but I think *Plessy v. Ferguson* was right and should be re-affirmed."[19]

The Vinson Court did a dance around *Brown v. Board of Education* in 1952 and it was, for all intents and purposes, postponed. Vinson died before the re-hearing, and now, in 1954, Warren was the boss. Warren thought, like Marshall would have, that a unanimous Court in a significant case would give the decision heft. By that time, Jackson was suffering from the heart disease that would finally kill him later that year. Warren's last conferee was Jackson. Jackson wanted to write either a concurrence or a dissent, being on the fence. Finally, he assented to Warren's request, and on May 17, 1954, he was wheeled into Court, so he could stand in unanimity on the signal case of the mid-twentieth-century Supreme Court.

In 1986, though, when Rehnquist was in hearings for his elevation to chief justice (he was already an associate justice), the memorandum to Jackson became public. His explanation was a bit thin:

"As best I can reconstruct the circumstances after some nineteen years, the memorandum was prepared by me at Justice Jackson's request; it was intended as a rough draft of a statement of *his* views. . . . He expressed concern that the conference should have the benefit of all of the arguments in support of the constitutionality of the 'separate but equal' doctrine, as well as those against its constitutionality.

"I am satisfied that the memorandum was not designed to be a statement of my views on these cases. . . . I am fortified in this conclusion because the bald, simplistic conclusion that *Plessy v. Ferguson* was right and should be re-affirmed is not an accurate statement of my own views at the time."[20]

Jackson's former secretary testified that these were not only Rehnquist's words, but that he meant them as his views, and that he only changed the facts to make sure of his confirmation, which came quite quickly. No matter which story was true, it certainly showed how vital and influential clerks can be to their justices.

Justice Horace Gray was the first member of the court to have a clerk—Thomas Russell, who had finished Harvard Law School as Gray climbed to the Supreme Court in 1882. In fact, all nineteen clerks Gray had for the rest of his term, which ended with his death in 1902, were from Harvard Law School. Before he became a Supreme Court justice, he was chief justice of the Massachusetts Supreme Judicial Court. There he hired the first clerk of any state's court, a young man who entered Harvard Law at twenty and is said to still have the highest grade point average of any student there, Louis Brandeis, who would eventually also become a Supreme Court associate justice.[21]

It became hardly coincidental that Harvard Law School was the preferred background of Supreme Court law clerks. Oliver Wendell Holmes Jr. had a twenty-nine-year term on the bench. He hired his first law clerk during his second year on the court—a young man from George Washington University's law school. He did not hire another one for three years, but when he did, it was a graduate of Harvard Law School, and the next twenty-seven—all of the rest of his clerks—graduated from Harvard. Felix Frankfurter's first twenty-three clerks were from Harvard. He appointed sixteen more, four of them from Penn, the University of Virginia, or Yale University law schools, but all the rest from Harvard.

Recent justices, whether conservative or liberal, cleave to the elite law school route to find clerks. Of her nearly one hundred clerks, Ruth Bader Ginsburg chose nearly all from Ivy League law schools, and in the late 2010s, nearly all also had two previous prestigious internships prior to the one under her. It was a similar situation with Ginsburg's fellow opera fan but strict originalist justice Antonin Scalia, whose clerks in his twenty-year stint on the bench were all from top-tier law schools. Only Clarence Thomas, among recent justices, hires at least half his clerks from non-Ivy law schools, though all of his have had previous federal court clerkships.[22]

On one hand, you cannot blame the justices, who themselves primarily went to Harvard or Yale Law Schools. They have a choice, and why not pick a year-long associate in whom they can see themselves at a younger age? There are certainly more women and people of color as clerks, but none who approaches being "of the people." There has been only one clerk from Rutgers Law School, for instance. A few have come from Duke, where President Richard Nixon got his degree, so it is clearly of some standing. The farther a law student is from the coasts, save for the Chicago area (University of Chicago, Northwestern University, and Notre Dame University), the vastly more unlikely it is that he or she will be a Supreme Court clerk.[23]

Should this matter? My contention is that, yes, it does. Marshall, who went to less than a month of law lectures at William and Mary College and existed long before the advent of Supreme Court clerks, had at least a hue of the common people. No matter where the early justices went to school, they also had to "ride the circuit," holding court, mostly in state capitals, but often far away from their usual Washington insularity. They saw cases where the plaintiffs and/or defendants were either aggrieved local citizens or businesses, or at least individual state governments. The cases were often filled with emotional speeches and, if important, spectators from local constituencies.

Even some dramatic and consequential cases came on the circuit. Perhaps the most dramatic case Marshall ever presided over was the treason trial of former vice president Aaron Burr, not in Washington, but in Richmond, where the case was situated. The location may have taken President Jefferson a bit out of the mix in a way it might not have if the case were heard in Washington, but it allowed people from a rather remote place at the time to see a major trial.[24]

The Court was not always a source of the "elite" in its early and middle days, but with the rise in the Court's docket, the clerks have more influence. Often, the justice uses them as a filter to see which cases should be heard. The elitism and collegiality of the clerks, and now the justices who also hail from Ivy schools, form a certain way of evaluating cases to be heard, not just the opinions in the end. If, say, either a Ginsburg or a Scalia chooses from that elite, she or he can expect—or if they are oblivious to it, maybe not—a different response politically, but not socially. Constituents from rural Arkansas, or even suburban Denver, do not crowd the chamber, as they did in the rural Burr trial or the Scopes evolution trial in Tennessee.

The website Oyez.org, from the Cornell Legal Information Institute, allows free access to the oral arguments of every Supreme Court case back to the fall of 1955. There is no doubt that the more the cases go toward the twenty-first century, the more arcane and elite the arguments sound. There are no passionate soliloquies like Daniel Webster's in *Dartmouth College v. Woodward*.

Perhaps the judicial branch of the federal government should be elite, as the Congress and president often campaign as the representatives "of the people." Though both Sonia Sotomayor and Clarence Thomas in their memoirs remember their relatively poor early years, they went to elite colleges and law schools, and their judicial bents are that way, though along different political lines.[25]

When the young men and women who populate their offices, and the offices of all their cohorts, come from elite backgrounds, the processes meld. It is no surprise that Scalia and Ginsburg were the best of friends, and that Elena Kagan and Neil Gorsuch go on the lecture tour together. Their main connection is the elite one that pervades their offices and the clerks who advise them and often write the first drafts of their opinions. Their politics are separate, but their thought processes are the same.

What will be preserved in the Courts of the future, it seems, whether they turn conservative or liberal, is this reinforcement, through clerks, of that elitism. Though it is at least comforting to know that our Supreme Court back offices are filled with intellectualism, perhaps a few North Dakota and Oklahoma, or even New Jersey voices in the courts would help things out.[26]

Chapter Eleven

Modest Proposals

THERE ARE ALWAYS DRUMBEATS TO TRANSFORM THE COUNTRY IN SOME way. There are spurts in constitutional amendments—long patches of none, then a flurry, like the Thirteenth through Fifteenth Amendments in the mid-nineteenth century and a bunch of unrelated ones in the early part of the twentieth century. The panning of the Electoral College goes back and forth between parties when the other one narrowly wins a presidential election. Supreme Court packing fury comes and goes, as it did most virulently after Franklin Roosevelt was elected in 1936, and in the late 2010s when progressives believed the Court's swing to the right was out of step with the populace.

There are other ideas, though, that on the surface seem far-fetched, but with a little explanation, well, maybe. Just maybe.

THE PROPOSALS

Secession

When I wrote the book *Worst. President. Ever.* about the horrendous presidency of James Buchanan, one of my defenses for my rating was that he let the nation dissipate by saying he could do nothing about the southern states starting to secede.[1]

Upon reflection, though, it is clear that the South did, indeed, win the Civil War. OK, so it did not do well in the battlefield in the end, and slavery was eliminated, but the white, segregationist South clearly existed for at least another ninety years.

Even today, much of that former Confederate contingent does not really like what comes out of Washington, or the North and the coasts which value progressive policies. Perhaps it is Lincoln who should be called Worst. President. Ever. Had he let the Confederacy secede, we would not have our sectional problems today—those former states being their own country.

Our country is large and unwieldy. Only India and maybe Canada among the other countries of our size and population—perhaps Brazil, Indonesia, Congo, China, and Russia—are democracies, and only Canada a really workable one. Canada always has the issue of the secession of Quebec along with other French-speaking citizens. Sometimes it even looks like it might happen. Would that be a good thing? Scotland is on a thin string in Great Britain. Who knows?

As with any major shift, it would take time to work out, but perhaps, say, Mississippi not ever having to deal with those pesky New Yorkers, and Texas loving being the most populous state in its own country would put each nation happily over the edge.

No More States

In almost every democracy, the federal government dominates over any regional issues. And most of those countries—look at Canada—have a reasonable number of districts, states, or provinces, in any case.

America has fifty state jurisdictions with sometimes senseless nuances of similar laws—where you can drink alcohol, how old and skilled do you have to be to drive a car, where and if you can gamble and on what—as small for instances.

Why put up with that? Why not just get rid of states altogether? Living in New Jersey most of my life has never stopped me from rooting for Philadelphia sports teams, but it does make me have to think about sales tax difference, toll bridges, drinking hours, and so forth.

Further, the elimination of states would solve the issue of the Electoral College. No more states—no more Electoral College, which was set up to try to make the presidential election more equitable among the continually debating states.[2]

There would have to be some maneuvering about how Congress would be shaped, but maybe the answer would be to have geographic sections with similar populations. Views shift over time—the map of the 1916 presidential election looks eerily like that of the 2016 election, except the parties are reversed—so dividing on current political persuasion would not work long-term. Those who love the popular vote as the method for determining victory in the election would revel in this change.

Eliminate the Senate

It works in Nebraska, where there is a unicameral (one house) legislature. Parties notwithstanding, there is always a complaint by one side or another that the smallest states in population—Delaware, Vermont, South Dakota, Alaska, for instance—have the same say in the Senate as California or Texas, with perhaps several dozen times more people.

There could still be the current states, with the current House of Representatives. The Constitution places no limit on how many members of Congress there are. Or the idea of a new country without states would work similarly here.

Besides, the Senate dining room has become a desolate place because not enough senators wanted to eat there and socialize any more. And the Democratic and Republican softball teams are mostly made up of younger representatives, rather than roly-poly oldster senators.[3]

A New Constitution

Or maybe just ditch the whole thing and start over. There is actually precedent for it. The Founders finally found that the Articles of Confederation were really no more than a peace treaty. Nine new states had their own military and three of them had executives called president. What we now call the Constitution is really just a reformation of the perceived mistakes of the Articles.[4]

Similarly, many states have had constitutional conventions to rehab their main documents. We amend the Constitution, but most scholars do believe that there needs to be at least some more clarification in places. There is not enough on how the judiciary is supposed to work. If *Roe v. Wade* taught the country anything, it was that there are lots of holes in the document just because it is more than two hundred years old. No one thought much about abortions, much less birth control, or the quick availability of it. There are no slaves, but there are computers and the internet today. Transportation and world commerce, just to name two things, are vastly different now.

Even if it were not completely thrown out, it would not be a bad idea to establish a periodic, maybe every twenty-five or even fifty years, over-haul of our sacred document.

FAVORITE AND UNLOVED AMENDMENTS

Second

Having changed meaning over the years, especially on its extremes, from the need for a state militia because no one trusted a federal army, to the right to own just about any explosive concoction or instrument available, it is time to rewrite it at least, and get rid of it at best. There is no piece of public policy jargon that comes out of politicians' mouths more often than "No one wants to abolish anyone's Second Amendment rights." That would be OK, except that no one knows what rights the Second Amendment really gives.

Fifth

What is this fervor about self-incrimination? If someone committed a crime, why does he or she get to opt not to give information that may convict them? It can be—literally—getting away with murder. I understand this may be severe to those who specialize in rights to privacy, but, really, if someone murdered your brother and is the only one who can give the right information, would you be happy if he or she "took the Fifth"?

Take the Fifth. Please.

Eighteenth

It really is not there anymore, since it made Prohibition constitutional and was erased a decade later by the Twenty-First Amendment.[5] Yet it seems so strange. Why would any product be banned by a constitutional amendment? Plenty of things are banned now just by congressional statutes or presidential orders. The amendment may have been overturned, but it sets the example of how not to ban things, instead of principles or actions, on moral grounds.

Third

Love this one. No military force can be quartered in my home. Imagine the grocery store bill, and the arguments of what football game to watch on Sunday. On the other hand, I know some families where it would be easier to house the Third Regiment than their kids and their pets.

Twenty-Second

Limits presidential terms to two. No matter how much you like the president, the third time around is a bit much. That Franklin Roosevelt got elected four times is amazing, but he had a mercurial candidate, Wendell Willkie, running against him the third time, and a truly awful candidate, Thomas Dewey, the last. It should have been in the Constitution in the first place, as most of the people at the Convention were afraid of potential monarchy.

Ninth

The shortest of amendments,[6] it protects the rights not specifically enumerated in the Constitution. In a way, it is the most forward-looking amendment, since it obviates the need to predict what sorts of principles and achievements will come about in the future. In practicality, though, it is a bit of a nothing burger. To decide a case because, solely, it involves a right to something not foreseen by the Founders, is too slight.

It is true that it also means that if the Constitution says something, it is meant to be followed and if not, it may be left for states to decide, but even that is a slim hole to step through.

Best and Worst Founders

Aaron Burr

This is a layup, but there are lots of guys following in the lane who can swat it away. Burr was brilliant but erratic. He had a coterie at times because he was smart, but he was also somewhat pliable. His maneuvering to try to become president through a technicality in the Electoral College system in 1800 was an outrage, but a brilliant outrage. He almost pulled it off until the Jeffersonians got the only voter from Delaware on a gift judgeship for his father-in-law as bait.

Burr probably was trying to find something more clever.

He made a bad career move in the Hamilton duel, while Hamilton probably made a good one. The Federalist Party was dissipating and being the leader of it did not seem all that enticing. Hamilton's future in politics would have been so much lesser than before, so he probably would have gone into business instead.

Burr did get to return to the vice presidency, and apparently his command of the Senate was smart, if manipulative. His excursions after his term in office in the western part of the country did not get him a presidency in a new country surrounding the Mississippi and New Orleans, but it did further energize the West in the minds of stodgy easterners, and also gave Andrew Jackson his second wind of fame.

Ben Franklin

Another figure both overrated and underrated. He was not the complete savior that some have made him out to be, but Franklin did produce a good aura for the late eighteenth century in Philadelphia.

He was away some of the time becoming what the French person's idea of an American was. He was ingenious about that, not just for occasionally wearing a coonskin hat, but for being forthright, hospitable, and not all that formal. The French wanted to meet real Americans, and if he were actually part of the elite and playing one of those real Americans, it was genius.[7]

At home in Philadelphia, he was the perfect spirit of the host. He had many parties, which were vital in getting all sides to speak to each other. He did his scientific experiments, those that made him an American Voltaire. In his sociability, he could be manipulative, but he made the Constitutional Convention delegates think, as they would say today, out of the box about his ideas, especially on taxes and Native American relations.[8]

Some rate him higher than Washington, but that is too much of a stretch.

George Washington

As in the section on the national myth in this volume, there would be no United States without George Washington. Though he suffered a bit of a letdown in his aura at the end of his presidential term, he always got something of a pass because of his war strategy—not losing was sometimes better than winning a battle or maneuver—and that it eventually gave us a country.

Then his ardor to have an all-inclusive Cabinet got the country a corralled Hamilton, Jefferson, and Madison. He was not crazy that they, for instance, went behind his back to broker the compromise that gave the capital to the District of Columbia in exchange for a central banking system, but he liked that it was near his property, raising its value for his dotage, and that they named it after him.

He was a leader in all ways, though, inspiring a cadre of soldiers who became politicians, and a cadre of politicians who became our Founders.

James Madison

A man not unwilling to change his mind, and not just for expediency. He was a Jeffersonian acolyte, but he codified his ideas, particularly in

The Federalist Papers, and he did not just put them in secret and sardonic letters, like Jefferson.

Jefferson counted on Madison to tell him what was going on in the Founding while he, Jefferson, was negotiating in Europe. Since the letters would take weeks to get there, Madison also filled them not just with news, but also with speculation. Reading them, it is apparent that no one knew more about the Founding, at least in philosophical and political terms, than Madison.

His diaries are the only ones by one of the main founders in real time during the Constitutional Convention. Since the proceedings were supposed to be secret, Madison technically violated the Founding Omerta, but he gave it in trade of not letting them be seen in his lifetime.[9]

His presidency was a little dicey. The British, after all, burned the White House. He did get one of the more able first ladies in his wife Dolley. He met her, as the story goes, through Aaron Burr.[10] Madison was short and shy, and Dolley was one of the more lovely widows in Philadelphia, her first husband, John Todd, dying young in a yellow fever epidemic. Burr apparently noticed Madison gazing at her one day in town and told him he knew Dolley from the time a few years back when he boarded at her father's tavern and the family lived in the building. Burr set up a meeting and the two were married a year later.

Maybe Burr gets brownie points there. Dolley outlived even Madison, who died in 1836, and became the woman everyone wanted at their parties when she retired to Washington. She had little money—her son by Todd having ripped her off in stealth and bad business dealings—but somehow Washington always wanted Dolley around.

Unlike some other Founders—Jefferson, Franklin, Marshall, and John Quincy Adams, for instance—when Madison retired, he really retired. He was rarely consulted on anything, despite his secretary of state, James Monroe, succeeding him in the White House. He sought no office and was happy just to be on his estate in Virginia, to read and rest, something he was rarely allowed to do during his Founding moments.

Roger Sherman

The only Founder to sign all four major Founding documents—the Continental Association, the Declaration of Independence, the Articles of Confederation, and the Constitution—Sherman rates as the most underrated Founder.[11]

The Continental Association is a little-talked-about document, drawn up and signed at the first Continental Congress meeting at Carpenters' Hall in Philadelphia in 1774. It more or less solidified the idea that the individual colonies could meet with the other colonies, and specifically it tied them together to boycott British goods surrounding the Intolerable Acts.[12]

Born in 1721, save for Benjamin Franklin, Sherman was the oldest Founder. He grew up in and around Boston, but when he was a young adult, he moved near his brother in New Milford, Connecticut, then but a village, where Sherman opened the first general store in the town. He soon became the clerk, the highest position in town, and then the surveyor of the county.

He served two separate terms in the Connecticut House of Representatives in the 1750s and 1760s, and then became a district judge. But he got the revolutionary fever and represented his state at all the major Congresses and meetings in the Revolutionary Period.

Sherman was one of the gang of five on the committee to draft the Declaration of Independence, with Franklin, Thomas Jefferson, John Adams, and Roger Livingston. His greatest contribution was, though, the Connecticut Compromise, the foundation of how Congress is structured. The Virginia plan, favored by the big states, had a bicameral (two-house) legislature with seats apportioned by population in both houses. The New Jersey plan, favored by smaller states, had a unicameral legislature with each state getting an equal number of seats.

Neither pleased the other side, as would be obvious. Sherman combined the two plans, with a lower house apportioned by population and an upper house, the Senate, with two senators from each state. It is a compromise that is often vilified, particularly by big states that do not like how the Senate is apportioned, but the Constitution's passage hinged on this, so there would be no United States without it. Sherman was not a big fan of the executive, which he wanted just to be the lead person doing the practical bidding of Congress. Nor did he want the people—perhaps thinking them the rabble—as part of the national legislative process. He thought that some version of an elected body, perhaps the state legislature, perhaps the lower house in Congress, should be appointing all of Congress in both houses.[13]

Sherman served in both the House and the Senate from Connecticut before dying in the typhoid fever epidemic that swept Philadelphia in 1793. Three of his grandsons became US senators and his great-great-great grandson was Archibald Cox, the first Watergate special prosecutor whom Richard Nixon fired because Cox was getting too close to the heart of the matter, in what came to be known as the Saturday Night Massacre.[14]

Alexander Hamilton
Go see the musical. It is a marker of why history is fun. No one has to agree with Lin-Manuel Miranda's view of America through his musical work, but it should move the viewer toward his or her own enlightenment.

CHAPTER TWELVE

Marshall and Burr, His Retreats to Richmond, and His Legacy

MARSHALL'S SUPREME COURT DECISIONS WERE, TO BE SURE, MONUMEN-
tal, but one that took him out of Washington, down to what might have
been thought of as an obscure circuit court in Richmond, was probably
his most public one.

Beveridge, in his four-volume biography of Marshall, full of flowery
language and a bit too praising of the subject, begins this saga with the
farewell speech of Aaron Burr, as vice president and also head of the Senate. He claims it was extemporaneous and took up much of the afternoon
of March 2, 1805, bringing many on the Senate floor to tears.

"From the unprecedented scene in the Senate Chamber when the
Vice President closed, a stranger would have judged that this gifted per-
sonage held in his hands the certainty of a great and brilliant career,"
wrote Beveridge. "Yet from the moment he left the Capitol, Aaron Burr
marched steadily toward his doom." To be sure, Jefferson did not want
him as vice president again, and he was succeeded by George Clinton,
also a New York politician, making the slight all the greater.[1]

That doom came over the next few years, culminating in what Beveridge called "the greatest criminal trial in American history." Burr's
prestige slithered downward starting from his quixotic battle to edge
out Jefferson, the obvious Republican nominee, in the 1800 presidential
election. Effectively silenced in an era when vice presidents were really

doing little except presiding over the Senate, he tried to keep in play his constituency in his home state of New York but was always thwarted by Alexander Hamilton, the Federalist with still a modicum of power as the party was spiraling to its own doom.[2]

Eventually that led to their duel and Burr's killing of Hamilton in it. Burr was never prosecuted for anything surrounding the duel, but his reputation went even further south afterwards. There was a residue of what was not quite affection for him, but a sense that Burr had energy and ideas. He championed opening up the West, so people there had, essentially, become his constituency.

Burr had tried to run as a Federalist candidate for governor of New York, but that was quixotic, as were meetings with New England Federalists to think about a secession of that area from the Union. He then looked west, his motives never clear. It is certain he met with James Wilkinson, who once declared himself "the Washington of the West," and was in the employ, sometimes secretly, of Spanish and English interests who wanted to divide the country East and West.[3]

Wilkinson had been appointed governor of Upper Louisiana and proposed to Burr, soon after he was out of government, that they invade Mexico in order to solidify a new nation west of the Alleghenies. Burr started down the Ohio River to see what he could gather. He stopped in Cincinnati, then a metropolis of seventeen hundred people. He got to Louisville, a burg even smaller, later, and rode from there on horseback to Frankfort and Lexington, dingy horse-bound towns inland. He went on to Nashville, meeting with the major general of the Tennessee Militia, a young strongman, Andrew Jackson. He finally met with Wilkinson at Fort Massac, down the Cumberland River from Nashville, and made it down to New Orleans on June 25, 1805.

There he was royalty, with balls and fancy repasts daily. The pashas of Louisiana all would be happy to support an invasion of Mexico, or a separation without that of the western states and territories. Burr continued circling the West and South, but finally word of his travels—and rumors, some wild with inaccuracies, of his motives—aggrieved Jefferson too much. He had Burr arrested for treason, and Marshall took the case to Richmond.[4]

The trial was watched by a full courtroom daily and people thronged the courthouse just to hear the proceedings first. Spittoons and sand pits for tobacco and its juices were scattered throughout the courtroom and grounds. Andrew Jackson was even curious enough to come and mingle with the throngs.

"Of all within the Hall of Delegates, and, indeed, among the thousand then in Richmond, only two persons appeared to be perfectly at ease," wrote Beveridge. "One of them was John Marshall, the other was Aaron Burr." Winfield Scott, who eventually did get to invade Mexico as an American general, wrote in his memoirs about his first impression of Marshall: "There he stood, in the hands of power, on the brink of danger, as composed, as immovable, as one of Canova's living marbles ... Marshall was the master spirit of the scene."[5]

The government employed a bevy of prestigious Virginia lawyers, the leading of whom was William Wirt, later the longest serving attorney general, making it through the twelve years of James Monroe's and John Quincy Adams's terms. Wirt gave a four-hour speech, hoping to prove that Burr, merely by being a significant figure, could, by his influence, induce people to fight for a separation of the states just by talking about it.[6]

Marshall, once again, was in both a political and judicial moment. As before and after, he found a way to more or less please, and anger, both sides. He said in his decision that Burr did not commit treason because he had to commit an "overt act" of war or its equivalent. Just talking about treasonous acts was not, in and of itself, treason. No witness had come up with proven overt acts, and in any case, the Constitution said there had to be two witnesses to any overt act.[7]

Republicans, particularly Jefferson, were angry about the decision, but in sum they got their wish. Burr was disgraced and would never again hold a public office. He went to Europe for several years, allegedly trying to collect money and support for his version of an invasion of Mexico. He came back to the United States in 1811, married well into the New York Jumel fortune, and then dissipated his wife's share of it. He died even later than Marshall, in September 1836, the longest living of the Founders, outliving James Madison by a few months—though both were retired by the time of Marshall's death a year earlier, making him the final working Founder.[8]

Marshall's reputation after the Burr trial, though, was intact, and he was able to make a significant ruling to add to the others he would make at the Supreme Court itself. Treason was not a crime to be taken lightly, and his calm and even demeanor was shown to the general public who gathered at the trial in Richmond, people who never would have seen him in the Supreme Court in Washington. As with the XYZ Affair, his popularity may have been ephemeral on the public national scene, but it was there again. And unlike the resolution of *Marbury*, his decisions, and the style of them, would not be surprising ever again, and he was now clearly the man who brought a judicial voice to the still new nation.

A few years prior to the Burr case, Marshall suffered through, with the rest of the Federalist justices and other federal judges, a political ordeal, that of the Jeffersonian Republicans' tactic of impeachment. It was the counter move of the Midnight Judges ploy that the Federalists used, packing the courts during the demise of the John Adams presidency.

Jefferson himself saw an opening to his gambit in the loud temper of Associate Justice Samuel Chase. Though Jefferson clearly was eventually aiming at Marshall, Chase was a more public target. Chase had made an inappropriate charge to a Baltimore grand jury denouncing the Republican repeal of the Judiciary Act of 1801, the law that had created the mass of new judgeships for the Federalists. Chase was entitled to his opinion, but in its proper place. Chase further chose not to dismiss cases under the Alien and Sedition Acts that Jefferson saw as confrontational.

The House brought up Chase on eight articles of impeachment in 1803, and by March 12, 1804, the House overwhelmingly voted to impeach him by a seventy-three to thirty-two vote.

Jefferson was confident his methods would be successful with Chase, and then he could move on to other Federalist justices and judges. His loyal cousin, Congressman John Randolph, would argue the case before the overwhelmingly Republican Senate, with Vice President Aaron Burr presiding. The fatal flaw in the setup of the case was that all of the cases in the articles of impeachment were from decisions Chase had made in lower courts, not the Supreme Court. Chase's attorneys were able to argue that conviction on impeachment charges had to come from improprieties while on the highest federal bench. These charges, Chase's advocates were able to say, were clearly just politically motivated, not of the substance needed for removal from office.[9]

Though the majority of senators—there were twenty-five Republicans and nine Federalists in the Senate by that time—voted to convict on each of the counts, there was never the necessary two-thirds vote on any of them, so Chase was acquitted on March 1, 1805.

Marshall and the rest of the Federalists then became safe, as the Jeffersonians did not try the move again. In fact, no other Supreme Court chief or associate justice has ever again been impeached.

———

Those soldiers and Navy men fighting in the War of 1812 were not the men of zeal and, at a turn, naïveté who fought in the Revolutionary War a generation or more before. What they were instead were defenders of America. If the Revolutionary War was one of liberation, this was an invasion of hostile forces.

Unlike the Vietnam War days, when it was the youth of the country who sought peace, it was older folks, especially those who saw some of the mistakes of the Revolutionary War, who did not want this war, especially on home soil. Marshall was among them. Just before the outbreak of the war, Marshall signed on for an adventure in the West.

The Virginia legislature, perhaps emboldened by, but surely fascinated with, the trial of Aaron Burr, appointed Marshall to head a group of "investigators" of western lands, mostly still within the state and uncharted. Marshall heartily accepted. Even at fifty-seven, he thought he could take on the mountains and unforded streams as he did in his youth along the fringes of the Appalachians. He would also get a reprieve from all the Washington talk of a war he disdained.

He came back after several months with a forward-looking plan, a fresh idea of the future. He saw the chance for the newly improved steamboats to go on what were still wild rivers. He wanted Virginia to build a modern trade route to the West, where towns would become established and wealth would come from settlement. The national government would also benefit, with ease of military passage to the West and a sense of a modern, expanding country, where immigrants and longtime Americans together would be looking to come to a vibrant new place.[10]

He came home to Richmond to write his report, but there he became depressed by news of the war. It had not gone well at first—eventually the White House would be burned with the British routing the capital—and New Englanders were touting a ceasefire or, worse, secession. Instead, the Massachusetts House of Representatives flew with the idea of a third party—The Peace Party—to run in the 1812 presidential election, or at least have it replacing the Federalist banner. Marshall was the first person anyone not from New York had thought of—the most prominent peacenik available.

In the end, though, the corrupt New York politician, DeWitt Clinton, got the nomination, mostly under the Federalist name. He did rather well, getting all of New England, save Vermont, New York, New Jersey, Delaware, and Maryland, but lost to the incumbent James Madison. Second-guessers said Marshall would have gotten North Carolina and Pennsylvania, winning the election.[11]

It was the real last gasp of anything associated with the Federalist Party. Marshall, though, was still chief justice, and that would have to be enough.

In time, the war turned, and by 1815, when peace was established, there was every bit a "new nation," as John F. Kennedy would announce it for his generation in his first inaugural address in 1961. They had defeated a foreign power and, with embargos, would not have to have Europe interfering with their doings. They had won the war in the West as well, taking New Orleans and putting a final stamp on any nation invading that way, thus giving all Americans an open eye to settlement and fortune in that direction.

The New Nation would set up Marshall with a chance to solidify his theory of nationalism from the bench in the coming years, which he took as a mission as his former political party fizzled out. And a populism, culminating in Andrew Jackson's rise, that he did not like pushed him more in that direction.

Marshall had built a stately home in Richmond and, in fact, spent much of his time there. With the Supreme Court meeting in Washington only several weeks a year, he was free to come back to his hometown. In a lot of ways, he strove, either intentionally or benignly, to have a part of him be the homespun, jovial, backslapper he was in Richmond, even when delivering the most important verdicts in the country's history down the road in Washington.

His wife, Polly, routinely criticized him when he would go out in his rough-hewn and often wrinkled dress, even to formal affairs. Some called his manners crude, but what they usually meant was that he did not hold back his emotions, especially his positive ones. He often told the story of when he was out near the market in Richmond, just chatting with passersby. A man who had not been in Richmond long, seeing his crude dress, offered him a coin if Marshall, whom he did not recognize, would carry home a turkey the man had just bought. He took the coin and the turkey and walked several paces behind his new employer, just so the man would not hear the laughter of townspeople who knew what was what.[12]

Marshall would walk everywhere. In some places, he would walk six miles for exercise in the morning. He owned a farm four miles from Richmond, and when he did not have anything large to carry out to it, he would walk there nearly every day he was home. Legend had it when he would ride out there, he would inevitably see children tired but walking on the road, so he would put them up on the horse, often one behind him and one in front.[13]

When he would go on the circuit trip to Raleigh, he drove a stick gig—sort of a one-horse shay—through the pines the 170 miles from Richmond, taking more or less a week to cover the crude trail. No doubt he did the thinking while alone on this trip—he mostly kept his servants and secretaries back in Richmond—that he needed to form his long and often convoluted decisions. He spent much of his time in Raleigh when not in court doing just what he did in Richmond—playing quoits, hanging out in taverns and finding the best folks, those up and down the economic scale—among the only several hundred living in the town to talk to.[14]

Marshall had a couple of big disappointments in life, especially when most of his life was so full. He would have loved his biography of George Washington to have been a hit. Washington was his primary hero, from the time he met him as a young officer at Valley Forge and the battles nearby. When Washington's nephew Bushrod arranged for Marshall to get Washington's extensive papers to use, it seemed like a no-brainer that it would be a successful mission.

As noted elsewhere in this book, it was not, for several reasons, not the least of which was Marshall's unusually sluggish writing. While he may have hoped the volumes would be up on every American's shelf next to the Bible and a cookbook, it was there only for a few thousand souls, most probably intimates of Marshall in the first place.

The other more serious disappointment was the mental and emotional long-term condition of his wife Polly. Marshall was struck by her when she was not yet fourteen at a party at her parents' home while he was at Williamsburg during his few weeks in law school at William & Mary College. He was twenty-five, but mostly acted like an adolescent, doodling her name on his law notes and mooning over her. What would seem an inappropriate age disparity in our day was, apparently, unopposed in theirs. There is a story that Polly told him to bug off one day, and he rode away thinking everything was over. Allegedly she reconsidered and had a cousin ride quickly after Marshall with a lock of her hair. Marshall made a locket with her hair, be it that lock or another, and she wore it until the day she died. Marshall took it off her that day and wore it the rest of his life as well.[15]

They married when she was fifteen and he was twenty-seven. They soon after started having children—ten of them, with six living to adulthood. In the beginning, all was fine, but then between the births of son Jaquelin Ambler, named after her father and their second child, in 1787, and daughter Mary in 1795, Polly had two miscarriages and lost two toddlers. While there were certainly some physical problems with all that, the worst affliction was the mental anguish it brought her. For the most part after that, she became much the recluse in the family home until she died in 1831.[16]

It apparently did not end Marshall's devotion to her. He wrote her numerous letters, especially when close by in Washington, but even when he was abroad as a diplomat, and he demanded letters back from her. He was said to have always complimented her to friends and never let on how sick she was. His devotion to Polly led him to be as much a feminist as there was back in those days, always approving of whatever work and study women did and never letting anyone defame or joke maliciously about women.

Those derogatory things were never allowed air at the Quoit Club in Richmond, which Marshall founded and delighted in attending, either to play quoits, at which he stayed adept into his seventies, or just to drink and dish gossip. He was chief justice of the Supreme Court, dignified and erudite on the bench, but he reveled just as much, maybe more, being the chieftain of his hangout in Richmond.[17]

As with many persons who attended little school, late in life Marshall became somewhat of a dilettante. He read all of Jane Austen's works when he was seventy-one, and constantly read poetry, silently alone or aloud to Polly at home. His children who lived to adulthood all were successful in law, business, farming, or, as it would be with women, marriage. When they were grown, he always took to children, playing marbles with those of relatives even in Washington and greeting them in as adult a way as possible into his dotage.

He was not a big fan of the formal run in Washington and avoided it when he could, putting up with it when he had to. He had his portrait drawn a few times but was never quite satisfied with how stilted it often looked. His longing for consensus was not solely for his court decisions. He wanted everyone at his table to be happy with one another, even if they held different political views. Everyone, he believed, deserved a place at that table, and though he owned slaves most of his life, he was conflicted, as were many Founders, over the existence of slavery in the first place.

He never really considered retiring from the Court. He loved its sessions, its puzzles, and, especially after Bushrod Washington, his early friend, died, he became a soulmate, intellectually and socially, with Joseph Story, even though Story was nominated to the Court by a Virginia rival, James Madison.

Story's ascension was fortuitous. Madison first nominated John Quincy Adams to fill the late William Cushing's seat. Adams was confirmed by the Senate but then refused the nomination. Madison continued to turn to Massachusetts, nominating Story, the Speaker of the House in that state legislature—and the youngest person ever to serve on the Court at age thirty-two.[18]

Marshall saw a younger version of himself in Story, and the two paired for most of the significant decisions of the post–War of 1812 era of the Marshall Court. Since Marshall was tangentially involved in the properties that *Martin v. Hunter's Lessee* would adjudicate, Story wrote that opinion. It confirmed the Marshall ideal that the Constitution came not from the states, but its citizens. "The Constitution of the United States was established, not by the states in their sovereignty capacities, but emphatically, as the preamble declares, 'by the people of the United States,'" Story wrote in his decision.

When Andrew Jackson came to power, Story and Marshall provided the line Jackson could not cross in his populism and states' rights platforms. Marshall and Story rarely strayed from the path of nationalism and provided the grist, in their decisions, that Supreme Court justices would use for the next two centuries, and presumably beyond.[19]

Marshall's end did not come quickly, though he mourned extensively when Polly died in 1831. He developed stones in his kidneys and bladder, and went to Philadelphia in what must have been an excruciatingly painful ride in 1831 to have them removed. They came about again in the summer of 1835, and he rode to Philadelphia again. His demise came soon after that last operation, and he was bled as was the order of the day, weakening him further.

Three of Marshall's sons made it to Philadelphia before he died. Tragically, his oldest son, Thomas, died the day before when, while in Baltimore racing to get to Philadelphia during a storm, he was smashed by bricks that blew down on him from a chimney. John Marshall did not hear that story before he died.[20]

Though it was said later that when Marshall died on July 6, 1835, the not-yet-called-Liberty Bell rang and cracked for the last time, that is a fiction. Bells might have tolled in the city, but mostly just laments came in the coming days in papers all over the country, even Republican ones that would not give Marshall much of the better of the doubt during his lifetime. Three days after his death, a steamboat carrying his body came to the Richmond wharf. A long procession marched to Marshall's house and then to the graveside of his wife, where he was buried. Flags in Virginia were at half-staff for several weeks in his memory.

Of all the honors he could have, and did have, the one the chief justice probably would have appreciated the most was the Quoits Club's resolution that "there should be no attempt to fill [his loss] ever, but that the number of the club should remain one less than it was before his death."[21]

CHAPTER THIRTEEN

Why We Study History, and How the Study of It Has Deeply Changed

I WENT UP TO THE ATTIC TO ONE OF MY "SAVE THESE" BINS OF BOOKS and pulled out *Greek and Roman Philosophy after Aristotle*, a paperback from 1966 that was a textbook of mine three years later, when I took a Carleton College freshman survey course on The Humanities.

On the flyleaf, printed in pencil, in my handwriting, is this: "Is Epicurean free will compatible with view of space & matter?" On page forty-seven, there is a star next to this underlined passage from Epicurus's Letter to Pythocles: "We do not seek to wrest by force what is impossible, nor to understand all matters equally well, nor make our treatment always clear as when we discuss human life or explain the principles of physics in general—" the rest of the sentence after that dash left clean of that underlining pencil.

I remember this section of the survey—there were other sections on art history and modern history—taught by one of my favorite professors, Maury Landsman, as exciting, something new that I had never seen before: Philosophy, with that capital "P." Yet I can say easily a half-century later that I probably have not thought of Epicurus, or his friend Pythocles, much if at all since those underlines and stars.

When it came time to declare a major at the end of sophomore year, a lot had passed. Carleton had gotten co-ed dorms. The Kent State murders of four students had unsettled a generation of students. I was playing rugby, a sport I had barely heard of, let alone played, before that year. I had long hair and a girlfriend from Beverly Hills.

And while I loved reading history and American literature, I made the decision to become a philosophy major. I had chosen it for what now appears to be the opposite of why current college students choose what they do. I surmised that I would read history and American literature books the rest of my life. Epicurus, not so much. If I did not take the advantage of reading and discussing him and his Greek and Roman buddies at Carleton, chances are they would not be on the nightstand later on.

"I think the way you thought about it is not as common any more," said Julian Zelizer, the Princeton University history professor who regularly appears on CNN as the network's historical consultant. "Four years any more to have the luxury of doing things you will never do later, as opposed to by twenty-one competing in the job market? That whole thing has changed over the years."[1]

In fact, that kind of change has decimated the philosophy major. At our Alumni Council meetings at Carleton in April 2019, the administration asked those of us on the council to go to what is now an informal ice cream sundae–making event the sophomores have at which they declare majors. They asked us to stand at tables that matched our majors when we were students, where the current students would get humorous buttons indicating theirs. For the better part of two hours, I hung out by the jar of Philosophy buttons. Not one student grabbed one, even in jest.

Clifford Clark, my old American history professor, who had recently retired, said things were no better in the history department of late.

"Until 2000, the biggest major at Carleton [where enrollment was about 450 students per grade], was English, second was biology which had maybe fifty, and then the third biggest was history," said Clark. "Now we have things that did not exist before, like computer science, film studies, neurobiology, and expansion in the number of data mining sciences.

"But English now has eighteen majors and history, instead of forty, has twenty majors," he said. "Parents are the ones often thinking about the cost of college, so the biggest major in the last thirty years has been business."

Clark did not want to put all of the onus on the rush to "practical" majors. Some of it, he said, lies in who went to college then, as opposed to now.

"As late as the 1960s, only 10 percent of the population went to college," he said. "If you went to a really selective college in that period, you were identifying yourself with a cohort of people who were hard-working, serious, self-disciplined, curious about knowledge and maybe interested in following that on to graduate school. Your major did not matter. The number of history majors who became doctors was pretty high.

"The nature of the job market has changed and that has created a new level of anxiety," he said. "No longer do you get out of college expecting a career, but because of the anxiety about the economy and jobs, history just falls off the chart."[2]

Although maybe this is not so new. I found this in a preface of a book in my home library:

"It is generally conceded, we believe, that the results of the study of history in our schools are very unsatisfactory. The pupils neither receive very distinct impressions nor acquire a love for the study of history that will lead them in later years to pursue the subject further. The attempt to enumerate all the minor events of history has obliged editors to condense their statements, to keep the books within the proper limits, as to rob them of that easy flow of language so necessary to any work of general interest or literary merit. The study thus becomes tedious and confusing to the child, who is not able to make a proper distinction between important and unimportant events."[3]

The source here is *Washington and His Country*, an introductory history book published in 1887, when our country had barely a century's worth of history to study.

So whither history? As I sit here writing the third major biography of John Marshall in the last three years, is it merely a fantasy that people any longer care, even in the Academy? I have picked him because I was enthralled, in high school, by my junior year history teacher, Walter Belfield, who taught us the "Great Man" theory of history, that it takes individuals, like Marshall, to move history, not the other way around.

In some ways, especially for young people, the change in the way Americans imbibe history came with the release of *The Civil War* series by filmmaker Ken Burns in 1990. Burns had honed his signature documentary style of cutting between and panning around still photographs in one-off documentaries for about a dozen years before *The Civil War*. In fact, Burns had Academy Award nominations for Best Documentary Feature both in 1982 (*Brooklyn Bridge*) and 1986 (*The Statue of Liberty*), but only cognoscenti saw them as groundbreaking, or even saw them at all.

When the Public Broadcasting System and Burns's sponsor, General Motors, though, decided to back Burns's idea for a vast-ranging multipart series on America's greatest internal conflict, it made Burns into a household name. Though some years earlier, ABC transferred Alex Haley's family history, *Roots*, to multi-episodic TV, it was still much like a fictional drama, with actors playing parts and movie-like quality. The historical value seemed secondary.

The Civil War, though, was prepared as an historical event. The nation's TV critics, of which I was one at the time for the *Asbury Park Press*, were given a boxed set before their summer meetings in Los Angeles, and Burns, his narrator David McCullough, the acclaimed popular historian, and actors like Sam Waterston, who voiced Abe Lincoln, and Jason Robards, who did the same for Ulysses S. Grant, were made available often and joyously.

The eleven-hour series ran from September 23 to September 28, and the Public Broadcasting System said thirty-nine million people saw at least one episode, the largest audience by far for any PBS production.[4]

It had taken Burns five years to make it, inspired as he was by Mathew Brady's photographs of the war and its times. One of the curious things about the series is that its main piece of music was a fiddle and piano tune called "Ashokan Farewell." Though written in 1982 and played by its composer, Jay Unger, and its arranger, Jacqueline Schwab, viewers assumed that it was a Civil War song and gobbled up copies of it and the other music played on the series.

The Civil War won a slew of awards: two Emmys, two Grammys, a Peabody, a DuPont-Columbia, and a $50,000 Lincoln Prize for history. The companion book, written by Burns and Geoffrey C. Ward, was a bestseller. In later years, the series was remastered twice, once for DVD and then again in a high-definition DVD format, each time selling hundreds of thousands of copies.

The series all but changed the presentation of history on television. The documentary form changed from merely informational, with a bunch of talking heads and grainy film footage, to something that also had to be entertaining—there had to be an "Ashokan Farewell" or a David McCullough, or even some Oscar-winner, narrating.

"Our idea," Burns said, "is you are meant to watch them in dark rooms in the company of strangers, your family, and friends. The television set is the new electronic campfire around which we sing our epic verses in Homeric fashion."[5]

Burns saw a deadening of history and hoped to revive it in photography and film.

"I've always described myself from the very beginning as an emotional archeologist. The combination of film, imagery, voice, music, and effect combine, if done honorably and authentically, to will the past alive," he said. "It reminds people that the word 'history' which for many people is a dull and boring word, is mostly made up of the word 'story.' With us, it's about trying to make old photographs come alive with complex movements, sound effects, period music, first person voices from the past, as well as third person narration—all of that makes you feel something."[6]

Zelizer acknowledges this is an era where popular histories, rather than academic ones, have more cachet, and that leads to people like him, who are on TV being asked about how the current news relates to history.

"But there have been public intellectuals before," said Zelizer. "Arthur Schlesinger was definitely an historian who was an academic, but also wrote for the public. . . . He was a celebrity, someone who was known in American life. Ken Burns didn't start that."[7]

About twenty years after the Burns series, the actor Lin-Manuel Miranda picked up a copy of *Hamilton*, a biography of the Founder written several years before by popular historian Ron Chernow. It is a long and rambling book, but it touched Miranda. He saw the chance to portray history from another angle and wrote that slice of history in the form of a hip-hop operetta. Sales not only of Chernow's *Hamilton*, but also a slew of American history books saw romance-novel-like increases. If *Hamilton* could become a musical, then why not James Garfield or Woodrow Wilson or Jimmy Carter or John Quincy Adams, or even Adams's wife, all of whom saw major biographies published in the wake of *Hamilton*?

There were critics who thought Miranda, in *Hamilton*, prostituted history for the sake of a story he wanted to tell. His case was brown and black playing white historical figures, rapping and jazzily singing through their lines. There is no doubt, however, that *Hamilton*, in its hit status, made people think about their history in a different way. What will be interesting, though, as *Hamilton* comes to the stage in high schools and community theaters that do not have enough minorities to play the figures as Miranda first saw them, whether the meaning of the musical will change as more white people get to play the historical characters.

Though Hal Holbrook made a virtual career channeling Mark Twain on stage, it was still more of a history-lite kind of thing. In 2017, though, Heidi Schreck wrote and performed what the *Washington Post* called an "autobiographical civics lesson," the Pulitzer-finalist and Tony-nominated *What the Constitution Means to Me*, inspired by Schreck's girlhood "career" of giving talks about the Constitution in American Legion contests. Those who did not already know got to learn about *Roe v. Wade*, feminism, immigration, and other historical issues wrapped up in drama form.

Schreck's play is primarily monologue and has a dramatic element to it. At the end, though, a high school debate champion (two alternated in the Broadway version) has a challenge with Schreck on an historical aspect of the Constitution and its relevance to today's world. I could see the puzzled looks from some audience members around me when I went to a performance. Clearly they didn't know about some aspects or passages in the Constitution that Schreck and her debate opponent were casually mentioning. I am hoping it inspired those people, and others who were familiar with the document, to try to discover more about the document, a seminal part of American history.[8]

Historians certainly are, if not in despair, at least worried about a culture that does not appreciate history. Robert Caro and his wife, Ina, went to live in the Hill Country of Texas to learn more about how Lyndon Johnson's early life there affected the rest of his life, a life that Caro has spent the better part of four decades chronicling—still not done, at this writing, with his fifth and presumably final volume on the former president. Even in the internet age, when more and more historical documents are there on the screen in a flash, it would be hard to imagine someone so eminent being caught up in history the same way.

"We, in our time, are raising a new generation of Americans who, to an alarming degree, are historically illiterate," said David McCullough in an address accepting the National Book Foundation Medal for Distinguished Contribution to American Letters. "Indifference to history isn't just ignorant, it's rude. It's a form of ingratitude. I'm convinced that history encourages, as nothing else does, a sense of proportion about life, gives us a sense of the relative scale of our own brief time on earth and how valuable that is."[9]

The speech was given in 1995, and McCullough has written many popular histories since then. Yet he obviously still believes what he said about the decline of history and its effects much later on, since an excerpt of that speech is included in his 2019 book, *The Pioneers: The Heroic Story of the Settlers Who Brought the American Ideal West.*

In that speech he lamentably looks back at two talks he gave to college history students. In the first, at a school with "a lively Ivy League setting," he was at a seminar of twenty-five senior history majors. He asked if anyone knew who George Marshall (no relation to John) was. Not a single student, "the cream of the crop," McCullough said, knew who the general who arranged the massive food distribution in postwar Europe, among other things, was. Then at "a large university in the Midwest," he told of a young woman who came up to him after his lecture thanking him, because before that she did not know that all the original thirteen colonies were on the Atlantic sea coast.

"[History] inspires courage and tolerance. It encourages a sense of humor. It is an aid to navigation in perilous times," McCullough continued in his National Book Foundation speech. "History shows that times of change are the times when we are most likely to learn. This nation was founded on change. We should embrace the possibilities in these exciting times and hold to a steady course, because we have a sense of navigation, a sense of what we've been through in times past."

He then evoked personal history as even more important.

"There's no one in this room who hasn't an ancestor who went through some form of hell. Churchill in his great speech in the darkest hours of the Second World War, when he crossed the Atlantic, reminded us, 'We haven't journeyed this far because we are made of sugar candy.'"

I had to admit I had never heard that line, which is unusual because I do love the quotes that are the frothiest. McCullough gave another quote, this one from Thomas Jefferson, "Any nation that expects to be ignorant and free, expects what never was and never will be."

"What it really comes down to is that history is an extension of life. It both enlarges and intensifies the experience of being alive," McCullough concludes. "It's like poetry and art. Or music. And it's ours, to enjoy. If we deny our children that enjoyment, that adventure in the larger time among the greater part of the human experience, we're cheating them out of a full life."[10]

Perhaps the first popular history written in the United States was David Ramsey's *History of the American Revolution*, published in 1789, only a few years after the war had finished. Ramsey was a surgeon in the Continental army and then a congressman from South Carolina under the Articles of Confederation. Ramsey felt limited, but complete, if those contradictory terms can be reconciled. He was covering a new country over a few years. To him, the issues were both fresh and personal. Though it was a history, the book was almost a memoir, since he had been so involved.

Now, though, history seems so much more complex and far off. Franklin, Madison, Washington, and Jefferson are merely characters wearing foppish or old-time military jackets and wigs. And there are now centuries of dead folks roadblocking a simple explanation of our history. Is it just too hard, like biochemistry? And was it easy, like arithmetic, in Ramsey's age?

Jill Lepore, the Harvard historian and *New Yorker* essayist, tried to bridge that gap in her one-volume history of the United States from 1492 on, *These Truths*. What better way to explain why we need to study history than producing the ultimate study guide. In 2011, several years before the publication of the book, she told an interviewer that it had been a goal of historians over the last fifty years "to write an integrated history of the United States, a history both black and white, a history that weaves together political history and social history, the history of presidents and the history of slavery."[11]

—◆—

When we stopped at Lexington, Virginia, for lunch on the way home from a college visit for my older daughter, I asked if we could make a quick side trip to the Washington & Lee University campus to see the graves of Robert E. Lee and his horse Traveler. I have always loved unusual historical sites, and the mound under which Traveler lies next to Lee's crypt indeed qualifies.

A few years later, my daughters having both gone to Davidson College, Lexington was just off I-81 through Virginia on our trips south. On one pass-through, I stopped to see my old Carleton College newspaper editor, Pam Luecke, who after a distinguished journalism career had come to teach at W & L. She took me to an adjunct unusual historical site. The presidential house for the university has a barn-type garage, whose door is always left open in case the ghost of Traveler wants to come back to visit the ghost of his master, Lee, who was the president of the university after his Civil War service.

In recent years, monuments to, especially, those who fought for the Confederacy, like Lee, or promoted slavery, like former vice president and US senator from South Carolina John Calhoun, have been hidden, torn down, changed names, and, in the most tragic consequence, caused deranged partisans to march in Charlottesville, Virginia, shouting racist taunts, which inspired a man to ram his car into a counter-protesting group, killing a woman.

While as a living citizen, I certainly do not think of white supremacy or its aligned malignant cousins as something to approve of, there is the historian in me that sees these pulling down of statues and renaming, as Yale did for Calhoun College and Minneapolis did for its Lake Calhoun, as a bit hasty and kneejerk.

I feel this allows every group strong enough to slay this kind of dragon to rewrite history to include only their views. It disallows context, which is something historical study hopes to provide. The tearing down of the Robert E. Lee statue in Charlottesville caused a tragic outcome. In other places, the legacies we do not admire about, say, our Founding Fathers, have been given the boost of historical updating and revision. The tour of Monticello, for instance, now no longer skips quickly over Jefferson's slaveholding. The updating of the re-creation of Ben Franklin's shop and living quarters in Philadelphia's Independence National Historic Park also admits Franklin's slaveholding.[12]

These are good things, and they give reason to use monuments as history teaching moments. American history, and thus our forebears, has gone through what the current day would call embarrassing times. Women got the vote only a century ago. It is hard to believe that people my age lived through a time when there were Jim Crow laws, but we did. Interracial marriage was declared legal, on a federal basis, only a half-century ago. And the big blot of slavery, together with the annihilation of the Native American culture, subsumes it all.

I would feel remiss without my trip to Traveler's grave, to allow me to think what times were in the aftermath of the Civil War for such as Lee. He was a traitor in some senses of the word and chose to fight for the right to own slaves rather than emancipate them. But he also served with distinction in the US Army, particularly in Texas, where he calmed the early chances for rebellion there. And he fostered a new wave of higher education in the South, just when it might have helped unite the country during Reconstruction.

Like many men who have become heroes to at least some, Lee held contradictions. If we take the "tear down" route, no one is safe. Even Barack Obama did not believe gay marriage should be legal when he took office, though he did come around to the majority view.

Should we tear down the Pyramids because they were built with slave labor—slaves owned by those interred there? In Berlin, there is no marker where Hitler's bunker was, supposedly to thwart neo-Nazis from gathering there, yet everyone of that ilk, and plenty more average citizens, know exactly where it was.

We watch movies that glorify the worst of historical figures—think of *Caligula* and any number of films of royal court misbehavior. We stand for *The Star Spangled Banner*, written by Francis Scott Key, a slaveholder, who as a Maryland lawyer defended the right of Washington, DC, to permit slavery.

I have been to Timbuktu, which is now in Mali, and saw the religious carvings and buildings there—which are no longer there after zealots bombed them or tore them down. It is not as if the ruins of Pompei and Ephesus and Petra, glorious as they are, were not built by slaveholding and war-mongering leaders.

Even the subject of this book, John Marshall, who did so much to elevate the Supreme Court to a place that often gave rights to the weak who could not get them otherwise, owned slaves and never sought to have women on equal grounds with men.

It is true that everyone is entitled to see history in his or her own way, but I would hope that instead of just discarding those who have major flaws, they decide to use that person, as I hope I have used Marshall in this book, to inspect the history of his time and how we can find value in it in ours.

Notes

INTRODUCTION

1. https://www.findagrave.com/memorial/2850/john-barry. Grave is at St. Mary's Catholic Churchyard, 252 S. 4th Street, Philadelphia.
2. Kane, *Facts About the Presidents*. Kane kept revising the book until he died at 103 in 2002. It went through seven editions.
3. Video and transcript of the April 23, 2019 panel at Mount Vernon, with Douglas Brinkley and Richard Norton Smith, with their stories here.

CHAPTER ONE

1. https://www.rottentomatoes.com/m/zelig/reviews.
2. Beveridge, *The Life of John Marshall*, 7. Beveridge's Marshall biography is four volumes and more than one thousand pages of print. It was not the first biography of Marshall but was the one with the greatest compendium of facts. Hereafter: Beveridge.
3. Beveridge. Beveridge's first chapter is a detailed account of Marshall's lineage and a short passage on the Braddock defeat.
4. Beveridge, 34–36.
5. Irving, *George Washington*. Irving's account of Washington's life is lively, so easy reading. He outlines Washington's and Thomas Marshall's relationship with Lord Fairfax, for whom Marshall especially developed a fondness.
6. The Franklin Institute, the institution that has long been tied to Franklin's science experiments, has a good description of the kite experiment: https://www.fi.edu/benjamin-franklin/kite-key-experiment.
7. Story, *Discourse on John Marshall*, 42. Joseph Story was Marshall's closest friend on the Supreme Court for the last decade of Marshall's life. Story listened to and wrote down Marshall's musings over the years and delivered a book, like Aristotle for Plato, with a lot of quotes from the subject.
8. Story, 50.
9. Beveridge, 62–65. Henry leading in the Stamp Act opposition and "liberty or death" speech.
10. Beveridge, 65.
11. Beveridge, 67–68.

CHAPTER TWO

1. Beveridge, 71 and onward. Beveridge is flowery in his language, but the facts are there.
2. Beveridge, 72.
3. Jean Edward Smith, *John Marshall: Definer of a Nation*, 62–65.
4. Beveridge, 75.
5. Beveridge, 80 and onward. That Marshall was dependent on his father for all of his military training becomes obvious. But he also looked around at others in command to see their different styles.
6. Irving, iii, 200–209.
7. Marshall, *Autobiography*, 157–58. In truth, Marshall's work here is a collection of letters and writings, not a true autobiography, but it is often the seminal place for quotes from Marshall.
8. A longer version of the battles and skirmishes between Brandywine and the encampment at Valley Forge may be found in Beveridge, 100–107.
9. Smith, 62–65. A concise passage on the setup of the encampment at Valley Forge.
10. Beveridge, 110.
11. Beveridge, 118–19.
12. Beveridge, 90.
13. Beveridge, 108 and onward. The juxtaposition between the fiesta that was British Philadelphia, while only miles away the ragged soldiers encamping in Valley Forge were in desperation, is vivid in Beveridge's few pages on it.
14. Marshall, Vol. I, 227.
15. Beveridge, 118.
16. Beveridge, 119.
17. Washington, *Writings*, letter of April 21, 1778.
18. Smith, 64–65.
19. Beveridge, 132.
20. Beveridge, 134–35.
21. Marshall, 255, letter from Lafayette to Marshall.
22. Beveridge, 146–47.
23. Lee, *Letters from the Federal Farmer*.
24. Beveridge, 255–58.
25. Talleyrand, *Memoirs of Talleyrand*, 176–77.
26. Beveridge, 261.
27. Beveridge, 265–66.
28. Beveridge, 268–69.
29. Hamilton, Jay, Madison, *The Federalist Papers*. A general reading yields many philosophical thoughts in a political document.
30. Beveridge, 270–90. A long discussion on how big and inaccessible most of revolutionary America was.

CHAPTER THREE

1. Smith, 71.
2. Beveridge, Vol. I, 151.
3. Beveridge, Vol. I, 151. Beveridge quotes from a cache of letters in the Marshall papers from "Mrs. Carrington," Mary Ambler's older sister, Eliza, which are the sources about the Marshalls' initial courtship.
4. Beveridge, Vol. I, 151.
5. Beveridge, Vol. I, 153.
6. Beveridge, Vol. I, 159.
7. Smith, 81.
8. Smith, 82.
9. Beveridge, Vol. I, 167.
10. Beveridge, Vol. I, 171.
11. Beveridge, Vol. I, 175. Beveridge spends a dozen pages on the details of Marshall's account books.
12. Beveridge, Vol. I, 183.
13. Beveridge, Vol. I, 203.
14. Beveridge, Vol. I, 205.
15. Madison, *Writings*, to Washington, December 14, 1787.
16. Beveridge, Vol. I, 207.
17. Page Smith, *John Adams*, 444.
18. Beveridge, Vol. I, 322.
19. Beveridge, Vol. I, 324.
20. Beveridge, Vol. I, 329 and forward about the size of the states.
21. Freeman, *George Washington*, 504.
22. Beveridge devotes a chapter to the Virginia debates, Vol. I, 319–56.
23. Winik, *The Great Upheaval*, 127–30.
24. Winik, 422 and onward.
25. Marshall, 155.
26. Winik, 462.
27. Marshall, 170.

CHAPTER FOUR

1. Beveridge, Vol. II, 57.
2. Smith, 571–72.
3. Beveridge, Vol. II, 48.
4. Beveridge, Vol. II, 53
5. Beveridge, Vol. II, 56.
6. Smith, 142–43.
7. Beveridge, Vol. II, 58.
8. Beveridge, Vol. II, 63
9. Marshall, 191.
10. Winik, 157–58.

11. Beveridge, Vol. II, 96.
12. George Washington, *Papers*, August 26, 1795.
13. Beveridge, Vol. II, 124.
14. Beveridge, Vol. II, 130.
15. Smith, 179–81.
16. Beveridge, Vol. II, 167 and onward, a dozen pages on Marshall's "other" life in Richmond.
17. Beveridge, Vol. II, 217 and onward, about Marshall and his feelings toward his compatriot envoys.
18. Smith, 201–10, on the negotiations, or lack thereof, in Paris.
19. Beveridge, Vol. II, 343.
20. Beveridge, Vol. II, 343–45, on the tumultuous greeting of Marshall in Philadelphia.
21. Jefferson, papers, to Madison, June 21, 1798.
22. Beveridge, Vol. II, 349–51, more fêting of Marshall in Philadelphia.
23. Beveridge, Vol. II, 352–53.
24. Beveridge, Vol. II, 378 and onward, the story of Washington and Marshall at Mount Vernon.
25. Smith, 239–44.
26. Beveridge, Vol. II, 392.
27. Beveridge, Vol. II, 418.
28. Beveridge, Vol. II, 441.
29. Smith, 265.
30. Beveridge, Vol. II, 494 and onward. A description of what Marshall supervised—the initial building of Washington, DC.
31. Census of the United States, 1800.
32. Census of the United States, 1800.
33. Beveridge, Vol. II, 500.

CHAPTER FIVE

1. Heidler and Heidler, *Henry Clay*, 10.
2. Strauss, *Worst. President. Ever.*, 38.
3. Boorstin, 167.
4. Boorstin, 170.
5. Hoffer, *The Supreme Court*, 63–67.
6. Hamilton, *Three Kentucky Presidents*, 1 and onward.
7. Dodd, *Jefferson Davis*, 133–35.
8. Dodd, 171–72.
9. Stahr, *Seward, Lincoln's Indispensable Man*, 21–26.
10. Taylor, *William Henry Seward: Lincoln's Right Hand*, 188–92.
11. Morris, *Fraud of the Century*, 208–9.
12. Morris, 235–36.
13. Morris, 255–56.
14. Kazin, *A Godly Hero*, 293–95.
15. Kazin, 10–11.

16. Kazin, 35–38, 51.
17. Kazin, 56–62.
18. Kazin, 63.
19. Kazin, 202–3.
20. Clements, *William Jennings Bryan: Missionary Isolationist*, 38.
21. Kazin, 179–81.
22. Kazin, 234–36
23. Kazin, 245–47.
24. Kazin, 294–97. The film, *Inherit the Wind*, is not an exact retelling of the Scopes Trial, but the character played by Fredric March, Matthew Harrison Brady, even to his use of the middle name, is clearly based on Bryan. His scenes with Spencer Tracy, as the defense lawyer, are priceless.
25. Franklin D. Roosevelt address at a memorial to William Jennings Bryan.
26. Simon, *FDR and Chief Justice Hughes*, 95–99.
27. Simon, 104.
28. Simon, 172–74.
29. Simon, 303.
30. Neal, *Dark Horse*, 52–54.
31. Neal, 144–45.
32. Neal, 260–63.
33. Dunn, *1940, FDR, Willkie, Lindbergh, Hitler*, 317.
34. Baker, *The Stevensons*, 317.
35. Martin, *Adlai Stevenson of Illinois*, 225–26.
36. McKeever, *Adlai Stevenson*, 160–61.
37. McKeever, 380–83.
38. Baker, 403.
39. Baker, 402.

CHAPTER SIX

1. Smith, 20.
2. Phone interview with historians at Independence National Historic Park, November 2018.
3. Smith, 328–32. A retelling of the negotiations and lack of success of the Marshall biography of Washington.
4. Boorstin, *The Americans*, 201.
5. Freeman, 577.
6. Page Smith, 1022.
7. Beveridge, Vol. II, 392.
8. George Will, *Washington Post*.
9. Crockett, *Biographical Directory of the United States Congress*.
10. Millard, *Destiny of the Republic*, an outstanding biography of a man who should have dominated more of American history, James Garfield.
11. Pafford, *Accidental President: Chester A. Arthur*, 25.
12. Rick Atkinson, *New York Times*, May 11, 2019.

13. Atkinson, May 11, 2019.
14. Visit to the Supreme Court building in Washington.

CHAPTER SEVEN

1. Hoffer, 41 and onward about Jay's frustration at having little to do on the first Court.
2. Hoffer, 37, 40.
3. Hoffer, 49.
4. Beveridge, Vol. II, 554.
5. Beveridge, Vol. II, 538.
6. Stone and McKean, *Great Decision*, 50–52.
7. Beveridge, Vol. II, 539. In a chart in a footnote, it is striking that the attorney general got only $1,500 a year, less than half of most of the rest of the Cabinet.
8. Beveridge, Vol. II, 560–62.
9. Beveridge, Vol. II, 561–62, though Beveridge does say "this tale is, probably, a myth."
10. Stone and McKean, 3.
11. Stone and McKean, 3–6.
12. Stone and McKean, 65–66.
13. Smith, 17.
14. Stone and McKean, 68–70.
15. Stone and McKean, 78–79.
16. Stone and McKean, 80.
17. Stone and McKean, 81.
18. Stone and McKean, 90. Stone and McKean present the beginnings of the Marshall and Jefferson terms in their respective jobs in parallel. They were in firm control of their jobs and were creating what became precedents for many decades.
19. Stone and McKean, 94.
20. Stone and McKean have the best and most detailed rendering of the lead-up to the Marbury case, 96 and onward.
21. Beveridge, Vol. III, 95–97.
22. Stone and McKean, 114–16.
23. Smith, 333.
24. Stone and McKean, 119.
25. Stone and McKean, 121–22.
26. Stone and McKean, 122–23.
27. Stone and McKean, 124.
28. Stone and McKean, 143.

CHAPTER EIGHT

1. Savage, "Acting Attorney General Matthew G. Whitaker Once Criticized Supreme Court's Power."
2. Savage.
3. Marcus, "Matthew Whitaker Is a Crackpot."

4. Hoffer, 97–100.

5. Schwartz, *History of the Supreme Court*, 105–25. There are many places to find commentary on *Dred Scott v. Sandford*, the most notorious of Supreme Court cases. Schwartz goes into complete analysis in these twenty pages.

6. Strauss, 153.

7. Tresolini and Shapiro, *American Constitutional Law*, 316–18.

8. Tresolini and Shapiro, 319–20.

9. Tresolini and Shapiro, 320–21.

10. Schwartz, 193–202.

11. Jeffrey Toobin, *The Nine*, 184.

12. Dershowitz, *Supreme Injustice*, 174–98.

13. Toobin, 200.

14. Legal Information Institute, Stevens Dissent.

15. National Constitution Center podcasts, *Abortion and the Constitution.*

16. *Abortion and the Constitution.*

17. *Abortion and the Constitution.*

18. Cole, "Keeping Up Appearances."

19. O'Connor, *Out of Order*, 137.

20. Schlesinger Jr., *Politics of Upheaval*, 456.

21. Hall, *Oxford Companion to the Supreme Court of the United States*, 146.

22. O'Connor, 136.

23. Douglas, *Autobiography*, 13.

24. O'Connor, 134–35.

25. O'Connor, 135.

26. Strauss, 150.

27. Schwartz, 73.

28. Tresolini and Shapiro, 345–50.

29. Hoffer, 102–3.

30. Denniston interview, June 2019.

31. Christensen, *Here Lies the Supreme Court*, 102.

32. Hall, 150.

33. Hoffer, 177.

34. Tresolini and Shapiro, 605.

35. Tresolini and Shapiro, 606.

36. Tresolini and Shapiro, 606–7.

37. Tresolini and Shapiro, 607.

38. Klugar, *Simple Justice*, 12.

39. O'Connor, 140–41.

40. O'Connor, 138–39.

41. O'Connor, 140–41.

42. From interview with Michael Zuckert, Nancy Reeves Dreux Professor of Political Science Emeritus, University of Notre Dame. Also, not coincidentally, my American Constitutional Law professor when I attended Carleton College as an undergraduate.

43. Rosen, *Supreme Court.*

44. Ibid.
45. O'Connor, 141.
46. Hoffer, 134.
47. Hoffer, 135.
48. Chemerinsky, *Case Against the Supreme Court,* 760.
49. Beth, *John Marshall Harlan* 81–109.
50. Chemerinsky, 761.
51. Chemerinsky, 761.
52. Schwartz, 163.
53. Rehnquist, "A Random Thought on the Segregation Cases."

CHAPTER NINE

1. Stone and McKean, 95.
2. Beveridge, Vol. III, 124.
3. Beveridge, Vol. III, 125.
4. Schwartz, 40–41.
5. Tresolini and Shapiro, 80–81.
6. Hoffer, 52–56.
7. Stone and McKean, 190.
8. Beveridge, 557 and onward.
9. Hoffer, 60–62.
10. Smith, 426.
11. Smith, 428.
12. Smith, 430.
13. Hoffer, 63–65.
14. Smith, 433–38.
15. Smith, 435.
16. Hoffer, 65–67.
17. Schwartz, 46.
18. Smith, 440–46.
19. Boorstin, ed. *An American Primer,* 242–44.
20. Boorstin, *An American Primer,* 239–40.
21. Smith, 456–62.
22. Smith, 458.
23. Hoffer, 66.
24. Smith, 459.
25. Smith, 462.
26. Speiser, *Founding Lawyers,* 19.
27. Smith, 475–77.
28. Schwartz, 47–49.
29. Visit to the National Archives.
30. Beveridge, Vol. II, 351.
31. Smith, 112–43.
32. Smith, 305–7.

33. The John Quincy Adams theory of the end of the founding comes primarily from an interview with James Traub, the author of *John Quincy Adams: Militant Spirit*. He would also, though, fall in with the next section, "Not Yet," a spirit congenial with Adams's ideals that the nation is always evolving.
34. Stewart interview.
35. Speiser, 61.
36. Alexander Hamilton as "Publius," *Federalist Number 78*.
37. Tresolini and Shapiro, 83.
38. Schwartz, 52.
39. Wood, "The Origins of Judicial Review Revisited, or How the Marshall Court Made More Out of Less," 789.

CHAPTER TEN

1. Kennedy Inaugural Address.
2. United States Constitution, Article III, Section 1.
3. US Constitution, same section.
4. Schwartz, 16.
5. Schwartz, 17.
6. Schwartz, 17.
7. Schwartz, 19.
8. Hoffer, 37.
9. Hoffer, 37.
10. O'Connor, 65.
11. Smith, 282.
12. Schwartz, 67–73.
13. Schwartz, 94.
14. O'Connor, 28.
15. Hoffer, 94–95.
16. Hoffer, 336.
17. O'Connor, 36–37.
18. Ward and Weiden, *Sorcerers' Apprentices*, 1–5.
19. Rehnquist.
20. Rehnquist.
21. Peppers and Ward, *In Chambers*, 1–3.
22. Biskupic, "Exclusive Club," CNN, October 8, 2018.
23. *List of Law Clerks of the Supreme Court of the United States*, Wikipedia. Though many researchers are loath to admit they have used Wikipedia, I found this list tantalizing. It had every clerk, when and who they clerked for, their non–Supreme Court clerkships, and their law schools. It was, for this author, fun reading.
24. Smith, 358–74.
25. Thomas, *My Grandfather's Son*, and Sotomayor, *My Beloved World*. I listened to both of these memoirs on CD, and they were more affecting for hearing how the authors read their words aloud. It gave more resonance than just reading the texts.

26. Peppers and Ward, "Section Three, The Modern Clerkship Institution." The essays here bring the conclusion that the Court is more "elite" than either "liberal" or "conservative." They are products of mostly the same law schools, legal backgrounds, and social status—if not as children, then as adults. It brings a different perspective to the current and recently past Courts.

CHAPTER ELEVEN

1. Strauss.
2. US Constitution, Article II, Section 1, Clause 3.
3. Parker, "On Senate Menu."
4. McDonald, *Intellectual Origins of the Constitution*, 276.
5. US Constitution, Eighteenth and Twenty-First Amendments.
6. US Constitution, Ninth Amendment.
7. Van Doren, *Benjamin Franklin*, 709–10.
8. Isaacson, *Benjamin Franklin: An American Life*, 311–12.
9. Madison, *The Constitutional Convention*.
10. Stewart, "The Surprising Raucous Home Life of the Madisons."
11. Marsden, *Roger Sherman*.
12. Hall, *Roger Sherman and the Creation of the American Republic*.
13. Madison, June 29, 1787.
14. National Constitution Center, *Saturday Night Massacre*.

CHAPTER TWELVE

1. Beveridge, Vol. III, 275.
2. Beveridge, Vol. III, 276.
3. Beveridge, Vol. III, 285.
4. Beveridge, Vol., III, 291–315.
5. Beveridge Vol. III, 406.
6. Beveridge Vol. III, 407–17.
7. Beveridge Vol. III, 504–9.
8. Beveridge Vol. III, 525 and onward.
9. Smith, 342–47.
10. Smith, 411–14.
11. Smith, 414.
12. Beveridge, Vol. IV, 62.
13. Beveridge, Vol. IV, 63.
14. Beveridge, Vol. IV, 64–65.
15. Smith, 85–86.
16. Smith, 102–3.
17. Smith, 160–61.
18. O'Connor, 24–25.
19. Smith, 519–20.

20. Smith, 523–24.
21. Smith, 524.

CHAPTER THIRTEEN

1. Zelizer interview, April 2019.
2. Clark interview, April 2019.
3. *Washington and His Country*, 1–5.
4. Ward, Burns, and Burns, *The Civil War*. Reading the book is good, but seeing the documentary, even now that other filmmakers mock his style, is better.
5. Burns interview from Television Critics Association, 1992 meeting.
6. Burns interview.
7. Zelizer interview.
8. *What the Constitution Means to Me*, performance, August 2019.
9. McCullough, 1995 National Book Foundation Medal acceptance speech.
10. McCullough, all quotes above from speech.
11. Carp, "History for a Post-Fact America."
12. Visits to Monticello and Independence National Historical Park. Dodd, 171–72; Taylor, *William Henry Seward: Lincoln's Right Hand*, 188–92; Morris, 235–36; Morris, 255–56; McKeever, 380–83.

BIBLIOGRAPHY

BOOKS

Amar, Akhil Reed, and Alan Hirsch. *For the People: What the Constitution Really Says About Your Rights.* New York: Simon & Schuster, 1998.

Becker, Carl L. *The Declaration of Independence: A Study in the History of Political Ideas.* New York: Vintage, 1961.

Beveridge, Albert J. *The Life of John Marshall.* 4 volumes. Boston: Houghton Mifflin, 1916-1919.

Biskupic, Joan. *The Chief: The Life and Turbulent Times of Chief Justice John Roberts.* New York: Basic Books, 2019.

Black, Hugo Jr. *My Father: A Remembrance.* New York: Random House, 1975.

Boorstin, Daniel, ed. *An American Primer.* Chicago: University of Chicago Press, 1966.

Boorstin, Daniel. *The Americans: The National Experience.* New York: Random House, 1965.

Brookhiser, Richard. *John Marshall: The Man Who Made the Supreme Court.* New York: Basic Books, 2018.

Brooks, David L., ed. *From Magna Carta to the Constitution: Documents in the Struggle for Liberty.* San Francisco: Fox & Wilkes, 1993.

Carmon, Irin, and Shana Knizhnik. *Notorious RBG, the Life and Times of Ruth Bader Ginsburg.* New York: Dey Street Books, 2015.

Dillon, John F. *Marshall: Life, Character, and Judicial Services.* 3 volumes. Chicago: Callaghan, 1903.

Ellis, Joseph, J. *American Creation.* New York: Vintage, 2007.

Flexner, John Thomas. *George Washington.* 2 volumes. Boston: Little, Brown, 1970.

———. *Washington, The Indispensable Man.* New York: Open Road Media edition, 2017.

Freeman, Douglas Southhall, John Alexander Carroll, and Mary Wells Ashworth. *George Washington.* 7 volumes. New York: Scribner's, 1957.

Ginsburg, Ruth Bader. *My Own Words.* New York: Simon & Schuster, 2016.

Gorsuch, Neil. *A Republic, If You Can Keep It.* New York: Crown Forum, 2019.

Hamilton, Alexander, James Madison, and John Jay. *The Federalist Papers (Mentor Book Edition)* New York: Penguin, 1961.

Hemingway, Mollie, and Carrie Severino. *Justice on Trial: The Kavanaugh Confirmation and the Future of the Supreme Court.* Washington, DC: Regnery, 2019.

Irons, Peter. *A People's History of the Supreme Court: The Men and Women Whose Cases and Decisions Have Shaped Our Constitution.* New York: Viking, 1999.

Irving, Washington. *Washington and His Country,* Boston: Ginn and Company, 1889.

Isaacson, Walter. *Benjamin Franklin: An American Life,* New York: Simon & Schuster, 2003.

Kane, Joseph Nathan. *Facts About the Presidents: A Compilation of Biographical and Historical Information.* New York: H. W. Wilson, 1959.

Luxenberg, Steve. *Separate: The Story of* Plessy v. Ferguson, *and America's Journey from Slavery to Segregation.* New York: W. W. Norton, 2019.

Marshall, John. *The Life of George Washington,* Philadelphia: C. P. Wayne, 1805–07.

———. *The Papers of John Marshall.* Rhodes, Irwin R., ed. Norman: University of Oklahoma Press, 1969.

McCullough, David. *John Adams.* New York: Simon & Schuster, 2001.

———. *The Pioneers: The Heroic Story of the Settlers Who Brought the American Ideal West.* New York: Simon & Schuster, 2019.

Meacham, Jon. *The Soul of America: The Battle for Our Better Angels.* New York: Random House, 2018.

O'Connor, Sandra Day. *Out of Order.* New York: Random House, 2013.

Rehnquist, William H. *The Supreme Court.* New York: Knopf, 2004.

Rosen, Jeffrey. *The Unwanted Gaze: The Destruction of Privacy in America.* New York: Random House, 2000.

Rubenstein, David. *The American Story: Conversations With Master Historians.* New York: Simon & Schuster, 2019.

Saunders, Jason L., ed. *Greek and Roman Philosophy after Aristotle.* New York: The Free Press, 1966.

Scalia, Antonin. *Scalia Speaks: Reflections on Law, Faith and Life Well Lived.* New York: Crown Forum, 2017.

Schwartz, Bernard. *A History of the Supreme Court.* New York: Oxford University Press, 1993.

Schreck, Heidi. *What the Constitution Means to Me.* Theater on Broadway, performance seen by author in November 2019.

Smith, Jean Edward. *John Marshall: Definer of a Nation.* New York: Henry Holt, 1996.

Sotomayor, Sonia. *My Beloved World.* New York: Knopf, 2013.

Speiser, Stuart M. *The Founding Lawyers and America's Quest for Justice.* Washington, DC: Pound Civil Justice Institute, 2010.

Stewart, David O. *Madison's Gift: Five Partnerships that Built America.* New York: Simon & Schuster, 2015.

Thomas, Clarence. *My Grandfather's Son: A Memoir.* New York: Harper, 2007.

Thomas, Evan. *First: Sandra Day O'Connor.* New York: Random House, 2019.

Toobin, Jeffrey. *The Nine: Inside the Secret World of the Supreme Court.* New York: Anchor, 2008.

———. *The Oath: The Obama White House and The Supreme Court.* New York: Anchor, 2012.

———. *Too Close to Call: The Thirty-Six Day Battle to Decide the 2000 Election.* New York: Random House, 2001.

Trachtman, Michael G. *The Supremes' Greatest Hits: The 44 Supreme Court Cases That Most Directly Affect Your Life.* New York: Sterling, 2009.

Tresolini, Rocco & Martin Shapiro. *American Constitutional Law.* New York, MacMillan, 1983.

Unger, Harlow Giles. *John Marshall: The Chief Justice Who Saved the Nation.* New York: Da Capo Press, 2014.

Winik, Jay. *The Great Upheaval: America and the Birth of the Modern World, 1788-1800.* New York: Harper, 2007.

Woodward, Bob, and Scott Armstrong. *The Brethren: Inside the Supreme Court.* New York: Simon & Schuster, 1979.

Zelden, Charles L. *Bush v. Gore: Exposing the Hidden Crisis in American Democracy.* Lawrence, Kansas: University Press of Kansas, 2010.

INTERVIEWS

Clark, Clifford, Professor of History emeritus, Carleton College. Personal interview with author, December 2019.

Denniston, Lyle, historian. Personal interview with author, January 2020.

Gerhardt, Michael, Samuel Ashe Distinguished Professor of Constitutional Law, University of North Carolina School of Law. Personal interview with author, December 2019.

Roosevelt, Kermit. University of Pennsylvania Law School. Personal interview with author, January 2016.

Stewart, David O., historian. Personal interview with author, December 2019.

Traub, James, historian. Personal interview with author, December 2019.

Zelizer, Julian, Professor of History, Princeton University. Personal interview with author, December 2019.

Zuckert, Michel, Reeves Dreux Professor of Political Science, Notre Dame University. Personal interview with author, November 2019.

INDEX

abolition, 105, 142–43, 148
abortion, 196. *See also Roe v. Wade*
Adams, Abigail, 67, 69, 72, 97, 98
Adams, Henry, 100
Adams, John
 death of, ix
 diplomatic service in Britain, 52
 1800 presidential election, 111–12
 1800 State of the Union address, 114
 elected vice president, 77, 173
 election as president, 59, 67–72, 180
 transfer of power to Jefferson, 173–74
 XYZ Affair, 1, 27, 61, 66, 124–25, 206
Adams, John Quincy, 82, 90, 174, 200,
  205, 212, 220
Affordable Care Act (Obamacare),
  130, 137
African Americans
 discrimination, 148–49
 Jim Crow laws, 87, 140, 143, 224
 separate but equal doctrine, 132, 143,
  147, 149, 189
 struggle for civil rights, 90, 103, 169
Agricultural Adjustment Act
  (1933), 140
Alaska, 81, 195
Allegiance (Roosevelt), 132
Alexander Hamilton (sailing ship), 61
Alger, Horatio, Jr., 102–03
Alien and Sedition Acts, 65–67,
  124–25, 184, 206
Allen, Woody, 1
Ambler, Eliza, 33–35, 37, 229n3
Ambler, Jacquelin, 33, 35, 39

Ambler, Mary Willis. *See* Marshall,
  Mary Willis Ambler
Ambler, Rebecca Burwell, 33
American Civil Liberties Union,
  87, 138
American Indians. *See* Native
  Americans
American Legion, 220
*American Moonshot: John F. Kennedy and
  the Great Space Race* (Brinkley), xi
The Americans (Boorstin), 95
Andre, John, 23
anti-Semitism, 140
Armstrong, Neil, xi
Arnold, Benedict, 24, 51
Arthur, Chester A., 103
Articles of Confederation, 25, 40–46,
  167, 171, 195, 201, 222
Arvey, Jacob, 91
Asbury Park Press, 218
"Asoken Farewell" (Unger), 218–19
Atkinson, Rick, 104
Aurora (newspaper), 95
Austen, Jane, 211

Bache, Benjamin, 95
Back-to-Africa movement, 47, 73
Bakeshop Act of 1895, 133
Bancroft, George, 99
Bank of North America, 172
Bank of the United States, 141, 161–63
The Bank of Virginia, 59
Barbary Wars, 120–21
Barlow, Joel, 123
Barnes, David, 109–10